Architecting Angular Applications with Redux, RxJS, and NgRx

Learn to build Redux style high-performing applications with Angular 6

Christoffer Noring

BIRMINGHAM - MUMBAI

Architecting Angular Applications with Redux, RxJS, and NgRx

Commissioning Editor: Ashwin Nair
Acquisition Editor: Reshma Raman
Content Development Editor: Nikhil Borkar
Technical Editor: Subhalaxmi Nadar
Copy Editor: Safis Editing
Project Coordinator: Ulhas Kambali
Proofreader: Safis Editing
Indexer: Rekha Nair
Graphics: Tania Dutta
Production Coordinator: Shraddha Falebhai

First published: March 2018

Production reference: 1230318

Published by Packt Publishing Ltd.
Livery Place
35 Livery Street
Birmingham
B3 2PB, UK.

ISBN 978-1-78712-240-6

www.packtpub.com

`mapt.io`

Mapt is an online digital library that gives you full access to over 5,000 books and videos, as well as industry leading tools to help you plan your personal development and advance your career. For more information, please visit our website.

Why subscribe?

- Spend less time learning and more time coding with practical eBooks and Videos from over 4,000 industry professionals

- Improve your learning with Skill Plans built especially for you

- Get a free eBook or video every month

- Mapt is fully searchable

- Copy and paste, print, and bookmark content

PacktPub.com

Did you know that Packt offers eBook versions of every book published, with PDF and ePub files available? You can upgrade to the eBook version at `www.PacktPub.com` and as a print book customer, you are entitled to a discount on the eBook copy. Get in touch with us at `service@packtpub.com` for more details.

At `www.PacktPub.com`, you can also read a collection of free technical articles, sign up for a range of free newsletters, and receive exclusive discounts and offers on Packt books and eBooks.

Foreword

Programming is all about solving problems, and effective problem solving is all about breaking down big problems into little ones; this makes the problem digestible. You can eat an elephant if you do it one bite at a time.

One of the more recent advancements in breaking down problems into smaller pieces is Redux-style state management, which for Angular means NgRx. Learning NgRx and knowing how to use it effectively in your applications will provide a high return on investment as you and your team will be able to keep your code clean and keep your velocity from degrading over time. This book will teach you how to use NgRx and use it effectively.

Joe Eames

Software craftsman

Contributors

About the author

Christoffer Noring, a software developer with over 10 years' experience, has successfully delivered software for industries ranging from telecom to aviation. He has worked on everything from databases to frontend. Frequently speaking on TDD, React, NativeScript, RxJS, and Angular, he writes books and blogs and holds the title of Google Developer Expert in Web Technologies and Angular.

Currently working for McKinsey as a full stack developer, he's the author and maintainer of *RxJS Ultimate*, and he has coauthored *Learning Angular - Second Edition*, a Packt title.

Thank you to my reviewers, Sachin, Andrew, Vince, Mashhood, and Ward, whose comments have been most helpful and have improved this book.
Sara, my wife, I wouldn't be in this place in my career without your valuable input and your saintly patience. Forever yours.
My brother, your suggestions and ongoing support have turned me into the writer I am today.
Mom and dad, thank you for your loving support and encouragement.

About the reviewers

Mashhood Rastgar is the founder and technical lead at Recurship, which is a JavaScript consultancy based in Karachi, Pakistan. He is also part of the Google Developer Experts for Web and Angular. Mashhood works startups working in EU and USA, to help them crawl through the technical maze and quickly build amazing products focused around the problems they are trying to solve. He specializes in using the latest technologies available to identify the best solutions. He is also a frequent international and local speaker at different web conferences.

Vinci Rufus is a Google Developer Expert and Senior Director with SapientRazorfish. He consults clients and teams on frontend architecture, mobile strategy, and user experience, primarily in the areas of content and commerce. His areas of interest involve progressive web apps, Angular, React, and web components. He is an author of *AngularJS Web Application Development Blueprints*.

> *A big shout out to my kids, Shannon and Jaden, and my nephew, Chris, who make it all worth it.*

Sachin Ohri is a technology architect with a keen interest in web-based technologies. He has been writing web applications for more than a decade, with technologies such as .NET, JavaScript, Durandal, Angular, and TypeScript. He works on providing technical solutions, including architectural design, technical support, and development expertise, to Fortune 500 companies. He holds various Microsoft certifications, such as Microsoft Azure Architect, Microsoft ASP.NET MVC web application, and Microsoft Programming with C#.

Andrew Leith Macrae first cut his programming teeth on an Apple IIe, poking bytes into the RAM. Over the years, he has developed interactive applications with Hypercard, Director, Flash, and more recently, Adobe AIR for mobile. He has also worked with HTML since there was HTML to work with and is currently working as a senior frontend developer at The Learning Channel, using Angular 4 with TypeScript.

Packt is searching for authors like you

If you're interested in becoming an author for Packt, please visit `authors.packtpub.com` and apply today. We have worked with thousands of developers and tech professionals, just like you, to help them share their insight with the global tech community. You can make a general application, apply for a specific hot topic that we are recruiting an author for, or submit your own idea.

Table of Contents

Preface

NgRx is an implementation of the popular pattern, Redux, that's meant for use with Angular. It is entirely possible to create an Angular application without NgRx. You might even be very successful in doing so. There are situations, though, where Redux can really help; you can get that help by using NgRx.

So, what is Redux and when do we need it? Redux is about adding predictability to your app. Predictability is about knowing who did what to the state in your application.

Single source of truth is a concept that Redux lives up to as it promotes adding all your data to one store. At any given moment, you will be able to tell what state your application is in. This is great if you want to save the state and come back to it (also called rehydration) like you would in a game where you create a save point and later resume your game from that save point.

It's not only about having a single source of truth; it's also about knowing who is allowed to change the content, or the state, of the store. A challenge you often face is that as an application grows, you need to add a lot of views and controllers, you gradually lose the overview of what code affects what state in the application. Redux helps you with this by ensuring that a view can't change the state directly but will have to dispatch actions that represent the intent of how you want the state to change.

Another thing that might happen is that a lot of user interaction kicks off a lot of changes to the state. Some of those actions should lead to immediate changes and some lead to asynchronous actions that will eventually change the state of the application. The important thing at this point is that we ensure that all those changes happen in the right order. Redux helps us with that by queuing up all the actions and ensures that our app changes its state in a predictable way.

A very important aspect of Redux is that when it changes the state, it does not mutate it. It replaces the state with a copy of the old state, but with the latest action applied to it. If we take our game analogy again, imagine that you have a game and you want to add a potion to your backpack. When you do that in Redux, we replace the main character; we replace it with a main character that has a potion in its backpack. The fact that we do things this way makes it easy for us to remember each previous state and return to an earlier state if we need to, which is known as time-travel-debugging. To enable us to replace the previous state with a new state, we are using something called pure functions. Pure functions ensure that we only create a copy of the data instead of mutating it.

There are a lot of benefits to knowing what state your app contains at a given point. However, not all the state in your app will need Redux. It comes down to preference. Some prefer to put all the state in the store, some prefer to put some state in the store, and some other state is fine if it only lives as local state in a specific component. Think of it this way, if you were to restore your app, what state would be okay to lose; the answer may be a drop-down selection made or something else, if anything. Having everything in the store will ensure that you don't, by mistake, make extra Ajax calls if the store already holds the data, so it is a way of helping you with caching as well.

Who this book is for

This book is intended for Angular developers who have written an app or two and are looking for a more structured way to handle data management. This means you ideally have a decent grasp of JavaScript, HTML, and CSS and know how to scaffold an Angular application using angular-cli, and you also know how to make AJAX requests using the HttpClient service in Angular.

What this book covers

Chapter 1, *Quick Look Back at Data Services for Simple Apps*, covers how to work with services and how Angular dependency injection helps out. It also brings up the MVC pattern and discusses cohesion and coupling.

Chapter 2, *1.21 Gigawatt – Flux Pattern Explained*, teaches what the Flux pattern is and what concepts it consists of. It shows how to implement the Flux pattern using stores, a dispatcher, and several views.

Chapter 3, *Asynchronous Programming*, looks at what asynchronous means and talks about callbacks, promises, async/await, and how the async library can help us create order in our asynchronous code.

Chapter 4, *Functional Reactive Programming*, compares declarative and imperative programming and looks at a subset of declarative programming, functional programming. We drill down into certain properties of functional programming, such as higher-order functions, immutability, and recursion. Furthermore, we look at how to make code reactive and what reactive means.

Chapter 5, *RxJS Basics*, introduces the RxJS library. Furthermore, it brings up concepts such as Observable, Producer, and Observer. It further discusses how the Observable is the asynchronous concept that we need to unify all our asynchronous concepts into one. We also touch on operators and what they are. Lastly, we attempt to build our own micro implementation of RxJS to further understand what's going on under the hood.

Chapter 6, *Manipulating Stream and Their Values*, focuses a lot on educating the reader on operators, the thing that gives RxJS its power. The reader should leave this chapter with a lot more knowledge about how to manipulate data as well as Observables.

Chapter 7, *RxJS Advanced*, goes deeper and tries to explain more advanced concepts in RxJS, such as hot and cold Observables, subjects, error handling, and how to test your RxJS code with Marble testing.

Chapter 8, *Redux*, demonstrates the Redux pattern and explains how it came from the Flux pattern and improved upon some of its paradigms and concepts. The reader will learn how it works in practice by learning to build their own Redux and also using the same, involving a couple of views.

Chapter 9, *NgRx – Reduxing that Angular App*, explores what NgRx is and what it consists of. It also shows the reader how to put it in to use by adding it to an Angular application. Concepts such as store are explained and demoed, and the reader will learn how to debug and handle side effects with the Effects library.

Chapter 10, *NgRx – In Depth*, covers the Entity library, which allows you to write way less code by reducing a lot of boilerplate. It also shows how you can put a router's state in the store. Furthermore, we look at how to test NgRx, how to build it yourself, and lastly, we cover Schematics, which will help us further by allowing us to scaffold the most common constructs we need to work with in NgRx.

To get the most out of this book

This book is about building Angular applications using NGRX. To get the most out of the book you need a basic understanding of the Angular framework and should be able to scaffold an Angular application using the Angular-CLI or be able to set up an Angular project through Webpack, if that is your preferred way. It's good to have a decent understanding of JavaScript and TypeScript. Most of all a curious mind is really all you need. It's a good idea to have NodeJs installed on your machine.

Download the example code files

You can download the example code files for this book from your account at
www.packtpub.com. If you purchased this book elsewhere, you can visit
www.packtpub.com/support and register to have the files emailed directly to you.

You can download the code files by following these steps:

1. Log in or register at www.packtpub.com.
2. Select the **SUPPORT** tab.
3. Click on **Code Downloads & Errata**.
4. Enter the name of the book in the **Search** box and follow the onscreen instructions.

Once the file is downloaded, please make sure that you unzip or extract the folder using the latest version of:

- WinRAR/7-Zip for Windows
- Zipeg/iZip/UnRarX for Mac
- 7-Zip/PeaZip for Linux

The code bundle for the book is also hosted on GitHub at
https://github.com/PacktPublishing/Architecting-Angular-Applications-with-Redux
-RxJs-and-NgRx. We also have other code bundles from our rich catalog of books and
videos available at https://github.com/PacktPublishing/. Check them out!

Conventions used

There are a number of text conventions used throughout this book.

CodeInText: Indicates code words in text, database table names, folder names, filenames,
file extensions, pathnames, dummy URLs, user input, and Twitter handles. Here is an
example: "We need to install webpack by typing the following in our terminal."

A block of code is set as follows:

```
interface IPrinter {
  print(IPrintable printable);
}
```

When we wish to draw your attention to a particular part of a code block, the relevant lines or items are set in bold:

```
interface IPrintable {
  String getContent();
}

interface IPrinter {
  print(IPrintable printable);
}
```

Any command-line input or output is written as follows:

```
npm install webpack webpack-cli --save-dev
```

Bold: Indicates a new term, an important word, or words that you see onscreen. For example, words in menus or dialog boxes appear in the text like this. Here is an example: "Let's add an item to our store by adding a value to our input element and pressing the **Save** button."

Warnings or important notes appear like this.

Tips and tricks appear like this.

Get in touch

Feedback from our readers is always welcome.

General feedback: Email feedback@packtpub.com and mention the book title in the subject of your message. If you have questions about any aspect of this book, please email us at questions@packtpub.com.

Errata: Although we have taken every care to ensure the accuracy of our content, mistakes do happen. If you have found a mistake in this book, we would be grateful if you would report this to us. Please visit www.packtpub.com/submit-errata, selecting your book, clicking on the Errata Submission Form link, and entering the details.

Piracy: If you come across any illegal copies of our works in any form on the Internet, we would be grateful if you would provide us with the location address or website name. Please contact us at copyright@packtpub.com with a link to the material.

If you are interested in becoming an author: If there is a topic that you have expertise in and you are interested in either writing or contributing to a book, please visit authors.packtpub.com.

Reviews

Please leave a review. Once you have read and used this book, why not leave a review on the site that you purchased it from? Potential readers can then see and use your unbiased opinion to make purchase decisions, we at Packt can understand what you think about our products, and our authors can see your feedback on their book. Thank you!

For more information about Packt, please visit packtpub.com.

1

Quick Look Back at Data Services for Simple Apps

Welcome to the first chapter of this book. You have hopefully picked up this book because you have experienced issues setting up the architecture of your Angular application. Your application has grown and in that process you slowly feel your are losing track of what your application knows at a given point, what we call the state of the application. There might be other issues, such as parts of your application not being in agreement with what they know. An update that happened in one part may not have been applied to some other part and you scratch your head, thinking should it be this hard and is there a better answer?

It's entirely possible you are just picking up this book as you have heard about NgRx as the way to structure your application and you are curious and want to know more.

Regardless of which motivation drives you to read this book, this book is about learning to structure your application and learning how to set up and communicate your application's state, and its changes, in a way that all parts of your application are in agreement on what is happening. The underlying architectural pattern for NgRx is Redux, which constrains data to live in only one place and ensures data is flowing in only one direction. We will have a chance to cover Redux in more depth in a dedicated chapter in this book.

To get to a point where we have learned to master NgRx, we first need to pick up some paradigms and patterns along the way. We need to build a good foundation of knowledge. A good foundation consists of learning concepts such as **Functional Reactive Programming (FRP)**, the architectural pattern Flux, and a new and exciting way of thinking about async concepts, Observables.

So why are these relevant for our learning journey of mastering NgRx? The Flux pattern has a lot in common with Redux and it is its shortcomings that led to Redux being created. NgRx itself is implemented using RxJS, which promotes a functional reactive style of programming. So you see, the foundations we are about to explore all help us grasp the theory and motivations behind NgRx.

In this chapter, we lay the foundations for the book by discussing the well-known **Model-View-Controller** (**MVC**) pattern. To verify we understand the MVC pattern, we use the Angular framework to make things easier. As interesting as it is to talk about architecture, if you don't see it applied to something real, it might be hard to grasp.

We continue diving into an application workflow in Angular and its Dependency Injection machinery. Before concluding the chapter, we will also have a look at how to fetch data through an API because, after all, that is where the data comes from and should flow to.

In this chapter, we will:

- Describe the building blocks of the MVC pattern
- Describe MVC in Angular and the core constructs that help support it
- Review the HTTP service and how to deal with Ajax

Model-View-Controller – the pattern we all know

Regardless of whether you have been a programmer for a year or 20 years, you have almost certainly encountered the MVC pattern in some way, shape, or form. The pattern itself, MVC, consists of three interconnected parts: model, view, and controller. More important than knowing all its parts is knowing what problem it solves. It solves the problem of separation of concerns by decoupling view logic, data logic, and business logic. The MVC pattern has given rise to, among others:

- **Model-View-Adapter** (**MVA**)
- **Model-View-Presenter** (**MVP**)
- **Model-View-ViewModel** (**MVVM**)

Cohesion and coupling – establishing a common language

Without a pattern like MVC, your code could turn out to be hard to maintain as it could have low cohesion and high coupling. Those are fancy words, so what do we mean? Cohesion is about focus and what the class should do. The lower the cohesion, the more different things are performed by a class and therefore it has no clear intention of what it should perform.

The following code shows what happens when a class has low cohesion; it does a lot more than storing data about an invoice, such as being able to log to a file or talk to a database:

```
Invoice
   details
   total
   date
   validate()
   print()
   log()
   saveToDatabase()
```

Now we have introduced new dedicated classes and moved methods out of the Invoice class to make sure that each and every class now has high cohesion, that is, is more focused on doing one thing well. We therefore now have the classes Invoice, Printer, Logger, and InvoiceRepository:

```
Invoice
   details
   total
   date
   validate()

Printer
   print(document)

Logger
   log()

InvoiceRepository
   saveToDatabase(invoice)
```

The point I am trying to make here is that a class should only do one thing well. This is illustrated by the unfocused Invoice class being split into four different classes that each do only one focused thing well.

So that deals with cohesion/focus. What about coupling? Coupling is about how strongly connected a software element is to another software element. Ultimately, the higher the coupling, the harder/more tedious it is to change. Let's look at the following example of high coupling written in Java:

```
// cohesion-and-coupling/invoice-system.java

class Printer {
  print(Invoice invoice) {
    String total ="";
    total += invoice.getTitle();
    total += invoice.getDetails();
    total += invoice.getDate();
    //print 'total'
  }
}

class Invoice {
  String title;
    String details;
    int total;
    Date date;
    public String getTitle() { return this.title; }
    public String getDetails() { return this.details; }
    public String getDate() { return this.date; }
}

public class Program {
  private Printer printer = new Printer();
  public void run(ArrayList list) {
    for(int i=0; i< list.length; i++) {
      Object item = list.getItem(i);
      if(item instanceof Invoice) {
        Invoice invoice = (Invoice) item;
        printer.print(invoice);
      }
    }
  }

  public static void main(String [] args) {
    ArrayList list = new ArrayList();
    list.add(new Invoice());
    Program program = new Program();
    program.run( list );
  }
}
```

There are multiple problems with this code, especially if you aim to change the code in any way. Let's say we wanted to print an email as well. It is tempting to think we would need an `Email` class and need to add another `print()` method override to the `Printer` class. We would also need to add branching logic to the `Program` class. Furthermore, testing the `Program` class cannot be achieved without causing a side-effect: calling the `run()` method would cause an actual call to a printer. The way we tend to work with tests nowadays is to run our tests every time the code changes, which it might do quite a lot as we are developing our program. We might end up with thousands of printed papers just developing our code. For that reason, we need to isolate ourselves from side effects when developing code and tests. What we want to test at the end of the day is that our code behaves correctly, not that the physical printer seems to work.

In the following code, we see an example of high coupling. We add another type, `Email`. The purpose of doing that is to see the effects of doing so, which is that we need to add code to several places at once. Having to do so is a sign of a code smell. The fewer changes you need to make, the better it usually is:

```java
// cohesion-and-coupling/invoice-systemII.java

class Email {
    String from;
    String to;
    String subject;
    String body;
    String getSubject() { return this.subject; }
    String getFrom() { return this.from; }
    String getTo() { return this.to; }
    String getBody() { return this.body; }
}

class Invoice {
    String title;
    String details;
    int total;
    Date date;
    String getTitle(){ return this.title; }
    String getDetails() { return this.details; }
    Date getDate() { return this.date; }
}

class Printer {
    print(Invoice invoice) {
        String total ="";
        total += invoice.getTitle();
        total += invoice.getDetails();
```

```
      total += invoice.getDate();
      //print 'total'
    }

  print(Email email) {
    String total ="";
    total += email.getSubject();
    total += email.getFrom();
    total += email.getTo();
    total += email.getBody();
  }
}

class Program {
  private Printer printer = new Printer();
  run(ArrayList list) {
    for(int i=0; i< list.length; i++) {
      Object item = list.getItem(i);
      if(item instanceof Invoice) {
        Invoice invoice = (Invoice) item;
        printer.print( invoice );
      } else if( item instanceof Email ) {
        Email email = (Email) item;
        printer.print( email );
      }
    }
  }

  public static void main(String [] args) {
    ArrayList list = new ArrayList();
    list.add( new Invoice() );
    list.add( new Email() );
    Program program = new Program();
    program.run( list );
  }
}
```

So let's rearrange the code a bit:

```
// cohesion-and-coupling/invoice-systemIII.java

class Email implements IPrintable {
  String from;
  String to;
  String subject;
  String body;
  String getSubject() { return this.subject; }
  String getFrom() { return this.from; }
```

```
    String getTo() { return this.to; }
    String getBody() { return this.body; }
    public String getContent() {
      String total = "";
      total += email.getSubject();
      total += email.getFrom();
      total += email.getFrom();
      total += email.getBody();
      return total;
    }
}

class Invoice implements IPrintable {
  String title;
  String details;
  int total;
  Date date;
  String getTitle() { return this.title; }
  String getDetails() { return this.details; }
  String getDate() { return this.date; }
  public String getContent() {
    String total = "";
    total += invoice.getTitle();
    total += invoice.getDetails();
    total += invoice.getDate();
    return total;
  }
}

interface IPrintable {
  String getContent();
}

interface IPrinter {
  print(IPrintable printable);
}

class Printer implements IPrinter {
  print( IPrintable printable ) {
    String content = printable.getContent();
    // print content
  }
}

class Program {
  private IPrinter printer;
  public Program(IPrinter printer) {
    this.printer = printer;
```

```
    }
    run(ArrayList<IPrintable> list) {
      for(int i=0; i< list.length; i++) {
        IPrintable item = list.getItem(i);
        printer.print(item);
      }
    }
    public static void main(String [] args) {
      ArrayList<IPrintable> list = new ArrayList<IPrintable>();
      Printer printer = new Printer();
      list.add(new Invoice());
      list.add(new Email());
      Program program = new Program(printer);
    }
  }
```

At this point, we have made our program open to extension. How can we say that, you ask? Clearly, we have removed the `printer` methods from `printer`. We also removed the switch logic from the method run in the `Program` class. We have also added the abstraction `IPrintable`, which makes anything printable responsible for telling a printer what the printable content is.

You can clearly see how we went from high coupling to low coupling when we introduced the types `Document` and `Note`. The only change they cause is themselves being added and implementing the `IPrintable` interface. Nothing else has to change. Success!

```
// invoice-systemIV.java

class Document implements IPrintable {
  String title;
  String body;

  String getContent() {
    return this.title + this.body;
  }
}

class Note implements IPrintable {
  String message;

  String getContent() {
    return this.message;
  }
}

// everything else stays the same
```

```
// adding the new types to the list
class Program {
  public static void main(String[] args) {
    list.add(new Note());
    list.add(new Document());
  }
}
```

OK, so to sum up our changes:

- We added the `IPrintable` interface
- We simplified/removed the branching logic in the `Program.run()` method
- We made each printable class implement `IPrintable`
- We added some code at the end of the previous snippet to demonstrate how easy it would be to add new types
- We injected an `IPrinter` through the `Program` class constructor to ensure that we can easily test the `Program` class

In particular note that we did not need to change any logic in either `Printer` or `Program`, when adding the `Document` and `Note` types. The only thing we needed to do was add `Document` and `Notes` as classes and ensure they implemented the `IPrintable` interface. To put emphasis on this, *any addition to a program should not lead to an overall system change in the code.*

Let's reiterate the last bullet of adding `IPrinter`. Testability is a very good measurement to see whether your code has low coupling. If you depend on abstractions rather than actual classes, you are able to easily switch out one concrete class for another, while maintaining high-level behavior.

Another reason for switching `Printer` to `IPrinter` is so that we remove side effects from the program when we test our code. Side effects are when we talk to files, mutate states, or talk over the network for example. Testing the `Program` class means we want to get rid of a side effect such as actual printing and have it call something fake, or we would have a large stack of papers every time we run our tests. So to instantiate our `Program` class for the purposes of testing, we would write something like this instead:

```
// cohesion-and-coupling/invoice-systemV.java

class FakePrinter implements IPrinter {
  print(IPrintable printable) { System.out.println("printing"); }
}

class Program {
```

```
FakePrinter fakePrinter;
Program(FakePrinter fakePrinter) {
  this.fakePrinter = fakePrinter;
}
public static void main(String[] args) {
  ArrayList<IPrintable> list = new ArrayList<IPrintable>();
  Printer printer = new FakePrinter();
  list.add(new Invoice());
  list.add(new Email());
  Program program = new Program(printer);
}
}
```

What we see from this code is how we shift from instantiating the `Printer` class (which prints to a real printer) to the `Program` class using an instance of `FakePrinter`. In a testing scenario, this is exactly what you would do, if wanting to test the `Program` class. What you most likely care about is the `print()` method being called with the correct arguments.

OK, so this was a pretty long way of expressing what low coupling is about. It is, however, important to establish what crucial terms such as coupling and cohesion are, especially when talking about patterns.

Explaining the components of MVC

Back to the MVC pattern. Using said pattern means we get high cohesion and low coupling; this is due to code being split into different layers with different responsibilities. View logic belongs in views, controller logic in controllers, and model logic in models.

The model

This is the crucial part of the application. This does not rely on any specific user interface but more defines the domain in which you operate. Rules, logic, and data live here.

The view

This can be anything from a native app view to a bar chart, or even a web page. The point is that it ultimately displays data from the model. There can be different views displaying the same thing, but depending on for whom they are designed, they might look different. An admin might see a totally different view than a user for the same information.

The controller

This is really the spider in the web. It is able to take input from the view or from the data and turn it into commands.

Interactions – the behavior between the components

All these three mentioned components act in different ways when talking to each other. A model stores data it is being given from the controller based on commands. A view changes its appearance based on changes happening in the model. A controller can send a command to the model based on a user interaction. One such example is a user deciding to browse between page-based records. A new set of data will need to be retrieved based on the new visual position.

These two basic flows are what mostly happens in an application-based on MVC:

- User interaction: Controller sends command to Model => Model changes => View is updated
- View asks for data: Controller sends command to Model => Model is created/changed => View is updated

MVC summary

A lot can be said about MVC and its many variants, but let's be content with what we have for now by summarizing the properties of the pattern that we identified:

- Low coupling
- High cohesion, separating presentation concerns from the model

- Simultaneous development is possible; due to the existence of many layers, people can work in parallel on a task
- Ease of change; because of how things are separated, adding future concepts or making alterations becomes easier

An MVC flow in Angular

Let's look at the following problems and how we solve them in Angular:

- Creating and rendering model data to the screen
- Learning how the MVC pattern maps to the Angular framework
- Learning how we can structure an Angular application in different building blocks
- Fetching data/persisting data

The model

The model in Angular is a plain class, as we are using TypeScript. It can look like the following code:

```
// mvc/MvcExample/src/app/product.model.ts

export class Product {
  constructor(
    private id: number,
    private title: string,
    private description: string,
    private created: Date
  ) {}

  method() {}

  anotherMethod() {}
}
```

It is a plain TypeScript file, or rather an ES2015 module, not to be confused with an Angular module. We will discuss in the next main section what an Angular module is, in terms of setup and how it is consumed. For now, remember the model is a simple thing.

The component – a controller and a building block

In the context of MVC, the component is the V and C, the view and the controller. The component allows you to define either a separate template file or an inline template. The template is the view part.

The controller in this context is a component class file that handles user interactions and also fetches the necessary data for the template to display.

Components have come to be a central concept for a lot of frameworks that are popular today, such as React, Vue.js, and Polymer. A component can take inputs, which are either data or methods. It consists of a piece of code and an HTML template, which render interesting data, living on the component. A component in Angular consists of three major parts:

- A decorator function
- A class
- A template

A component consists of a controller class and a template. It can play two different roles in an Angular application: either it can be the responder to the route or it can serve as a building block. In the first case, Angular will instantiate it when a new route happens and respond with that component. In the latter case, the component is created directly by existing as a child component within another component.

We will explain next what we meant by the previous paragraph.

First responder to a route

As mentioned, a component can be used as a responder to a route. So let's say the application routes to the /products route as a result of a user interaction, or programmatically. Angular's way of dealing with this is to associate the /products route with a component. With the help of a component's class and HTML markup, we are able to produce a piece of HTML containing our markup and data rendered together. Pointing out a component as a responder to a route, is done when defining the so-called route map, like so:

```
// example of what routing might look like

export const appRoutes: Routes = [
```

```
  {
    path: '',
    component: HomeComponent
  },
  {
    path: 'payments',
    component: ProductsComponent,
    data: { title: 'Products' }
  }
]
```

Essentially, a route is defined as an object with `path` properties, pointing out our route, and a `component` property pointing to the responding component. We can attach other properties to the route, such as `data`, to give the responding components some initial data to render.

Used as a building block

Using a component as a building block means it will be part of another component's template. Essentially, it will be seen as that component's child. This line of thinking is quite natural and means that we can think of our application as a hierarchical tree of components. A component in Angular consists of a controller class and a template as we have mentioned previously. A typical component looks like so:

```
// an example component

@Component({
  selector: 'example-component'
})
export class ExampleComponent {}
```

The `@Component` decorator function adds metadata to the class. This instructs Angular on how to create the component so that Angular can place the component in the DOM. This enables you to use it as a responder to a route or as your own custom element. The property `selector` is what decides what your component should be called, if used as a custom element. Example usage looks like the following:

```
// an example container component
@Component({
  selector: `
  {{ title }}
  <example-component>
  `
})
```

```
export class ContainerComponent {
  title ="container component";
}
```

The fact that components can be used this way makes it easy to think about an app as consisting of a hierarchical tree of components. A Todo application could therefore look like the following:

```
AppComponent
  TodoList
    TodoItem
    TodoItem
    TodoItem
    ...
```

Let's start to create this app, starting with the AppComponent. As this is the topmost component, it is also referred to as the root component. The AppComponent should render the TodoListComponent in its own template, like so:

```
// mvc/MvcExample/src/app/app.component.ts

import { Component } from "@angular/core";

@Component({
  selector: "app-root",
  template: `
  <todo-list></todo-list>
  `,
  styleUrls: ["./app.component.css"]
})
export class AppComponent {
  title = "app";
}
```

The next step is defining the TodoListComponent and knowing that it should be able to render a number of TodoItemComponent instances within its template. The size of a list is usually unknown. This is exactly what the structural directive *ngFor is for. So that is what we will utilize in the following code as we define the TodoListComponent:

```
// mvc/MvcExample/src/app/todo-list.component.ts

import { Component } from "@angular/core";

@Component({
  selector: "todo-list",
  template: `
```

```
    <h1>{{title}}</h1> <custom></custom>
    <div *ngFor="let todo of todos">
      <todo-item [todo]="todo" ></todo-item>
    </div>
`  . // the view
})
export class TodoListComponent { // the controller class
    title: string;
    todos = [{
      title: "todo1"
    },{
      title: "todo1"
    }]
}
```

Here, we can see that we render out a list of `todo` items by looping out the todos array in the template, like so:

```
<div *ngFor="let todo of todos">
    <todo-item [todo]="todo" ></todo-item>
</div>
```

We can see in the preceding code that we are rendering out the `todo-item` selector, which points to a `TodoItemComponent` that we are yet to define. Worth noting is how we pass it a `todo` object and assign it to an input property on the `TodoItemComponent`. The definition for said component is as follows:

```
// mvc/MvcExample/src/app/todo-item.component.ts

import { Component, Input } from "@angular/core";
@Component({
    selector: "todo-item",
    template: `<h1>{{todo.title}}</h1>`
})
export class TodoItemComponent {
    @Input() todo;
}
```

Reasoning about which components should exist as part of which other components is something you are going to dedicate a lot of time to.

Components from an architectural standpoint

You are encouraged to create a lot of components in your Angular application. With the former section's example of creating a `todo` list application it was tempting to create an application that just consisted of one component, the `AppComponent`. This would have meant that one component would have been responsible for a ton of things, such as displaying `todo` items, saving said items, removing them and so on. Components are meant to be used to solve one thing well. That's why we created a `TodoItemComponent` which only job in life was to display a `todo` item. Same thing goes for the `TodoListComponent`. It should only care about displaying a list, nothing else. The more you split down your applications into small and focused areas the better.

NgModule – our new facade (and some other bits)

So far, we have talked about components in terms of them being dedicated to solving one task well. However, there are other constructs that can be used in Angular, such as pipes, directives, and services. A lot of our components will find themselves belonging to a common theme, such as products or user management and so on. When we realize what constructs belong to the same theme, we also realize that some of these constructs are constructs we want to use elsewhere in the application. Conversely, some constructs are only meant to be used in the context of the mentioned theme. To protect the latter constructs from unintended use, we would like to group them in a facade-like way and put a protective layer between the constructs and the rest of the application. The way to do that in pure ES2015 modules is to create a facade file, in which public constructs are exported and others are not, like so:

```
// an old facade file, index.ts

import { MyComponent } from 'my.component';
import { MyService } from 'my.service';

export MyComponent;
export MyService;
```

Imagine we have a directory consisting of the following files:

```
/my
  MyComponent.ts
  MyService.ts
  MyOtherService.ts
  index.ts
```

The intent of creating a facade file here is to ensure there is only one place from where you import all the constructs you need. In this case that would be the `index.ts` file. A consumer of the preceding directory would do the following:

```
// consumer.ts

import * as my from './my';
let component = new my.MyComponent();
let service = new MyService();
```

`MyOtherService` is not being exposed by the `index.ts` file though, so attempting to access it like we do in `consumer.ts` would lead to an error. You could theoretically specify the full path to the construct but you are supposed to be using the barrel. Barrels are usually meant to be used to easily access your constructs without having to write import statements that are five miles long, like so:

```
// index.ts
import { Service } from '../../../path-to-service';
import { AnotherService } from '../../path-to-other-service';
export Service;
export AnotherService;

// consumer.ts

// the long and tedious way
import { Service } from '../../../path-to-service';
import { AnotherService } from '../../path-to-other-service';

// the easier way using a barrel
import * as barrel from './index';
let service = new barrel.Service();
let anotherService = new barrel.AnotherService();
```

As you can see that barrel, `index.ts` is the one that is responsible for knowing where all your constructs are located. This also means that were you to move files around, changing directories for certain constructs, the barrel file is the only one where updating the paths to these constructs is needed.

The Angular way of dealing with this is to use Angular modules. An Angular module looks like the following:

```
// mvc/MvcExample/src/app/my/my.module.ts

import { NgModule } from "@angular/core";
import { MyComponent } from "./my.component";
import { MyPipe } from "./my.pipe";
```

```
@NgModule({
    imports: [],
    exports: [MyComponent],
    declarations: [MyComponent, MyPipe],
    providers: []
})
export class MyModule {}
```

The effect of putting `MyComponent` and `MyPipe` into the declarations property of the module is so that these components can be freely used within `MyModule`. For example, you can use `MyPipe` within the `MyComponent` template. However, if you want to use `MyComponent` outside of this module, in a component belonging to another module, you will need to export it. We do that by placing it in the array belonging to the `exports` property:

```
exports: [MyComponent]
```

Angular takes the concept of a module way beyond grouping. Some instructions in our `NgModule` are meant for the compiler so that it knows how to assemble the components. Some other instructions we give it are meant for the Dependency Injection tree. Think of the Angular module as a configuration point, but also as the place where you logically divide up your application in to cohesive blocks of code.

On the object sent to the `@NgModule` decorator, there are properties you can set that have different meanings. The most important properties are:

- The `declarations` property is an array that states what belongs to our module
- The `imports` property is an array that states what other Angular modules we are dependent on; it could be basic Angular directives or common functionality that we want to use inside of our module
- The `exports` property is an array stating what should be made available for any module importing this module; `MyComponent` is made public whereas `MyPipe` would become private for this module only
- The `providers` property is an array stating what services should be injectable into constructs belonging to this module, that is, to constructs that are listed in the declarations array

Using ES2015 modules

So far, we have mentioned that models are just plain classes. An ES2015 module is just one file. Within that file lives both public and private constructs. Things that are private are only visible within that file. Things that are public can be used outside said file. In Angular, Es2015 modules aren't used only for models but for all imaginable constructs such as components, Directives, Pipes, Services, and so on. This is because ES2015 modules are an answer to how we split our project into smaller parts, which provides us with the following benefits:

- Many small files makes it easier to parallelize the work you do and have many developers work on it at the same time
- The ability to hide data by, making some parts of your application public and some other private
- Code reuse
- Better maintainability

We have to remember what web development used to look like to understand these statements. When the web was young our JavaScript code more often than not consisted of one file. That quickly became a huge mess. There have been different techniques over the years to find a way to split up our app into many small files. Many small files have made it easier to maintain and also to get a good overview of what is going on, among many other benefits. There have been other issues though. As all these small files had to be stitched back together before being shipped with the app, a process called bundling, we suddenly had one giant file where functions and variables could by mistake affect each other due to naming collisions. A way to attack that problem is to deal with something called information hiding. This to ensure the variables and functions we created are only visible to certain other constructs. There are multiple ways, of course, to address this issue. ES2015 has a private by default way about them. Everything declared in an ES2015 is private by default unless you explicitly export it, thereby making it publicly accessible to other modules that import the aforementioned module.

So how does this connect to the previous statements? Any module system really allows us to maintain visibility in our project as it grows with us. The alternative is one file which is complete chaos. As for several developers working at the same time, any way of logically dividing up the app makes it easier to divide up the workstreams between developers.

Consuming a module

In ES2015, we use the `import` and `from` keywords to import one or several constructs like so:

```
import { SomeConstruct } from './module';
```

The imported file looks like this:

```
export let SomeConstruct = 5;
```

The basic operations involved, working with ES2015 modules, can be summarized as follows:

- Define a module and write the business logic of the module
- Export the constructs you want to make public
- Consume said module with an `import` keyword from a consumer file

Of course there is a bit more to it than that, so let's look at what else you can do in the next subsection.

An Angular example

We have been using ES2015 imports extensively throughout this chapter already, but let's emphasize when that was. As mentioned, all constructs used ES2015 modules, models, services, components, and modules. For the module, this looked like this:

```
import { NgModule } from '@angular/core';

@NgModule({
  declarations: [],
  imports: [],
  exports: [],
  providers: []
})
export class FeatureModule {}
```

Here, we see that we import the functionality we need and we end up exporting this class, thereby making it available for other constructs to consume. It's the same thing with modules, like so:

```
import { Component } from '@angular/core';

@Component({
```

```
    selector: 'example'
})
export class ExampleComponent {}
```

The pipe, directive, and filter all follow the same pattern of importing what they need and exporting themselves to be included as part of an NgModule.

Multiple exports

So far, we have only shown how to export one construct. It is possible to export multiple things from one module by adding an export keyword next to all constructs that you wish to export, like so:

```
export class Math {
  add() {}
  subtract() {}
}

export const PI = 3.14
```

Essentially, for everything you want to make public you need to add an export keyword at the start of it. There is an alternate syntax, where instead of adding an export keyword to every construct, we can instead define within curly brackets what constructs should be exported. It looks like this:

```
class Math {
  add() {}
  subtract() {}
}

const PI = 3.14

export {
  Math, PI
}
```

Whether you put export in front of every construct or you place them all in an export {}, then end result is the same, it's just a matter of taste which one to use. To consume constructs from this module, we would type:

```
import { Math, PI } from './module';
```

Here, we have the option of specifying what we want to import. In the previous example, we have opted to export both Math and PI, but we could be content with only exporting Math, for example; it is up to us.

The default import/export

So far, we have been very explicit with what we import and what we export. We can, however, create a so-called default export, which looks somewhat different to consume:

```
export default class Player {
  attack() {}
  move() {}
}

export const PI = 3.13;
```

To consume this, we can write the following:

```
import Player from './module';
import { PI } from './module'
```

Note especially the first row where we no longer use the curly brackets, { }, to import a specific construct. We just use a name that we make up. In the second row, we have to name it correctly as PI, but in the first row we can choose the name. The player points to what we exported as default, that is, the Player class. As you can see, we can still use the normal curly brackets, { }, to import specific constructs if we want to.

Renaming imports

Sometimes we may get a collision, with constructs being named the same. We could have this happening:

```
import { productService } from './module1/service'
import { productService } from './module2/service'; // name collision
```

This is a situation we need to resolve. We can resolve it using the as keyword, like so:

```
import { productService as m1_productService }
import { productService as m2_productService }
```

Thanks to the as keyword, the compiler now has no problem differentiating what is what.

The service

We started this main section talking about how ES2015 modules are for all constructs in Angular. This section is about services, and services are no different when it comes to using ES2015 modules. Services we use should be declared in a separate file. If we intend to use a service, we need to import it. It needs to be imported for different reasons though, depending on what type of service it is. Services can be of two types:

- Services without dependencies
- Services with dependencies

Service without dependencies

A service without dependencies is a service whose constructor is empty:

```
export Service {
  constructor(){}
  getData() {}
}
```

To use it, you simply type:

```
import { Service } from './service'
let service = new Service();
service.getData();
```

Any module that consumes this service will get their own copy of the code, with this kind of code. If you, however, want consumers to share a common instance, you change the `service` module definition slightly to this:

```
class Service {
  constructor() {}
  getData() {}
}
const service = new Service();
export default service;
```

Here, we export an instance of the service rather than the service declaration.

Service with dependencies

A service with dependencies has dependencies in the constructor that we need help resolving. Without this resolution process, we can't create the service. Such a service may look like this:

```
export class Service {
  constructor(
    Logger logger: Logger,
    repository:Repository
  ) {}
}
```

In this code, our service has two dependencies. Upon constructing a service, we need one `Logger` instance and one `Repository` instance. It would be entirely possible for us to find the `Logger` instance and `Repository` instance by typing something like this:

```
import { Service } from './service'
import logger from './logger';
import { Repository } from './repository';

// create the service
let service = new Service( logger, new Repository() )
```

This is absolutely possible to do. However, the code is a bit tedious to write every time I want a service instance. When you start to have 100s of classes with deep object dependencies, a DI system quickly pays off.

This is one thing a Dependency Injection library helps you with, even if it is not the main motivator behind its existence. The main motivator for a DI system is to create loose coupling between different parts of the system and rely on contracts rather than concrete implementations. Take our example with the service. There are two things a DI can help us with:

- Switch out one concrete implementation for another
- Easily test our construct

To show what I mean, let's first assume `Logger` and `Repository` are interfaces. Interfaces may be implemented differently by different concrete classes, like so:

```
import { Service } from './service'
import logger from './logger';
import { Repository } from './repository';

class FileLogger implements Logger {
```

```
  log(message: string) {
    // write to a file
  }
}

class ConsoleLogger implements Logger {
  log(message: string) {
    console.log('message', message);
  }
}

// create the service
let service = new Service( new FileLogger(), new Repository() )
```

This code shows how easy it is to switch out the implementation of Logger by just choosing FileLogger over ConsoleLogger or vice versa. The test case is also made a lot easier if you only rely on dependencies coming from the outside, so that everything can therefore be mocked.

Dependency Injection

Essentially, when we ask for a construct instance, we want help constructing it. A DI system can act in one of two ways when asked to resolve an instance:

- **Transient mode**: The dependency is always created anew
- **Singleton mode**: The dependency is reused

Angular only creates singletons though which means every time we ask for a dependency it will only be created once and we will be given an already existing dependency if we are not the first construct to ask for that dependency.

The default behavior of any DI framework is to use the default constructor on a class and create an instance from a class. If that class has dependencies, then it has to resolve those first. Imagine we have the following case:

```
export class Logger { }

export class Service {
  constructor(logger: Logger) { }
}
```

The DI framework would crawl the chain of dependencies, find the construct that does not have any dependencies, and instantiate that first. Then it would crawl upwards and finally resolve the construct you asked for. So with this code:

```
import { Service } from './service';

export class ExampleComponent {
  constructor(srv: Service) { }
}
```

The DI framework would:

- Instantiate the logger first
- Instantiate the service second
- Instantiate the component third

Dependency Injection in Angular using providers

So far we have only discussed Dependency Injection in general, but Angular has some constructs, or decorators, to ensure that Dependency Injection does its job. First imagine a simple scenario, a service with no dependencies:

```
export class SimpleService {}
```

If a component exists that requires an instance of the service, like so:

```
@Component({
  selector: 'component'
})
export class ExampleComponent {
  constructor(srv: Service) {}
}
```

The Angular Dependency Injection system comes in and attempts to resolve it. Because the service has no dependencies, the solution is as simple as instantiating `Service`, and Angular does this for us. However, we need to tell Angular about this construct for the DI machinery to work. The thing that needs to know this is called a provider. Both Angular modules and components have access to a providers array that we can add the `Service` construct to. A word on this though. Since the arrival of Angular modules, the recommendation is to not use the providers array for components. The below paragraphs are merely there to inform you how providers for components work.

This will ensure that a `Service` instance is being created and injected at the right place, when asked for. Let's tell an Angular module about a service construct:

```
import { Service } from "./Service";

@NgModule({
  providers: [Service]
})
export class FeatureModule{}
```

This is usually enough to make it work. You can, however, register the `Service` construct with the `component` class instead. It looks identical:

```
@Component({
  providers: [Service]
})
export ExampleComponent {}
```

This has a different effect though. You will tell the DI machinery about this construct and it will be able to resolve it. There is a limitation, however. It will only be able to resolve it for this component and all its view child components. Some may see this as a way of limiting what components can see what services and therefore see it as a feature. Let me explain that by showing when the DI machinery can figure out our provided service:

Everybody's parent – it works: Here, we can see that as long as the component highest up declares `Service` as a provider, all the following components are able to inject `Service`:

```
AppComponent // Service added here, Can resolve Service
  TodosComponent // Can resolve Service
    TodoComponent // Can resolve Service
```

Let's exemplify this with some code:

```
// example code on how DI for works for Component providers, there is no
file for it
// app.component.ts
@Component({
  providers: [Service] // < - provided,
  template : `<todos></todos>`
})
export class AppComponent {}

// todos.component.ts
@Component({
  template : `<todo></todo>`,
  selector: 'todos'
})
```

```
export class TodosComponent {
  // this works
  constructor(private service: Service) {}
}

// todo.component.ts
@Component({
  selector: 'todo',
  template: `todo component `
})
export class TodoComponent {
  // this works
  constructor(private service: Service) {}
}
```

TodosComponent – will work for its children but not higher up: Here, we provide Service one level down, to TodosComponent. This makes Service available to the child components of TodosComponent but AppComponent, its parent, misses out:

```
AppComponent // Does not know about Service
  TodosComponent // Service added here, Can resolve Service
    TodoComponent // Can resolve Service
```

Let's try to show this in code:

```
// this is example code on how it works, there is no file for it
// app.component.ts
@Component({
  selector: 'app',
  template: `<todos></todos>`
})
export class AppComponent {
  // does NOT work, only TodosComponent and below knows about Service
  constructor(private service: Service) {}
}

// todos.component.ts
@Component({
  selector: 'todos',
  template: `<todo></todo>`
  providers: [Service]
})
export class TodosComponent {
  // this works
  constructor(private service: Service) {}
}
```

```
// todo.component.ts
@Component({
  selector: 'todo',
  template: `a todo`
})
export class TodoComponent {
  // this works
  constructor(private service: Service) {}
}
```

We can see here that adding our `Service` to a component's `providers` array has limitations. Adding it to an Angular module is the sure way to ensure it can be resolved by all constructs residing inside of that array. This is not all though. Adding our `Service` to an Angular module's providers array ensures it is accessible throughout our entire application. How is that possible, you ask? It has to do with the module system itself. Imagine we have the following Angular modules in our application:

```
AppModule
SharedModule
```

For it to be possible to use our `SharedModule`, we need to import it into `AppModule` by adding it to the `imports` array of `AppModule`, like so:

```
//app.module.ts

@NgModule({
  imports: [ SharedModule ],
  providers: [ AppService ]
})
export class AppModule{}
```

We know this has the effect of pulling all constructs from the `exports` array in `SharedModule`, but this will also concatenate the providers array from `SharedModule` to that of `AppModule`. Imagine `SharedModule` looking something like this:

```
//shared.module.ts

@NgModule({
  providers : [ SharedService ]
})
export class SharedModule {}
```

After the import has taken place, the combined providers array now contains:

- `AppService`
- `SharedService`

So the rule of thumb here is if you want to expose a service to your application, then put it in the Angular module's `providers` array. If you want to limit access to the service, then place it into a component's `providers` array. Then, you will ensure it can only be reached by that component and its view children.

Up next, let's talk about cases when you want to override the injection.

Overriding an existing construct

There are cases when you want to override the default resolution of your construct. You can do so at the module level, but also at the component level. What you do is simply express which construct you are overriding and with which other construct. It looks like this:

```
@Component({
  providers: [
     { provide: Service, useClass : FakeService }
  ]
})
```

The `provide` is our known construct and `useClass` is what it should point to instead. Let's imagine we implemented our `Service` like so:

```
export class Service {
  no: number = 0;
  constructor() {}
}
```

And we added the following override to a component:

```
@Component({
  providers: [{ provide : Service, useClass: FakeService }]
})
```

The `FakeService` class has the following implementation:

```
export class FakeService {
  set no(value) {
    // do nothing
  }

  get no() {
    return 99;
  }
}
```

Now the component and all its view child components will always get `FakeService` when asking for the Service construct.

Overriding at runtime

There is a way to decide what to inject for/into a construct at runtime. So far, we have been very explicit about when to override, but we can do this with a bit of logic added to it by using the `useFactory` keyword. It works like the following:

```
let factory = () => {
  if(condition) {
    return new FakeService();
  } else {
    return new Service();
  }
}

@Component({
 providers : [
    { provide : Service, useFactory : factory }
 ]
})
```

This factory can in itself have dependencies; we specify those dependencies with the `deps` keyword like so:

```
let factory = (auth:AuthService, logger: Logger) => {
  if(condition) {
    return new FakeService();
  } else {
    return new Service();
  }
}

@Component({
  providers : [
    { provide : Service, useFactory : factory,
      deps: [AuthService, Logger] }
  ]
})
```

Here, we highlighted the `condition` variable, which is a Boolean. There can be a ton of reasons why we would want to be able to switch the implementation. One good case is when the endpoint don't exist yet and we want to ensure it calls our `FakeService` instead. Another reason could be that we are in testing mode and by just changing this one variable we can make all our services rely on a fake version of themselves.

Overriding constants

Not everything, though, is a class that needs to be resolved; sometimes it is a constant. For those cases, instead of using `useClass`, we can use `useValue`, like so:

```
providers: [ { provide: 'a-string-token', useValue: 12345678 } ]
```

This is not really a class type, so you can't write this in a constructor:

```
constructor(a-string-token) . // will not compile
```

That wouldn't compile. What we can do instead is to use the `@Inject` decorator in the following way:

```
constructor( @Inject('a-string-token') token) // token will have value
12345678
```

The `useValue` is no different from `useClass` when it comes to how to override it. The difference is of course that we need to type `useValue` in our instruction to override rather than `useClass`.

Resolving your dependencies with @Injectable

We took a little deep dive into DI in the previous section, but almost forgot about a very important decorator, `@Injectable`. `@Injectable` is not strictly mandatory to use for services in general. However, if that service has dependencies, then it needs to be used. Failure to decorate a service with `@Injectable` that has dependencies leads to an error where the compiler complains that it doesn't know how to construct the mentioned service. Let's look at a case where we need to use the `@Injectable` decorator:

```
import { Injectable } from '@angular/core';

@Injectable()
export class Service {
  constructor(logger:Logger) {}
}
```

In this case, Angular's DI machinery will look up `Logger` and inject it into the `Service` constructor. So, providing we have done this:

```
providers: [Service, Logger]
```

In a component or module, it should work. Remember, when in doubt, add `@Injectable` to your service if it has dependencies in the constructor or will have in the near future. If your service lacks the `@Injectable` keyword and you try to inject it into a component's constructor, then it will throw an error and your component will not be created.

This section set out to explain how DI works from a general standpoint and how it works in Angular. For the latter, it covered how to register constructs to work with Angular's DI machinery, but also how to override it. It is clear that the DI machinery is quite sophisticated. It can be scoped to the application level, by adding constructs to the providers array of Angular modules, but also to the component level and its view children. The main reason for describing the DI machinery was to teach you the possibilities of it, so you know how to best use it to your advantage when you define the architecture of your app.

Fetching and persisting data with HTTP – introducing services with Observables

So far, we have gone through a data flow where the component is our view to the outside world, but also the controller. The component uses a service to get the data, but also to persist it. The data, however, has up until this point lived in the service and that's not a very likely place for it to reside. Almost certainly, that data should be fetched and persisted to an endpoint. That endpoint is an exposed URL to a backend system published somewhere on the internet. We can use HTTP to reach said endpoint. Angular has created a wrapper on top of the vanilla way of fetching data through HTTP. The wrapper is a class that wraps the functionality of an object called `XmlHttpRequest`. The Angular wrapper class is called the `HttpClient` service.

Fetching data with the HTTP service

There is more than one way to communicate over HTTP. One way is using the `XmlHttpRequest` object, but that is a quite cumbersome and low-level way of doing it. Another way is to use the new fetch API, which you can read more about here: `https://developer.mozilla.org/en-US/docs/Web/API/Fetch_API`.

Angular has its own abstraction, the HTTP service, which can be found in the `HTTPModule`. To use it, simply import the `HttpModule`:

```
import { HttpClientModule } from '@angular/common/http';

@NgModule({
  imports: [HttpClientModule]
})
```

Then, inject the `HttpClient` service where you want to use it, like so:

```
import { HttpClient } from '@angular/common/http';

@Component({
  selector: 'consumer',
  template: ``
})
export class ConsumerComponent {
  constructor(private http:HttpClient) {}
}
```

At this point, we are ready to use it. Let's see a quick overview of what methods this HTTP service has:

- `get('url', <optional options param>)` fetches the data for us
- `post('url', payload,<optional options param>)` creates a resource
- `put('url', payload,<optional options param>)` updates a resource
- `delete('url',<optional options param>)` removes a resource
- `request` is a raw request where you can configure exactly what call you want to make, what headers you want to add, and so on

When we use `http.get()` we get a construct back called an Observable. An Observable is just like the `Promise`, an asynchronous concept that enables us to attach callbacks to when the data arrives some time in the future, as well as attaching callbacks to an error when an error occurs. The RxJS implementation of the Observable comes packed with a number of operators that help us transform the data and interact with other Observables. One such operator is called `toPromise()` and enables us to convert an Observable to a Promise. With this, we can make HTTP calls in two different ways, or flavors. The first way is where we use the `toPromise()` operator and convert our `Observable` to a `Promise`, and the other is using our Observable and dealing with the data that way.

A typical call comes in two different flavors:

- **Using promises**

```
// converting an Observable to a Promise using toPromise()
http
  .get('url')
  .toPromise()
  .then(x => x.data)
  .then(data => console.log('our data'))
  .catch(error => console.error('some error happened', error));
```

This version feels familiar. If you need to brush up on Promises, have a look at the following link before continuing: `https://developer.mozilla.org/en-US/docs/Web/JavaScript/Reference/Global_Objects/Promise`. We recognize the `.then()` method as the method that is called when the data arrives and the `.catch()` method that is called when something goes wrong with our request. This is what we expect when, dealing with promises.

- **Using RxJS**

```
// calling http.get() and gets an Observable back
http
  .get('url')
  .map( x => x.data )
  .subscribe( data => console.log('our data', data))
  .catch( error => console.error('some error happened', error))
```

The second version looks different. Here, we are using the `.map()` method in much the same way as we used the `.then()` method. This statement needs some explanation. Let's have a look at the promise flavor code one more time and highlight what we are saying:

```
http
  .get('url')
  .toPromise()
  .then(x => x.data)
  .then(data => console.log('our data'))
  .catch(error => console.error('some error happened', error));
```

The highlighted portion is the method that is called when the data first arrives from the service. What we do inside of this call is to create a projection of the data, like so:

```
.then(x => x.data)
```

The subsequent call to `then()` just deals with printing the data to the console:

```
.then(data => console.log('our data'))
```

Let's now have a look at how the RxJS version differs by highlighting the projection part and the part where we print out our result:

```
http
  .get('url')
  .map( x => x.data )
  .subscribe( data => console.log('our data', data) )
  .catch( error => console.error('some error happened', error) )
```

The first line of our highlighted portion of the code indicates our projection:

```
.map( x => x.data )
```

The call to subscribe is where we print our data, like so:

```
.subscribe( data => console.log('our data', data) )
```

When we use `http.get()`, we get a construct back called an Observable. An Observable is just like the Promise, an asynchronous concept that enables us to attach callbacks to when the data arrives some time in the future, as well as attaching callbacks to when an error happens.

The Observable is part of a library called RxJS and this is what is powering the `HttpClient` service. It is a powerful library meant for more than just a simple request/response pattern. We will spend future chapters exploring the RxJS library further and discover what a powerful paradigm the Observable really is, what other important concepts it brings, and the fact that it isn't really only about working with HTTP anymore, but all async concepts.

Summary

We started this chapter by trying to explain how important it was to get a good foundation in application architecture in general, and for that reason we had a look at the MVC pattern. We then continued describing how the MVC pattern was somewhat used in Angular, even though it was called MVW, model view whatever. We did this to understand that the Angular framework consists of a lot of constructs that help us organize our application in a way that makes it easy to extend, maintain, and parallelize the work.

Angular brought a lot of new things to it though, such as ES2015 modules, which attempted to solve the problem of how to split up the code in a manageable way. After that, we argued that although ES2015 modules were great, there was a lot of ceremony attached to them when it came to creating complex objects. To help relieve us of that ceremony, we described how Angular Dependency Injection could be the solution to said problem. In reality, you will use ES2015 to import your constructs. What Angular DI helps us with is creating the dependencies needed for our constructs.

Lastly, we tied the knot of explaining the MVC pattern by simply stating that data doesn't really live permanently, in either the model, the controller, or the view, but can be retrieved and persisted by talking to an endpoint, reachable through HTTP. We concluded the chapter by describing how the Angular 4.x HTTP service can help us with just that.

All of this is interesting from an educational standpoint. It doesn't describe the elephant in the room, how do we manage our data when things gets complicated? The concerns we have to deal with are:

- Bidirectional data flow
- Lack of predictability (a change can lead to cascading changes)
- Spread out state (there is no one source of truth and our components can sit on a state that is partially updated)

Let's keep these concerns in mind as we move on to Chapter 2, *1.21 Gigawatt – The Flux Pattern Explained*.

2

1.21 Gigawatt – Flux Pattern Explained

Let's first off explain our title. What do we mean by 1.21 Gigawatt? I'm going to quote the character Doc Brown from the movie *Back to the Future* (`http://www.imdb.com/name/nm0000502/?ref_=tt_trv_qu`):

> *"Marty, I'm sorry, but the only power source capable of generating 1.21 gigawatts of electricity is a bolt of lightning."*

Why are we talking about the movie Back to the Future? This is where the name Flux comes from. It's time for another quote from the same movie:

> *"Yes! Of course! November 5, 1955! That was the day I invented time-travel. I remember it vividly. I was standing on the edge of my toilet hanging a clock, the porcelain was wet, I slipped, hit my head on the sink, and when I came to I had a revelation! A vision! A picture in my head! A picture of this! This is what makes time travel possible: the **flux** capacitor!"*

So as you can see, there is an explanation for the name Flux. It obviously allows us to travel in time. At least for Redux, which we will write about later in this book, time travel is possible through something called time-travel debugging. Whether that needs a bolt of lightning is for you to find out dear reader.

Flux is an architectural pattern created by Facebook. It came about as it was perceived that the MVC pattern simply did not scale. It did not scale for large code bases as they tended to become fragile, generally complicated as more and more features were added, and most of all, unpredictable. Now let's hang on that word for a second, unpredictable.

Large systems were thought to become unpredictable due to their bidirectional data flow between models and views when the number of models and views really grew, as depicted in the following diagram:

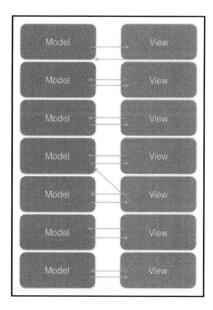

Here, we can see that the number of models and views is starting to grow. Everything is somewhat under control as long as one model talks to one view and vice versa. This is, however, seldom the case. In the preceding diagram, we see that suddenly a view can talk to more than one model and vice versa, which means we have a cascading effect on the system and we suddenly lose control. Sure, it doesn't look so bad with just one deviating arrow, but imagine that this one is suddenly ten arrows, then we have a real problem on our hands.

It is the very fact that we allow bidrectional data flows to happen that things get complicated and we lose predictability. The medicine or cure for that is thought to be a simpler type of data flow, a unidirectional flow. Now, there are some key players involved in enabling undirectional data flow, which brings us to what this chapter is meant to teach us.

In this chapter, we will learn:

- What an action and an action creator are
- How the dispatcher plays a central role in your application as a hub for messages
- State management with a store

- How to put our knowledge of Flux into practice by coding up a Flux application flow

Core concepts overview

At the core of the Flux pattern is a unidirectional data flow. It uses some core concepts to achieve this flow. The main idea is when an event is created on a UI, through the interaction of a user, an action is created. This action consists of an intent and a payload. The intent is what your are trying to achieve. Think of the intent as a verb. Add an item, remove an item, and so on. The payload is the data change that needs to happen to achieve our intent. If we are trying to add an item, then the payload is the newly created item. The action is then propagated in the flow with the help of a dispatcher. The action and its data eventually end up in a store.

The concepts that make up the Flux pattern are:

- Action and action creators, where we set up an intention and a payload of data
- The dispatcher, our spider in the web that is able to send messages left and right
- The store, our central place for state and state management

All these together form the Flux pattern and promote unidirectional data flow. Consider the following diagram:

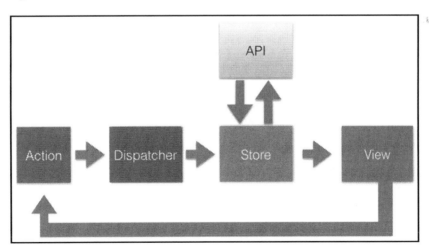

What is depicted here is a undirectional data flow. The data flows from **View** to **Action**, from **Action** to **Dispatcher**, from **Dispatcher** to **Store**. There are two possible ways that the flow is triggered:

- The application is loaded a first time, in which the data is pulled from the **Store** to populate the view.
- A user interaction happens in the view that leads to an intent to change something. The intent is encapsulated in an **Action**, and thereafter sent to the **Store**, via the **Dispatcher**. At the **Store**, it may be persisted in a database, through an **API** or saved as an application state, or both.

Let's dive into each concept in more detail, together with highlighting some code examples, in the upcoming sections.

A uniform data flow

Let's introduce all parties involved in our uniform data flow by starting from the very top and slowly work our way down, concept by concept. We will build an application consisting of two views. In the first view, the user will select an item from a list. This should result in an action being created. This action will then be dispatched, by the dispatcher. The action and its payload will end up in a store. The other view meanwhile listens to changes from the store. When an item is selected, the second view will be made aware and can therefore indicate in its UI that a specific item has been selected. On a high level, our application and its flow will look like the following:

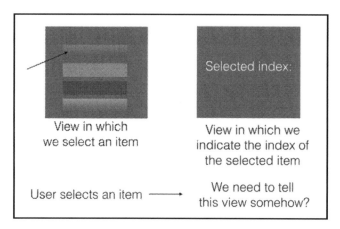

Action – capture the intent

An action is something as simple as an intent with accompanying data, that is, a message. How does an action come about though? An action comes about when a user interacts with a UI. The user may select a specific item in a list or a press a button with the intention of submitting a form. Submitting the form should, in turn, lead to a product being created.

Let's look at two different actions:

- Selecting an item in a list, here we are interested in saving the index of our selected item
- Saving a todo to a todo list

An action is represented by an object. The object has two properties of interest:

- The type: This is a unique string that tells us the intention of the action, for example, SELECT_ITEM
- The data: This is the data we mean to persist, for example, the numerical index of a selected item

Given our first example action, a code representation of that action would look like the following:

```
{
    type: 'SELECT_ITEM',
    data: 3 // selected index
}
```

OK, so we have prepared our action, which we can also think of as a message. We want the message to be sent so that the selected item is highlighted in the UI. As this is a undirectional flow, we need to follow a charted course and pass our message over to the next party, which is the dispatcher.

Dispatcher – the spider in the web

Think of the dispatcher as the spider in the web that handles messages being passed to it. You can also think of the dispatcher as a mailman who promises that your message will reach its target destination. A dispatcher lives, for one thing, to dispatch messages to anyone who will listen. There is usually just one dispatcher in a Flux architecture and a typical usage looks something like this:

```
dispatcher.dispatch(message);
```

Listening to the dispatcher

We have established that the dispatcher dispatches a message to anyone who will listen. Now it is time to be that listener. The dispatcher needs a `register` or `subscribe` method so that you, who listens, have the ability to listen for incoming messages. The setup for that usually looks something like this:

```
dispatcher.register(function(message){});
```

Now, when you set up a listener this way, it will have the capability to listen to any message type being sent. You want to narrow this down; usually, a listener is specified to only handle a few message types around a certain theme. Your listener most likely looks something like this:

```
dispatcher.register((message) => {
  switch(message.type) {
    case 'SELECT_ITEM':
      // do something
  }
});
```

OK, so we are able to filter out only the message types we care about, but before actually filling in some code we need to think about who this listener is. The answer is simple: it is the store.

The store – managing state, data retrieval, and callbacks

It's easy to think of the store as the place where our data lives. That is, however, not all it is. What the store's responsibilities are can be expressed by this list:

- Holder of state
- Manages the state, able to update it if need be
- Able to handle side effects such as fetching/persisting data through HTTP
- Handles callbacks

As you can see, that is a bit more than just storing the state. Let's now reconnect to what we were doing when we set up a listener with the `dispatcher`. Let's move that code into our store file, `store.js`, and let's persist our message content in our store:

```
// store.js
```

```
let store = {};

function selectIndex(index) {
  store["selectedIndex"] = index;
}

dispatcher.register(message => {
  switch (message.type) {
    case "SELECT_INDEX":
      selectIndex(message.data);
      break;
  }
});
```

OK, so now the store is being told about the new index, but an important piece is missing, how do we tell the UI? We need a way to tell the UI that something has changed. A change means that the UI should reread its data.

The view

To tell the view that something has happened and act on it, three things need to happen:

- The view needs to register with the store as a listener
- The store needs to send off an event conveying that a change has happened
- The view needs to reload its data

Starting with the store, we need to build it out so that you can register as a listener to its events. We therefore add the addListener() method:

```
// store-with-pubsub.js

function selectIndex(index) {
  store["selectedIndex"] = index;
}

// registering with the dispatcher
dispatcher.register(message => {
  switch (message.type) {
    case "SELECT_INDEX":
      selectIndex(message.data);
      // signals to the listener that a change has happened
      store.emitChange();
      break;
  }
```

```
    });

class Store {
  constructor() {
    this.listeners = [];
  }

  addListener(listener) {
    if (!this.listeners["change"]) {
      this.listeners["change"] = [];
    }
    this.listeners["change"].push(listener);
  }

  emitChange() {
    if (this.listeners["change"]) {
      this.listeners["change"].forEach(cb => cb());
    }
  }

  getSelectedItem() {
    return store["selectedIndex"];
  }
}

const store = new Store();
export default store;
```

In the preceding code, we also add the ability to emit an event with the addition of the `emitChange()` method. You can easily switch out this implementation to use an `EventEmitter` or similar. So now is the time to hook up our view to the store. We do so by calling the `addListener()` method like so:

```
// view.js

import store from "./store-with-pubsub";

class View {
  constructor(store) {
    this.index = 0;
    store.addListener(this.notifyChanged);
  }

  // invoked from the store
  notifyChanged() {
    // rereads data from the store
    this.index = store.getSelectedItem();
```

```
  // reloading the data
  render();
 }
 render() {
   const elem = document.getElementById('view');
   elem.innerHTML = `Your selected index is: ${this.index}`;
 }
}

let view = new View();

// view.html
<html>
  <body>
    <div id="view"></div>
  </body>
</html>
```

In the preceding code, we implement the `notifyChanged()` method, which when called invokes the `getSelectedItem()` method from the store and thereby receives the new value.

At this point, we have described the whole chain: how one view receives a user interaction, turns that into an action, which is then dispatched to a store, which updates the store's state. The store then emits an event that the other view is listening to. When the event is received, in the view the state from the store is reread and the view is then free to render this state, which it just read in, the way it sees fit.

We have described two things here:

- How to set up the flow
- How the information flows in Flux

Setting up the flow can be depicted with the following diagram:

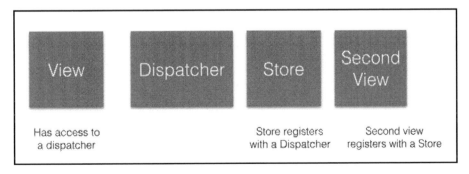

As for the second scenario, how the information flows through the system, it can be depicted in the following way:

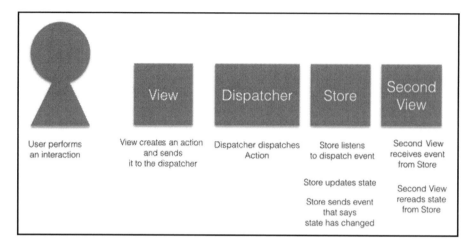

Demoing a uniform data flow

Ok, so we have described the parts our application consists of:

- A view where a user is able to select an index
- A dispatcher that allows us to send a message
- A store that contains our selected index
- A second view where the selected index is read from the store

Let's build a real app from all of this. The following code is found in the code repository under `Chapter2/demo`.

Creating a selection view

First off we need our view in which we will perform the selection:

```
// demo/selectionView.js

import dispatcher from "./dispatcher";

console.log('selection view loaded');
```

```
class SelectionView {
  selectIndex(index) {
    console.log('selected index ', index);
    dispatcher.dispatch({
      type: "SELECT_INDEX",
      data: index
    });
  }
}

const view = new SelectionView();
export default view;
```

We have bolded the `selectIndex()` method above that we intend to use.

Adding the dispatcher

Next off we need a dispatcher that is able to take our message, like so:

```
// demo/dispatcher.js

class Dispatcher {
  constructor() {
    this.listeners = [];
  }

  dispatch(message) {
    this.listeners.forEach(listener => listener(message));
  }

  register(listener) {
    this.listeners.push(listener);
  }
}

const dispatcher = new Dispatcher();
export default dispatcher;
```

Adding the store

The store will act as the data source for our state but will also be able tell any listeners when a change to the store happens:

```
// demo/store.js

import dispatcher from './dispatcher';

function selectIndex(index) {
  store["selectedIndex"] = index;
}

// 1) store registers with dispatcher
dispatcher.register(message => {
  switch (message.type) {
    // 3) message is sent by dispatcher ( that originated from the first
view)
    case "SELECT_INDEX":
      selectIndex(message.data);
      // 4) listener, a view, is being notified of the change
      store.emitChange();
      break;
  }
});

class Store {
  constructor() {
    this.listeners = [];
  }

  // 2) listener is added by a view
  addListener(listener) {
    if (!this.listeners["change"]) {
      this.listeners["change"] = [];
    }

    this.listeners["change"].push(listener);
  }

  emitChange() {
    if (this.listeners["change"]) {
      this.listeners["change"].forEach(cb => cb());
    }
  }

  getSelectedItem() {
```

```
        return store["selectedIndex"];
    }
}

const store = new Store();
export default store;
```

Adding a selected view

This view will register itself with the store and ask for updates to its content. If there are any updates it will be notified and the data from the store will be read and this view will communicate what the store value now is:

```
// demo/selectedView.js

import store from "./store";

console.log('selected view loaded');

class SelectedView {
  constructor() {
    this.index = 0;
    store.addListener(this.notifyChanged.bind(this));
  }

  notifyChanged() {
    this.index = store.getSelectedItem();
    console.log('new index is ', this.index);
  }
}

const view = new SelectedView();
export default SelectedView;
```

Running the demo

Before we can run our demo we need an application file, app.js. The app.js file should require in our views and also carry out the selection:

```
// demo/app.js

import selectionView from './selectionView';
import selectedView from './selectedView';
```

```
// carry out the selection
selectionView.selectIndex(1);
```

To run our demo we need to compile it. Above we are using ES2015 modules. To compile those we will use webpack. We need to install webpack by typing the following in our terminal:

npm install webpack webpack-cli --save-dev

Once we have done so we need to create webpack.config.js file where we tell Webpack how to compile our files and where to place the resulting bundle. That file looks like the following:

```
// webpack.config.js

module.exports = {
  entry: "./app.js",
  output: {
    filename: "bundle.js"
  },
  watch: false
};
```

This tells Webpack that app.js is the entry point to our application and it should crawl all the dependencies when creating the output file, bundle.js. Webpack will by default place bundle.js in the dist directory.

One more thing, we need an HTML file that we will name index.html. We will place under the dist folder. It should look like this:

```
// demo/dist/index.html

<html>
  <body>
    <script src="bundle.js"></script>
  </body>
</html>
```

Finally, to run our application, we need to compile it with Webpack and start a HTTP server and start up a browser. We will do all that with the following command from the demo directory:

webpack && cd dist && http-server -p 5000

Now, start a browser and navigate to `http://localhost:5000`. You should see the following:

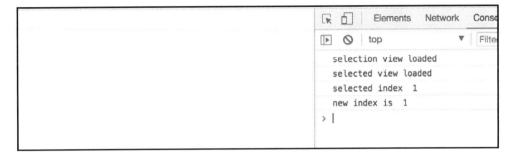

All of this demonstrates how to views can be made to communicate using a dispatcher and a store.

Adding more actions to our flow

Let's do a reality check here. We haven't built the Flux flow as prettily as we could make it. The overall picture is correct but it'd be nice if we can clean it up a bit to make room for more actions so we get a real sense of how the application should grow from here.

Cleaning up the view

The first order of business is to have a look at our first view and how it reacts to user interactions. It looks like this currently:

```
// first.view.js

import dispatcher from "./dispatcher";

class FirstView {
  selectIndex(index) {
    dispatcher.dispatch({
      type: "SELECT_INDEX",
      data: index
    });
  }
}

let view = new FirstView();
```

Adding a few more actions into the mix means we would extend the view with a few methods like this:

```
// first.viewII.js

import dispatcher from "./dispatcher";

class View {
  selectIndex(data) {
    dispatcher.dispatch({
      type: "SELECT_INDEX",
      data
    });
  }

  createProduct(data) {
    dispatcher.dispatch({
      type: "CREATE_PRODUCT",
      data
    });
  }

  removeProduct(data) {
    dispatcher.dispatch({
      type: "REMOVE_PRODUCT",
      data
    });
  }
}

let view = new View();
```

OK, so now we get how we can add actions. It looks a little ugly though with all these calls to the `dispatcher` and magic strings, so we clean this up a bit by creating a file with constants, called `product.constants.js`, which consists of the following code:

```
// product.constants.js

export const SELECT_INDEX = "SELECT_INDEX",
export const CREATE_PRODUCT = "CREATE_PRODUCT",
export const REMOVE_PRODUCT = "REMOVE_PRODUCT"
```

Let's do one more thing. Let's move the `dispatcher` into a `product.actions.js`; this is generally known as an action creator. This will contain the `dispatcher` and refer to our `product.constants.js` file. So let's create said file:

```
// product.actions.js

import {
  SELECT_INDEX,
  CREATE_PRODUCT,
  REMOVE_PRODUCT
} from "./product-constants";
import dispatcher from "./dispatcher";
import ProductConstants from "./product.constants";

export const selectIndex = data =>
  dispatcher.dispatch({
    type: SELECT_INDEX,
    data
  });

export const createProduct = data =>
  dispatcher.dispatch({
    type: CREATE_PRODUCT,
    data
  });

export const removeProduct = data =>
  dispatcher.dispatch({
    type: REMOVE_PRODUCT,
    data
  });
```

With these constructs, we can clean up our view considerably to look like this:

```
// first.viewIII.js

import {
  selectIndex,
  createProduct,
  removeProduct
} from 'product.actions';

function View() {
  this.selectIndex = index => {
    selectIndex(index);
  };
```

```
  this.createProduct = product => {
    createProduct(product);
  };

  this.removeProduct = product => {
    removeProduct(product)
  };
}

var view = new View();
```

Cleaning up the store

There are improvements we can make to on the store. There is no need to write all the code we do currently. In fact, there are libraries out there that do a better job of handling certain functionality.

Before we apply all those changes we have in mind, let's recap what our store can do and what features still need to be in place after the cleanup work.

Let's remind ourselves, what our store is capable of so far:

- Handles state changes: It handles the state changes; the store is able to change the state regardless of whether it is creating, updating, listing, or removing state.
- Subscribable: It lets you subscribe to it; it's important for the store to have a subscription functionality so a view, for example, can listen to the store's state when it changes. A suitable reaction by the view is, for example, rerendering based on new data.
- Can communicate a state change: It can send an event that its state has been changed; this goes together with being able to subscribe to the store, but this is the very act of actually notifying a listener that a state has changed.

Adding EventEmitter

The two last bullets can really be condensed into one theme, namely eventing, or the ability to register to and fire off events.

So what does a cleanup of the store look like, and why would we need to clean it up? The reason for cleaning it up is it makes for simpler code. There is a standard library that is often used when constructing a store, called `EventEmitter`. The library handles just what we mentioned previously, namely it is able to register and fire off events. It is a simple implementation of the pub-sub pattern. Basically, `EventEmitter` allows you to subscribe to certain events and also allows you to trigger events. For more information on the pattern itself, have a look at the following link: `https://en.wikipedia.org/wiki/Publish%E2%80%93subscribe_pattern`.

You could definitely write your own code for this, but it's nice to be able to use a dedicated library so you can focus on other things that matter, such as solving business problems.

We decided to use the `EventEmitter` library and we do so in the following way:

```
// store-event-emitter.js

export const Store = (() => {
  const eventEmitter = new EventEmitter();
  return {
    addListener: listener => {
      eventEmitter.on("changed", listener);
    },
    emitChange: () => {
      eventEmitter.emit("changed");
    },
    getSelectedItem: () => store["selectedItem"]
  };
})();
```

This makes our code a little cleaner because we no longer need to hold an internal list of subscribers. There are more changes we can make though, so let us talk about that in the next section.

Adding to and cleaning up the register method

One of the store's jobs has been to handle eventing, especially when the store wants to convey to a view that a change has happened to its state. In the `store.js` file, other things were happening as well, things like registering ourselves with the `dispatcher` and being able to receive dispatched actions. We used these actions to alter the state of the store. Let's remind ourselves what that looked like:

```
// store.js

let store = {};
```

```
function selectIndex(index) {
  store["selectedIndex"] = index;
}

dispatcher.register(message => {
  switch (message.type) {
    case "SELECT_INDEX":
      selectIndex(message.data);
      break;
  }
});
```

Here, we are only supporting one action, namely SELECT_INDEX. There are two things we need to do here:

- Add the other two actions, CREATE_PRODUCT and REMOVE_PRODUCT, and the accompanying functions createProduct() and removeProduct()
- Stop using magic strings and start using our constants file
- Use the store we created in the store-event-emitter.js file

Let's implement the suggested changes from our preceding list:

```
// store-actions.js

import dispatcher from "./dispatcher";
import {
  SELECT_INDEX,
  CREATE_PRODUCT,
  REMOVE_PRODUCT
} from "./product.constants";

let store = {};

function selectIndex(index) {
  store["selectedIndex"] = index;
}

export const Store = (() => {
  var eventEmitter = new EventEmitter();
  return {
    addListener: listener => {
      eventEmitter.on("changed", listener);
    },
    emitChange: () => {
      eventEmitter.emit("changed");
    },
```

```
      getSelectedItem: () => store["selectedItem"]
  };
})();

dispatcher.register(message => {
  switch (message.type) {
    case "SELECT_INDEX":
      selectIndex(message.data);
      break;
  }
});

const createProduct = product => {
  if (!store["products"]) {
    store["products"] = [];
  }
  store["products"].push(product);
};

const removeProduct = product => {
  var index = store["products"].indexOf(product);
  if (index !== -1) {
    store["products"].splice(index, 1);
  }
};

dispatcher.register(({ type, data }) => {
  switch (type) {
    case SELECT_INDEX:
      selectIndex(data);
      break;
    case CREATE_PRODUCT:
      createProduct(data);
      break;
    case REMOVE_PRODUCT:
      removeProduct(data);
  }
});
```

Further improvements

There are definitely more improvements we can make to this code. We did use ES2015 imports to import other files, but most of our code was written in ES5 so why not use most of what ES2015 gives us? Another improvement we can make is introducing immutability and making sure our store is not mutated but transitions from one state to another.

Let's have a look at the store file, primarily because that is where we can add the most ES2015 syntax. Our revealing module pattern looks like this currently:

```
// store-event-emitter.js

var Store = (function(){
  const eventEmitter = new EventEmitter();

  return {
    addListener: listener => {
      eventEmitter.on("changed", listener);
    },
    emitChange: () => {
      eventEmitter.emit("changed");
    },
    getSelectedItem: () => store["selectedItem"]
  };
})();
```

It can be replaced with a simple class and instead of instantiating an `EventEmitter`, we can inherit from it. In all fairness, we could have used ES2015 inheritance or the merge library to not have to create a separate `EventEmitter` instance, but this shows how elegant ES2015 can make things:

```
// store-es2015.js

import { EventEmitter } from "events";
import {
SELECT_INDEX,
CREATE_PRODUCT,
REMOVE_PRODUCT
} from "./product.constants";

let store = {};

class Store extends EventEmitter {
  constructor() {}
    addListener(listener) {
    this.on("changed", listener);
```

```
  }

  emitChange() {
    this.emit("changed");
  }

  getSelectedItem() {
    return store["selectedItem"];
  }
}

const storeInstance = new Store();

function createProduct(product) {
  if (!store["products"]) {
    store["products"] = [];
  }
  store["products"].push(product);
}

function removeProduct(product) {
  var index = store["products"].indexOf(product);
  if (index !== -1) {
    store["products"].splice(index, 1);
  }
}

dispatcher.register(({ type, data }) => {
  switch (type) {
    case SELECT_INDEX:
      selectIndex(data);
      storeInstance.emitChange();
      break;
    case CREATE_PRODUCT:
      createProduct(data);
      storeInstance.emitChange();
      break;
    case REMOVE_PRODUCT:
      removeProduct(data);
      storeInstance.emitChange();
  }
});
```

Adding immutability

The other thing we can undertake is adding immutability. The reasons for using immutability in the first place are to make your code more predictable, and some frameworks can use this for simpler change detection and can rely on reference checking over dirty checking. This was the case when AngularJS got its whole change detection mechanism changed when Angular was written. From a practical standpoint, this means that there are functions we can target in our store and apply immutable principles on. The first principle is to not mutate but create an entirely new state, instead of where the new state is *the old state + the state change*. A simple example of this is the following:

```
var oldState = 3;
var newState = oldState + 2
```

Here, we are creating a new variable, newState, rather than mutating our oldState variable. There are functions that will help us with this, called Object.assign and the function filter. We can use these for updating scenarios, as well as adding or removing things from a list. Let us use these and rewrite part of our store code. Let's highlight the code we mean to change:

```
// excerpt from store-actions.js

const createProduct = product => {
  if (!store["products"]){
    store["products"] = [];
  }
  store["products"].push(product);
};

const removeProduct = product => {
  var index = store["products"].indexOf(product);
  if (index !== -1) {
    store["products"].splice(index, 1);
  }
};
```

Let's apply Object.assign and filter(), and remember to not mutate things. The end result should look like this:

```
// excerpt from our new store-actions-immutable.js

const createProduct = product => {
  if (!store["products"]) {
    store["products"] = [];
  }
  store.products = [...store.products, Object.assign(product)];
```

```
};

const removeProduct = product => {
  if (!store["products"]) return;

  store["products"] = products.filter(p => p.id !== product.id);
};
```

We can see that the `createProduct()` method uses an ES2015 construct, namely the spread parameter, `...`, which takes a list and turns its members into a comma-separated list of items. `Object.assign()` is used to copy over all the values from an object so we store the value of an object rather than its reference. The `removeProduct()` method becomes very simple when we use the filter method. We simply create a projection that does not include the product that we should remove; removing has never been this easy or elegant. We haven't mutated anything.

Summarizing

Our cleanup started with the view; we wanted to remove a direct connection to the dispatcher and also stop having to use magic strings as this is quite error prone, and it's easy to misspell. Instead, we can rely on constants. To remedy this, we created an action creator class that talked to the dispatcher instead.

We also created a constants module to remove the magic strings.

Furthermore, we improved the store by starting to use `EventEmitter`. Finally, we further improved the store by adding more actions to it and also started to refer to the constants.

At this point, our solution is ready for more actions to be added to it and we should feel pretty clear on what files we need to add to, as we support more and more user interactions.

Lastly, we added improvements around ES2015 and immutability, which made our code look a lot cleaner. With this foundation, we are now ready to go from static data to involve working with side effects and Ajax in the upcoming section.

Let us summarize all our improvements in a diagram showing the constructs added to our flow:

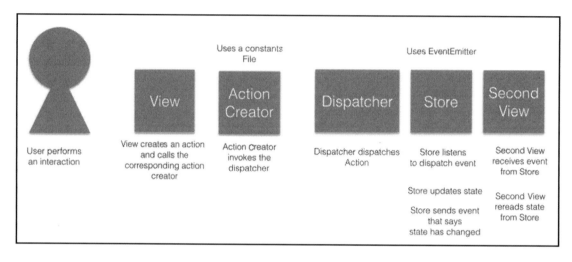

It is clear that using an action creator isn't strictly necessary but it does clean up the code quite a bit, and the same goes for using an `EventEmitter` in the store; it's nice but not necessary.

Adding AJAX calls

So far, we have only been dealing with static data in our Flux flow. The time has now come to add real data connections to the flow and thereby real data. It is time to start talking to APIs through AJAX and HTTP. Fetching data is quite easy nowadays, thanks to the fetch API and libraries such as RxJS. What you need to think about when incorporating it in the flow is:

- Where to place the HTTP call
- How to ensure that the store is updated and interested views are notified

We have a point at which we register the store to the `dispatcher`, with this piece of code:

```
// excerpt from store-actions-immutable.js

const createProduct = (product) => {
  if (!store["products"]) {
    store["products"] = [];
  }
```

```
      store.products = [...store.products, Object.assign(product)];
}

dispatcher.register(({ type, data }) => {
  switch (type) {
    case CREATE_PRODUCT:
      createProduct(data);
      store.emitChange();
      break;
      /* other cases below */
  }
})
```

If we do this for real, that is, call an API to persist this product, `createProduct()` would be where we would do the API call, like so:

```
// example use of fetch()

fetch(
  '/products' ,
  { method : 'POST', body: product })
  .then(response => {
    // send a message to the dispatcher that the list of products should be
reread
}, err => {
  // report error
});
```

Calling `fetch()` returns a `Promise`. Let's use async/await however, as it makes the call much more readable. The difference in code can be seen in the following example:

```
// contrasting example of 'fetch() with promise' vs 'fetch with
async/await'

fetch('url')
  .then(data => console.log(data))
  .catch(error => console.error(error));

  // using async/await
  try {
    const data = await fetch('url');
    console.log(data);
  } catch (error) {
    console.error(error);
  }
```

Replacing what happens in `createProduct()` with this adds code with a lot of noise so it is a good idea to wrap your HTTP interactions in an API construct like so:

```
// api.js

export class Api {
  createProduct(product) {
    return fetch("/products", { method: "POST", body: product });
  }
}
```

Now let us replace the `createProduct()` method content with the call to our API construct like so:

```
// excerpt from store-actions-api.js

import { Api } from "./api";

const api = new Api();

createProduct() {
  api.createProduct();
}
```

That's not really enough though. Because we created a product through an API call, we should dispatch an action that forces the product list to be reread. We don't have such an action or supporting method in a store to handle it, so let's add one:

```
// product.constants.js

export const SELECT_INDEX = "SELECT_INDEX";
export const CREATE_PRODUCT = "CREATE_PRODUCT";
export const REMOVE_PRODUCT = "REMOVE_PRODUCT";
export const GET_PRODUCTS = "GET_PRODUCTS";
```

Now let's add the required method in the store and the case to handle it:

```
// excerpt from store-actions-api.js

import { Api } from "./api";
import {
  // other actions per usual
  GET_PRODUCTS,
} from "./product.constants";

const setProducts = (products) => {
  store["products"] = products;
```

```
}

const setError = (error) => {
  store["error"] = error;
}

dispatcher.register( async ({ type, data }) => {
  switch (type) {
    case CREATE_PRODUCT:
      try {
        await api.createProduct(data);
        dispatcher.dispatch(getProducts());
      } catch (error) {
        setError(error);
        storeInstance.emitError();
      }
      break;
    case GET_PRODUCTS:
      try {
        const products = await api.getProducts();
        setProducts(products);
        storeInstance.emitChange();
      }
      catch (error) {
        setError(error);
        storeInstance.emitError();
      }
      break;
  }
});
```

We can see that the CREATE_PRODUCT case will call the corresponding API method createProduct(), which on completion will dispatch the GET_PRODUCTS action. The reason for doing so is that when we successfully manage to create a product, we need to read from the endpoint to get an updated version of the products list. We don't see that in detail, but it is being invoked through us calling getProducts(). Again, it is nice to have a wrapper on everything being dispatched, that wrapper being an action creator.

The full file looks like this:

```
// store-actions-api.js

import dispatcher from "./dispatcher";
import { Action } from "./api";
import { Api } from "./api";
import {
  CREATE_PRODUCT,
  GET_PRODUCTS,
  REMOVE_PRODUCT,
  SELECT_INDEX
} from "./product.constants";

let store = {};

class Store extends EventEmitter {
  constructor() {}
  addListener(listener) {
    this.on("changed", listener);
  }

  emitChange() {
    this.emit("changed");
  }

  emitError() {
    this.emit("error");
  }

  getSelectedItem() {
    return store["selectedItem"];
  }
}

const api = new Api();
const storeInstance = new Store();

const selectIndex = index => {
  store["selectedIndex"] = index;
};

const createProduct = product => {
  if (!store["products"]) {
    store["products"] = [];
  }
  store.products = [...store.products, Object.assign(product)];
};
```

```
const removeProduct = product => {
  if (!store["products"]) return;
  store["products"] = products.filter(p => p.id !== product.id);
};

const setProducts = products => {
  store["products"] = products;
};

const setError = error => {
  store["error"] = error;
};

dispatcher.register(async ({ type, data }) => {
  switch (type) {
    case "SELECT_INDEX":
      selectIndex(message.data);
      storeInstance.emitChange();
      break;
    case CREATE_PRODUCT:
      try {
        await api.createProduct(data);
        storeInstance.emitChange();
      } catch (error) {
        setError(error);
        storeInstance.emitError();
      }
      break;
    case GET_PRODUCTS:
      try {
        const products = await api.getProducts();
        setProducts(products);
        storeInstance.emitChange();
      } catch (error) {
        setError(error);
        storeInstance.emitError();
      }
      break;
  }
});
```

An even bigger solution

So far, we have been describing a solution that consists of only a product's topic and communication has only taken place from one view to another. In a more realistic application, we would have a lot of topics such as user management, orders, and so on; exactly what they are called is dependent on the domain of your application. As for views, it is quite possible that you will have a ton of views listening to another view, as in this example:

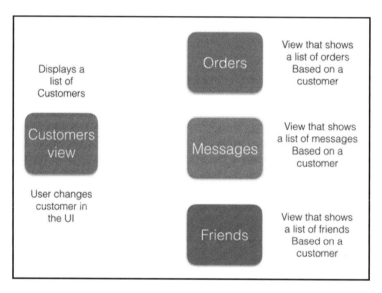

This describes an application that contains four different view components around their own topic. The **Customers view** contains a list of customers and it allows us to alter which customer we currently want to focus on. The other three supporting views show **Orders**, **Messages**, and **Friends** and their content depends on which customer is currently highlighted. From a Flux standpoint, the **Orders**, **Messages**, and **Friends** views can easily register with the store to know when things gets updated so they can fetch/refetch the data they need. However, imagine that the supporting views themselves want to support CRUD actions; then they would need their own set of constants, action creator, API, and store. So now your application would need to look something like this:

```
/customers
  constants.js
  customer-actions.js
  customer-store.js
  customer-api.js
/orders
```

```
    constants.js
    orders-actions.js
    orders-store.js
    orders-api.js
/messages
    constants.js
    messages-actions.js
    messages-store.js
    messages-api.js
/friends
    constants.js
    friends-actions.js
    friends-store.js
    friends-api.js
/common
    dispatcher.js
```

Two interesting situations exist here:

- You have a self-contained view; all CRUD actions happen within it
- You have a view that needs to listen to other views

For the first situation, a good rule of thumb is to create its own set of constants, action creator, API, and store.

For the second situation, ensure your view registers itself with the store of that topic. For example, if the friends view needs to listen to the customer view, then it needs to register itself with the customer store.

Summary

We set out trying only to explain the Flux architecture pattern. It would have been very easy to start mentioning how it fits with React and how there are nice libraries and tools that support Flux and React. That would, however, have taken our focus away from explaining the pattern from a more framework-agnostic viewpoint. Therefore, the rest of this chapter set out to explain core concepts such as actions, action creator, dispatcher, store, and uniform data flow. Little by little, we improved the code to start using constants, action creators, and a nice supporting library such as EventEmitter. We explained how HTTP fits into this and, lastly, we discussed how we could build out our application. There is a lot more that can be said about Flux, but we chose to limit the scope to understanding the fundamentals so we can compare its approach as we dive into Redux and NgRx in later chapters, which is the main focus of this book.

3
Asynchronous Programming

To learn what asynchronous code is, let's first cover what synchronous code is. With synchronous code, you have one statement being executed after another. The code is predictable; you know what happens and when. This is because you can read the code from top to bottom like this:

```
print('a')
print('b')
print('c')

// output
a, b, c
```

Now, with asynchronous code you lose all the nice predictability that the synchronous code offers. In fact, there is very little you know about asynchronous code other than that it finishes executing, eventually. So asynchronous, or async, code looks more like this:

```
asyncPrint('a')
asyncPrint('b')
asyncPrint('c')

// output
c, b, a
```

As you can see, the order in which a statement finishes is not determined by when a statement occurs in the code. Instead, there is a time element involved that decides when a statement has run its course.

Asynchronous code runs in an event loop. This means that async code runs in the following order:

1. Run async code
2. Wait for the response to be ready, then fire an interrupt
3. Run the event handler

An important thing to stress here is that async code is non-blocking—other operations can take place while async code is running. Therefore, async code is a good candidate to be used when dealing with I/O, long-running tasks, and network requests.

In this chapter, we will:

- Learn what asynchronous programming is and how it differs from synchronous programming
- Explain the callback model
- Describe promises and how they completely reformed how we write asynchronous code
- Look at which other asynchronous libraries exist and in what cases they should be used
- Discover the new standard async/await

The callback pattern

Previously, we described what asynchronous and synchronous code looks like when you encounter it in your everyday life as a developer. What might be of interest is to know how an operating system looks at such code and how it deals with it. An operating system deals with asynchronous code by thinking of it in terms of the following concepts:

- Events, these are messages that signals to the operating system that a certain type of action has occurred
- Event handler, this is the piece of code that should run when an event has occurred
- Event queue, this is where all events and their event handlers are placed, waiting to be executed

Let's illustrate this flow in the following diagram:

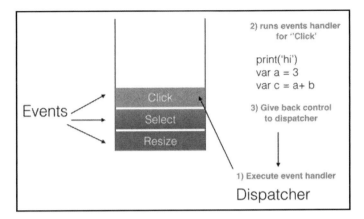

What we can see in the preceding image is how events are being picked from an event queue. Here, the **CLICK** event is being run when a Dispatcher tells it to and its corresponding event handler is executed. The event handler runs the associated lines of code in the event handler and when that's done, gives control back to the Dispatcher. Thereafter, the cycle begins anew for the next event in the queue. This is what it usually looks like in a single-threaded system, where only one event handler is executed at a time. There is also such a thing as a multithreaded system. In a multithreaded system, multiple threads exist. This means we might have several event handlers being executed at once. But even though there are multiple threads, there is only one active thread. The system itself is still single-threaded. Confused? Here is the thing: threads in a multithreaded system are cooperative, which means they can be interrupted. This means that the active thread is changed after a unit of work has been carried out. This creates an effect where it seems like everything happens in parallel. Let's illustrate this for clarity:

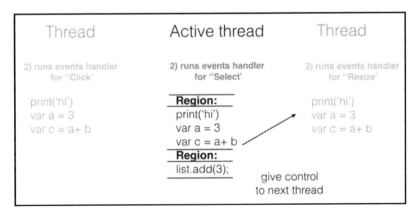

Here, we can see that a piece of code is divided into different regions. When a certain region has been executed, it gives control to the next **Thread**, which becomes the new **Active thread**. Once that thread has executed code through one of its regions, it gives control to the next thread. With the arrival of multiple CPUs, we are able to go from perceived parallelism (described previously) to actual parallel execution. In such a reality, one thread per CPU exists and we therefore have multiple active threads.

These are the different ways you can execute asynchronous code. We will focus on single-threaded execution, as this is how it is implemented in JavaScript and on the web.

The callback pattern on the web

The way to go about it is to attach functions to future events. When the event occurs, our attached function gets executed. An example of this is XMLHttpRequest, which looks like this:

```
const xhr = new XMLHttpRequest();
xhr.open('GET','/path', true);
xhr.onload = () => {
  // run me when the request is finished
}

xhr.send(null);
```

What we can see here is that all lines are executed synchronously except for xhr.onload. Attaching the function to onload happens synchronously, but running the function that onload is pointing to doesn't happen until the request finishes. We can also define other events, such as onreadystatechange, and attach a function to that as well:

```
xhr.onreadystatechange = () => {}
```

As the web is single-threaded, this is how we deal with asynchronous code. The onreadystatechange object and its callback are registered with the operating system. Once the asynchronous part has been completed the operating system is woken up by an event being dispatched. Thereafter, the callback is invoked.

The callback pattern in Node.js

Node.js is single-threaded, just like the web. To handle long running operations it also uses a callback pattern. The callback pattern in Node.js has a a few more details to it and can be described as having the following properties:

- There is only one function to handle success and error responses
- The callback is called only once
- The function is the last parameter of the calling function
- The callback consists of the parameter's errors and results, in that order, which is also called error-first

Let's now showcase what the calling code looks like, with a callback supplied as the function's last argument:

```
callAsync('1',2, (error, response) => {
  if(error) {
    console.error(error);
  } else {
    console.log('response', response);
    // do something with the response
  }
})
```

This piece of code fulfills all the properties laid out by the pattern, namely that the last parameter in the function call is the callback function. Furthermore, the callback function has the error as the first parameter and the response as the second parameter. In addition, the body of the callback function checks whether there is an error first and then, in the absence of an error, deals with the response we get back.

For reference, let's also look at how `callAsync()` is implemented:

```
function callAsync(param, param2, fn) {
  setTimeout(() => {
   if(param > param2) {
     fn(null, 'success');
   } else {
     fn('error', null);
   }
  }
}
```

The preceding implementation is just a mockup but it does show off two important aspects. One aspect is the time factor the `setTimeout()` function represents and the fact that the function takes time to complete.

The other aspect is our third parameter, `fn()` which is invoked differently. We call `fn(null, 'success')` when everything is alright and `fn('error', null)` when an error has occurred. The way we invoke `fn()` is how we communicate success and failure.

Problems with structuring async code – callback hell

In the previous section, we introduced the callback pattern as a way to deal with asynchronous calls. The pattern offers a structured way of dealing with such calls, in that we can always know what to expect in its method signature; the error is the first parameter, the second parameter is the response, and so on. But the pattern does have its shortcomings. The shortcomings might not be obvious at first, because you might only call the code like this:

```
openFile('filename', (err, content) => {
  console.log( content );
  statement4;
  statement5;
})

statement2;
statement3
```

What we see here is how we invoke the method `openFile()`. Once that runs to completion, the callback is called and, inside of the callback, we continue invoking `statement4` and `statement5`.

This looks okay in the sense that it is still readable. The problem arises when you need to do several async calls one after another and those calls are dependent upon each other. It might be that you first need to log in to a system and then fetch the other data, or it might mean that you need to make a call as to whose data needs to be used as input for the next call, like in this example:

```
getData('url', (err, data) => {
  getMoreData('newurl/'+ data.id, (moreData) => {
    getEvenMoreData('moreurl/'+ moreData.id, () => {
      console.log('done here');
    })
  })
})
```

The anti-pattern we see emerging here is that of tabulation and lost readability. For each call we make, we see the code is tabbed one step in; it's nested. When we have three calls like this, we can see that the code doesn't look very nice; it is readable, but not very pleasing to the eye. Another drawback is it's also technically hard to get right, in that we might struggle to place the parentheses and curly brackets in the correct place. Throw a few `if...else` clauses in there and you will have a hard time matching all the symbols.

There are several ways you can address this problem:

- Keep the code shallow and use named functions over anonymous ones
- Reduce the cognitive load and move functions into their own modules
- Use more advanced constructs, such as promises, generators, and async functions from ES7 and other async libraries

Keeping the code shallow is about giving our anonymous functions a dedicated name and breaking them out into their own functions; this will make our code look like this:

```
function getEvenMoreDataCallback(err, evenMoreData) {
  console.log('done here');
}

function getMoreDataCallback(err, moreData){
  getEvenMoreData('moreurl/'+ moreData.id, getEvenMoreDataCallback);
}

function getDataCallback(err, data){
  getMoreData('newurl/'+ data.id, getMoreDataCallback);
}

getData('url', getDataCallback)
```

This clearly flattens out the code and makes it more easier to read. It also removes the need to match curly brackets correctly as the functions are only one level deep.

This gets the code part out of the way, but there is still a cognitive load as we have to process three function definitions and one function call. We can move them out to their own dedicated modules, like this:

```
let getDataCallback = require('./datacallback');
getData('url', getDataCallback);
```

And for the other method, it would look like this:

```
function getEvenMoreDataCallback(err, evenMoreData) {
  console.log('done here');
}
```

And this:

```
var getEvenMoreDataCallback = require('./evenmorecallback');

function getMoreDataCallback(err, moreData){
  getEvenMoreData('moreurl/'+ moreData.id, getEvenMoreDataCallback);
}
```

Now we have removed quite a lot of the cognitive code. It may not have paid for itself in this case, as the methods were not that long, but imagine the methods spanned 30 or 40 lines in size; putting them in a separate module would have made a lot more sense.

The third option is to deal with this kind of code using more advanced constructs. We will address these in the upcoming sections.

Promises

Promises came about as a response to the callback hell problem described in the previous section. They have quite a long history, stretching back to the early 80s, when the legendary *Barbara Liskov* coined the term `Promise`. The idea of a `Promise` is to flatten out async code. A promise is said to have the following states:

- **Pending**: This means it has not yet been decided or that the data is not available yet
- **Fulfilled**: The data has come back
- **Rejected**: An error happened during the operation

Thenables

Something important to know is that a `Promise` returns straight away, but the result is not available straight away. Promises are also known as *thenables*, because you need to register a callback with its `then()` method once the data has been received, like so:

```
const promise = new Promise((resolve, reject) => {
  // either call resolve() if we have a success or reject() if it fails
```

```
});

// the 'promise' variable points to a construct
// that will eventually contain a value

promise((data) => {  // <- registering a callback on then()
  // our data has arrived at this point
})
```

In the preceding code, we demonstrated how to create a promise and how to register it with the then() method. The promise variable instance contains a construct that is returned straight away. The callback in the then() method gets invoked once the data is ready for us to use. In that sense, a Promise resembles a callback pattern.

A Promise is really just a wrapping around an asynchronous construct.

In short, to use Promises we need to:

- Create the promise and make sure to call resolve() or reject() when the data has arrived or an error has occurred
- Register a callback with its then() method
- Register a callback to handle errors as well, as that is the responsible thing to do

To put a promise to use, we need to instantiate it and make it part of a method, like so:

```
function getData() {
  return new Promise((resolve, reject) => {
    setTimeout(() => {
      resolve('data');
    },1000);
  })
}
```

We see that; when we instantiate a Promise object, its constructor takes two parameters, resolve and reject. Let's connect this to the states we know a promise can have, namely, pending, fulfilled, and rejected. When getData() is initially called, the promise returned and has the state pending. After a second, the promise will be fulfilled, because we called the resolve() method. Let's look at the getMoreData() method to see how we can put a Promise into a rejected state:

```
function getMoreData() {
  return new Promise((resolve, reject) => {
    setTimeout(() => {
      reject('error from more data')
    },1000);
```

```
    })
  }
```

In this case, we call the `reject()` method after a second. This will put the promise into a rejected state. To get the data from a `promise` instance, we need to call the `then()` method on it, like so:

```
promise.then( successCallback, <optional error call back> );
```

A promise's `then()` method takes two callbacks: the first callback is the data callback and the second callback is an optional error callback. Let's put this in use on our defined `getData()` method, like so:

```
getData().then( (data) => {
  console.log('data', data);
})
```

It's clear that we can't just call `getData()` on the method straight away to get the data, but we need to call `.then()` on the `promise` it returns. Once we provide a callback, we are able to get the data and deal with it as we see fit.

Handling rejected promises

For a rejected promise, we have two ways of handling it: we can either use the second callback in the `.then()` method, or we can use the `.catch()` method. Here are the two versions available to us:

```
// alternative 1
getMoreData().then(
  data => {
    console.log('data',data);
  },
  err => {
    console.log('error',err);
  }
)

// alternative 2
getMoreData().then(data => {
  console.log('data', data);
})
.catch((err) => {
  console.log('error', err);
});
```

In the first case, we have a second callback added to the `then()` method, and in the second version, we chain a `catch()` method to the existing `then()` method. They are equivalent so you can use either one, but only one.

Chaining – dealing with several promises

The most powerful feature of the promise lies in its ability to chain calls, thereby making code look synchronous. A chain looks like this:

```
getData()
  .then(getMoreData)
  .then(getEvenMoreData)
  .catch(handleError)
```

This makes the code very easy to read. You are able to tell in which order things happen; namely, `getData()` followed by `getMoreData()`, followed by `getEvenMoreData()`. Not only are we able to run the methods in the order that we want, but we are also able to access the data from the previous `promise`, like so:

```
function getData() {
  return new Promise((resolve, reject) => {
    setTimeout(() => {
      resolve('data');
    })
  })
}

function getMoreData(data) { // data is from getData
  return new Promise((resolve, reject) => {
    setTimeout(() => {
      resolve('data');
    })
  })
}

getData().then(getMoreData)
```

We can also see how we can add the `.catch()` method to the end to handle errors. The nature of chained promises are such that an error propagates all the way down to the `catch()` method.

It is, however, quite possible to handle an error at a specific level, like so:

```
getData()
  .then(getMoreData, (err) => {}) // local error handler
  .then(getEvenMoreData )
  .then(data => {} )
  .catch(handleError ) // global error handler
```

Now we have two error handlers, one at a local level `.then(getMoreData, (err) => {})` as the second argument in the `then()` method. This has a different effect than only adding `.catch()` to the bottom of our call chain. If only the `.catch()` method at the bottom exists, then the chain is short-circuited. As it stands, the current chain will call the local error function, the `.catch()` method, and the last `.then()` method when a `promise` is rejected from the `getMoreData()` method. The data parameter in the last `.then()` method will, however, not be set if the `promise` is rejected. Chaining is powerful and gives us the following:

- An ordered way of calling async methods
- The previously resolved promise data as input to our method
- The ability to handle errors globally as well as per promise, though with different results

Asynchronous libraries

So far, we have discussed callback patterns and how using promises gives your code that badly needed sense of order. Writing asynchronous code isn't just about stopping yourself from drowning in messy code, it's about being productive as well. Libraries exist out there that will make you really productive if you mean business about taking asynchronous coding head on. The best known libraries at the time of writing are:

- **Async**: This is by far the best known. It can be found at https://caolan.github.io/async/.
- **Step**: This library sells itself as a library that will help you with serial execution, parallel execution, and promises to make error handling painless. It can be found at https://github.com/creationix/step.
- **Node fibers**: This is a very different library than the first two and can be thought of more as bringing a light-thread support to JavaScript. It can be found at https://github.com/laverdet/node-fibers.

Async library

We have so far shown callbacks and Promises. We went from the problem with callbacks, namely callback hell, and how Promises solved that. However, there is a library called **async**, which is an alternative to callbacks and promises. So why would we want to use the async library instead? The async library is meant to operate on collections in an asynchronous context. The library authors themselves say this about it:

> *Async is a utility module which provides straight-forward, powerful functions for working with asynchronous JavaScript*

So, if your asynchronous code starts to become unmanageable and you find yourself wanting to operate on asynchronous collections rather than a few calls here and there, this library might be for you. In most scenarios, promises are most likely what you want though.

The async library comes with a lot of nice functionality. The idea of the async library is to make your code look a lot better so you can focus on building things instead of struggling to see what the code is doing.

To use it, simply install it by typing:

```
npm install async --save
```

async.map()

Let's have a look at an example where `async` shines and is able to remove unnecessary code. The following example shows how we call the `fs.stat()` method that will asynchronously tell us about a file, such as its size, when it was created, and so on. A normal call `fs.stat()` would look like this:

```
// async-demo/app.js

const fs = require('fs');

const basePath = __dirname + '/files/';
const files = ['file1.txt', 'file2.txt', 'file3.txt'];

fs.stat(basePath + 'file1.txt', (err, result) => {
  if(err) {
    console.log('err');
  } else {
    const { size, birthtime } = result;
    console.log('Size',size);
    console.log('Created', birthtime);
```

```
    }
  });
```

What if we wanted to make several calls and wanted to know the stats of several files? Firing off a number of calls- one per file- would mean our calls would come back at different times, depending on the size of the file. What if we don't care about the response until everything comes back? This is what the async library can help us with. There is a map() function that will allow us to fire off several calls at once and only return once all the calls are done, like so:

```
// app-map.js

const async = require('async');
const fs = require('fs');
const basePath = __dirname + '/files/';
const files = ['file1.txt', 'file2.txt', 'file3.txt'];
const mappedFiles = files.map( f => basePath + f);

async.map(mappedFiles, fs.stat,(err, results) => {
  if(err) {
    console.log('error', err);
  }else {
    // looping through our results array
    results.forEach(({size, birthtime}) => {
      console.log('Size',size);
      console.log('Created', birthtime);
    });
  }
});
```

So, what makes this so great? First off, our code aims to find out some file statistics about every file. Let's look at what life would look like without the async library:

```
// example of running a callback method in a forEach()

['file1','file2','file3'].forEach( f => {
  var states = [];
  fs.stat(f, (err, stat) => {
    console.log('stat', stat);
    states.push( stat );
  })
})
```

We can see that we need to introduce a states array just to collect all the results and even then, we probably need to add some logic to know that we are on the last item in the array and can therefore start processing based on the fact that we now have all the results. Conversely, using `async.map()` means we have access to a function that collects the result in an array and also waits until the full array has been processed and all the results have come back.

So, the takeaway from all this is that `async.map()` helps us call a list of asynchronous calls into one call enabling us to process all the results once every single call is done, not before.

async.parallel()

Another important method in this library is `async.parallel()`, which lets us send off a lot of statements in parallel, like so:

```
// async-demo/app-parallell.js

const async = require('async');

function getMessages(fn) {
  setTimeout(() => {
    fn(null, ['mess1', 'mess2', 'mess3']);
  }, 3000);
}

function getOrders(fn) {
  setTimeout(() => {
    fn(null, ['order1', 'order2', 'order3']);
  }, 5000);
}

async.parallel([
  getMessages,
  getOrders
], (error, results) => {
  if(error) {
    console.log('error', error);
  } else {
    console.log('results', results);
  }
});
```

What we can see from the previous code is that it allows us to kick off several calls in parallel. We specify the calls in an array that we provide to the `async.parallell([])` method. From what you can discern here, the functions we provide take one parameter, `fn`, which is the callback, for example `getOrders(fn) {}`.

async.series()

Another scenario is that you might want to actually have the calls happen one after another. For that, we get the `async.series()` method, which we call like this:

```
async.series([
    function login(){}
    function loadUserDetails() {}
],(result) => {})
```

Running the code like this guarantees the order in which it will be run, but also ensures that the chain of calls does not continue if there is an error.

There are a ton of useful functions in this library and we urge you to have a look at the documentation at `https://caolan.github.io/async/docs.html`.

Async/await

The async/await is part of the ECMAScript standard ES2017. This construct provides a synchronous-looking experience when dealing with async. Currently, you need something like Babel to run it in the frontend, but for Node.js it is sufficient to run it on version >= 8. Async/await is currently implemented with a concept called generators in the background. Generators are functions that can be exited and re-entered later. To read more about generators, have a look at the following link: `https://developer.mozilla.org/en-US/docs/Web/JavaScript/Reference/Statements/function*`. It is the new way of dealing with asynchronous code and it really helps make our code look synchronous, which takes away a lot of the cognitive pain associated with asynchronous programming.

Let's remind ourselves of our old example, illustrating the callback hell situation:

```
getData()
  .then( data => {
    getMoreData(moreData => {
      getEvenMoreData(() => {
        // do stuff
      })
    })
  });
```

We clearly see the downsides to calling the code this way. The async/await plays the role of a savior, in that it really cleans things up here. However, let's first explain the different parts and how we can work towards refactoring the previous example. A method using async/await is usually the highest-level method; the highest level in the sense that it is the first method to be called in a chain of `async` methods. In the previous example, this would be the `getData()` method. Let's transform `getData()` to look like this:

```
async function getData() {
  // more to come
}
```

What we need to realize at this point, is that we need to refactor the other two methods, `getMoreData()` and `getEvenMoreData()`, into methods that return promises instead of being callback-based. Why is that, you might wonder? Well, when we use async/await, we want to call the code in a certain way. As hinted at earlier, we will use the keyword `async` in front of our `getData()` function. What's more is that we want to use the keyword `await` in the following way:

```
async function getData() {
  let data = await getMoreData();
  let otherData = await getEvenMoreData();
}
```

Looking at the preceding code, we realize that there is a mismatch in our existing method signature. The mismatch is not the main reason we need to switch our implementation to being promise-based. The real reason is the fact the `await` keyword is able to unwrap promises but not callback based methods. Unwrapping means it can take the resulting value of our asynchronous operation and return it.

The current state of our methods before changing them into promises is:

```
function getMoreData(cb) {
  setTimeout(() => cb('more data'), 3000);
}
function getEvenMoreData(cb) {
  setTimeout( () => cb('even more data'), 3000 );
}
```

Turning them into promise-based methods means they should now look something like this:

```
function getMoreData() {
  return new Promise((resolve, reject) => {
    setTimeout(() => resolve('more data'))
  });

}

function getEvenMoreData() {
  return new Promise((resolve, reject) => {
    setTimeout(() => resolve('more data'))
  });
}
```

At this point, we are ready to return back to our `getData()` method and add the missing code. When we call `getMoreData()` and `getEvenMoreData()`, we can now use the keyword `await` to wait for the promise to resolve, like so:

```
async function getData() {
  var data = await Promise.resolve('data');
  var moreData = await getMoreData(data);
  var evenMoreData = await getEvenMoreData(moreData);
  return evenMoreData;
}
```

What we get now is completely synchronous-looking code. How do we retrieve the data from `getData()` though? Easy—it returns a `promise`. So, we can call it like this:

```
getData().then((result) => console.log('result', result) );
```

The async/await is a truly powerful construct, in that it takes away a lot of the cognitive pain caused by callback hell and further improves upon the concept of promises.

Summary

In this chapter, we have covered asynchronous code, when it is used, and for what purposes. It is clear that asynchronous code becomes harder and harder to read and maintain as it grows, giving rise to patterns such as callback hell. There are several techniques to deal with this, as described throughout this chapter. Changing your coding style a little is one way. Looking at constructs such as promises, especially in conjunction with async/await, is another way. Using async/await means we suddenly get something that can be likened to order in your async code. We have tried to keep things as framework free as possible as it is important to understand all the mentioned concepts without mixing them up with concepts from a specific application framework. One thing can be said though: Angular allows you to use whichever asynchronous method you want to organize your code. Doing HTTP calls, for example, uses an Angular service that is strongly tied to the RxJS library, but you are free to use a promise-based style such as the `fetch()` API. It is also possible to leverage async/await with Angular using Babel and the transformer that supports it.

This chapter has laid a foundation for what asynchronous coding is. The next chapter will build on that foundation by introducing the concept of **Functional Reactive Programming** (**FRP**). It deals more with how to reason around the fact that data arrives seemingly when it wants to. As messy as that sounds, even that can be modeled to create a sense of structure and order if we think of our data as a stream. More on that in the next chapter.

4
Functional Reactive Programming

According to Wikipedia, **Functional Reactive Programming (FRP)** is a programming paradigm for reactive programming, which uses the building blocks of functional programming. OK, that sounds fancy, but what does it mean? To understand the whole sentence we need to break it apart a bit. Let's try to define the following:

- A **programming paradigm** is an overarching theory, or way of working, centered around how a program should be organized and structured. Object-oriented programming and functional programming are examples of programming paradigms.
- **Reactive programming**, in short, is programming with asynchronous data streams. Asynchronous data streams are streams of data whose values can arrive at any point in time.
- **Functional programming** is a programming paradigm that takes a more mathematical approach, in that it sees a functional call as a mathematical computation and thereby avoids changing states or dealing with mutable data.

So, in short, our Wikipedia definition means we have a functional programming approach to values that might arrive at any point in time. That doesn't really mean much, but hopefully things will have been cleared up a bit by the end of this chapter.

In this chapter, we will learn about:

- The differences between declarative and imperative programming
- Asynchronous data streams
- How these streams can be manipulated

Functional programming versus imperative programming

We will discuss and describe two different styles of programming, imperative programming and declarative programming. Functional programming is a subset of declarative programming. The easiest way to explain what declarative programming is to compare it to its opposite, imperative programming. Imperative programming focuses on *how* the program should achieve its result. Functional programming, on the other hand, is a declarative programming paradigm, which means its focus is on what the programming should accomplish, or the what. This is an important distinction.

Imperative programming versus declarative programming

Imperative programming is made up of statements that help change the program's state. As mentioned before, it focuses on the *how* rather than the *what*. Let's have a look at what this can look like in code to make it more clear:

```
let sum = 0;

function updateSum(records) {
  for( let i = 0; i< records.length; i++ ) {
    sum += records[i];
  }
}

updateSum([1,2,3,4]);
```

The preceding code has the following effect: the variable `sum` is updated when we call `updateSum()`. We can also see that the function is very explicit about *how* the summation should happen.

Declarative programming is more focused on *what* to achieve. It's easy to think of this as being more high-level, because you say *what* you want to achieve. Let's look at some SQL code. SQL is a declarative programming language:

```
// content of table 'orderitem'
-------------------
id  price productId
-------------------
1     100   1
```

```
1      50   11

SELECT
  SUM(price) as total
FROM orderitem

// result of the query
150
```

Here, we are querying a table for a number of records while telling SQL what we want to summarize. We are clearly carrying out the same type of action, which is to summarize something. The difference is that with our declarative example we tell SQL what we want done; we trust SQL to know to summarize.

First-class higher-order functions

The term first class means that the language itself treats functions as values; they can be passed around as example arguments to other functions. A higher-order function is a function that takes other functions as parameters. Let's look at an example to make this clearer:

```
function project(obj, fn) {
  return fn(obj);
}

project( { name : 'chris', age: 37 }, (obj) => obj['name'] ); // 'chris'
project({ name : 'chris', age: 37 }, (obj) => obj['age'] ) // 37
```

Here we can see that the second argument in our `project()` function is a function. The function is being applied to the first argument. We can also see that, depending on what input argument we give the higher-order function as its second argument, the higher-order function will behave differently.

Pure functions

A pure function is a function that does not have a side-effect. Nothing the function does will ever affect a variable outside of it. This means that the input argument, when used in a computation, should not cause a side-effect, such as talking to the filesystem or opening a network connection, for example. Let's look at an example:

```
function notAPureFunction(filePath) {
  const fileContent = fs.readFileSync(filePath);
```

```
    const rows = fileContent.split (',');
    let sum = 0;
    rows.forEach(row => { sum += row; });
    return sum;
}
```

As we can see, our function opens up a file, loops through its rows, and calculates a sum of all the row contents. Unfortunately, the function talks to the filesystem, which is considered a side-effect. It may look a little bit contrived, but in a longer function it is not an impossibility to see both calculations—logging and talking to a database—take place, or so has been my experience. Such code is far from ideal, and suffers from separation of concerns and a whole lot of other issues. When it comes to pure functions though, it is a good idea to isolate the pure parts into their own functions, which would result in this:

```
function calculateSum(rows) {   // now it's pure
    let sum = 0;
    rows.forEach(row => { sum += row; });
    return sum;
}

function getRows(filePath) {   // still not pure, but some things needs to
perform side-effects
    const fileContent = fs.readFileSync(filePath);
    const rows = fileContent.split (',');
}
```

As you can see, we now have two functions. We managed to isolate the pure parts into a function called `calculateSum()` and we ended up creating the `getRows()` function, which performs side-effects. Most programs have side-effects in some form, but your job as a programmer is to keep those functions away from pure functions as much as possible.

In reality, we have described two things here:

- **Pure functions**: They are more like mathematical computations that do not have side-effects.
- **Single responsibility principle** (SRP): Part of doing functional programming well is writing small and focused functions. Even though this is not a strict property of functional programming or pure functions, it is an important principle that will help you have the right mindset while adopting the functional programming lifestyle.

One thing we didn't mention was why pure functions play an integral role in functional programming. They are predictable through their computational nature, which makes them easy to test. Building a system that mostly consists of many small predictable functions makes the whole system predictable.

Recursion

"To understand the word recursion see the word recursion."

This is a standing joke at most engineering schools and it explains what it is in a very short way. Recursion is a mathematical concept. Let's explain it a bit more. The official definition says the following:

Recursion is the process a procedure goes through when one of the steps of the procedure involves invoking the procedure itself. A procedure that goes through recursion is said to be 'recursive'.

Ok, what does that mean in human speak? It says that at some point in running our function, we will call ourselves. This means we have a function that looks something like this:

```
function something() {
  statement;
  statement;
  if(condition) {
    something();
  }
  return someValue;
}
```

We can see that the function `something()` at some point in its body calls itself. A recursive function should abide to the following rules:

- Should call itself
- Should eventually meet an exit condition

If a recursive function doesn't have an exit condition, we will run out of memory as the function will call itself for all eternity. There are certain types of problems that are more suitable than others to apply recursive programming to. Examples of these are:

- Traversing trees
- Compiling code

- Writing algorithms for compression
- Sort lists

There are many more examples, but it's important to remember that, although it's a great tool, it shouldn't be used everywhere. Let's look at an example where recursion really shines. Our example is a linked list. A linked list consists of nodes that know about the node they are connected to. The code for the `Node` structure looks like this:

```
class Node {
  constructor(
    public left,
    public value
  ) {}
}
```

Using such a structure as a `Node`, we can construct a linked list consisting of several linked nodes. We can connect a set of node instances in the following way:

```
const head = new Node(null, 1);
const firstNode = new Node(head, 2);
const secondNode = new Node(firstNode, 3);
```

A graphical representation of the preceding code would be the following diagram. Here, we can clearly see what our nodes consist of and how they are connected:

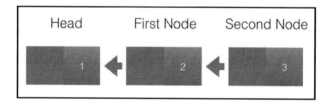

Here, we have a linked list where we have three connected node instances. The head node is not connected to the node to the left. The second node however is connected to the first node and the first node is connected to the head node. The following type of operations on a list might be interesting to do:

- Find the head node, given any node in the list
- Insert a node at a given point in the list
- Remove a node from a given point in the list

Let's have a look at how we can solve the first bullet point. Firstly, we will use an imperative approach and thereafter we will use a recursive approach to see how they differ. More importantly, let's discuss why the recursive approach might be preferred:

```
// demo of how to find the head node, imperative style

const head = new Node(null, 1);
const firstNode = new Node(head, 2);
const secondNode = new Node(firstNode, 3);

function findHeadImperative (startNode)  {
  while (startNode.left !== null) {
    startNode = startNode.left;
  }
  return startNode;
}

const foundImp = findHeadImperative(secondNode);
console.log('found', foundImp);
console.log(foundImp === head);
```

As we can see here, we are using a `while` loop to traverse through the list until we find the node instance whose `left` property is null. Now, let's show the recursive approach:

```
// demo of how to find head node, declarative style using recursion

const head = new Node(null, 1);
const firstNode = new Node(head, 2);
const secondNode = new Node(firstNode, 3);

function findHeadRecursive(startNode) {
  if(startNode.left !== null) {
    return findHeadRecursive(startNode.left);
  } else {
    return startNode;
  }
}

const found = findHeadRecursive(secondNode);
console.log('found', found);
console.log(found === head);
```

In the preceding code, we check whether `startNode.left` is null. If that is the case, we have reached our exit condition. If we haven't reached the exit condition yet, we keep on calling ourselves.

Ok, so we have an imperative approach and a recursive approach. Why is the latter so much better? Well, with the recursive approach, we start off with a long list and we make the list shorter every time we call ourselves: a bit of a *divide and conquer* approach. One thing that clearly stands out with the recursive approach is that we defer execution by saying, no, our exit condition isn't met yet, keep processing. Keep processing means we call ourselves as we do in our `if` clause. Is the point of recursive programming that we get fewer lines of code? Well, that could be the result, but more importantly: it changes our mindset toward how we go about solving problems. In imperative programming, we have a *let's solve the problem from top to bottom mindset*, whereas in recursive programming, our mindset is more, define when we are done and slice down the problem to make it easier to deal with. In the preceding case, we discarded the part of our linked list that wasn't interesting anymore.

No more loops

One of the more significant changes when starting to code in a more functional way is that we get rid of `for` loops. Now that we know about recursion, we can just use that instead. Let's have look at a simple imperative piece of code that prints an array:

```
// demo of printing an array, imperative style

let array = [1, 2, 3, 4, 5];

function print(arr) {
  for(var i = 0, i < arr.length; i++) {
    console.log(arr[i]);
  }
}

print(arr);
```

The corresponding code using recursion looks like this:

```
// print.js, printing an array using recursion

let array = [1, 2, 3, 4, 5];

function print(arr, pos, len) {
  if (pos < len) {
    console.log(arr[pos]);
```

```
        print(arr, pos + 1, len);
    }
    return;
}

print(array, 0, array.length);
```

As we can see, our imperative code is still there in spirit. We still start at 0. Moreover, we keep going until we come to the last position of our array. Once we hit our break condition, we exit the method.

Reoccurring pattern

We haven't really sold recursion as a concept at this point. We kind of get it, but are probably not convinced why good old `while` or `for` loops can't be used in its place. Recursion shines when it solves problems that look like a reoccurring pattern. An example of that is a tree. A tree has some similar concepts to it such as consisting of nodes. A node without children connected to it is called a leaf. A node with children but that has no connection to an upward node is called a root node. Let's illustrate this with a diagram:

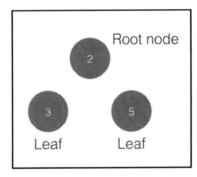

There are a few interesting operations that we would want to carry out on a tree:

- Summarise the node values
- Count the number of nodes
- Calculate the width
- Calculate the depth

To attempt to solve that, we need to think about how to store a tree as a data structure. The most common way of modeling it is by creating a representation of a node as having a value, and a `left` property and a `right` property, then both those properties point to nodes in turn. Therefore, the code for said Node class might look like this:

```
class NodeClass {
  constructor(left, right, value) {
    this.left = left;
    this.right = right;
    this.value = value;
  }
}
```

The next step is thinking how to create the tree itself. This code shows how we can create a tree with a root node and two children, and how to bind these together:

```
// tree.js

class NodeClass {
  constructor(left, right, value) {
    this.left = left;
    this.right = right;
    this.value = value;
  }
}

const leftLeftLeftChild = new NodeClass(null, null, 7);
const leftLeftChild = new NodeClass(leftLeftLeftChild, null, 1);
const leftRightChild = new NodeClass(null, null, 2);
const rightLeftChild = new NodeClass(null, null, 4);
const rightRightChild = new NodeClass(null, null, 2);
const left = new NodeClass(leftLeftChild, leftRightChild, 3);
const right = new NodeClass(rightLeftChild, rightRightChild, 5);
const root = new NodeClass(left, right, 2);

module.exports = root;
```

Worth highlighting is how the instances `left` and `right` do not have children. We can see that because we set their values to `null` on creation. Our root node, on the other hand, has the object instances `left` and `right` as children.

Summarise

Thereafter, we need to think about how to summarise the nodes. Just looking at it, it looks like we should summarise the top node and its two children. So, a code implementation would start off like this:

```
// tree-sum.js

const root = require('./tree');

function summarise(node) {
   return node.value + node.left.value + node.right.value;
}

console.log(summarise(root)) // 10
```

What happens if our tree grows and suddenly looks like this:

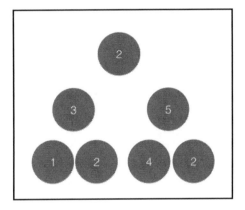

Let's add to the preceding code so it looks like this:

```
// example of a non recursive code

function summarise(node) {
   return node.value +
      node.left.value +
      node.right.value +
      node.right.left.value +
      node.right.right.value +
      node.left.left.value +
      node.left.right.value;
}

console.log(summarise(root)) // 19
```

This is technically working code, but it can be improved. What we should see at this point, looking at the tree, are reoccurring patterns in the tree. We have the following triangles:

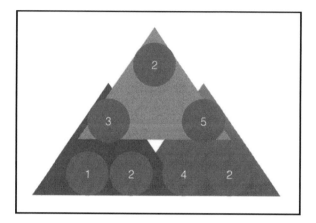

One triangle is made up of **2, 3, 5**, another one is made up of **3, 1, 2**, and the last one is made up of **5, 4, 2**. Every triangle computes its sum by taking the node itself, plus its left child and its right child. Recursion is all about this: discovering a reoccurring pattern and codifying it. We can now implement our `summarise()` function with recursion, like so:

```
function summarise(node) {
  if(node === null) {
    return 0;
  }
  return node.value + summarise(node.left) + summarise(left.right);
}
```

What we are doing here is expressing our reoccurring pattern as *node + left node + right node*. When we call `summarise(node.left)` we simply run through `summarise()` again for that node. The preceding implementation is short and elegant, and is able to traverse the entire tree. Recursion is truly elegant once you find that your problem can be seen as a repeating pattern. The full code looks like this:

```
// tree.js

class NodeClass {
  constructor(left, right, value) {
    this.left = left;
    this.right = right;
    this.value = value;
  }
}
```

```
const leftLeftLeftChild = new NodeClass(null, null, 7);
const leftLeftChild = new NodeClass(leftLeftLeftChild, null, 1);
const leftRightChild = new NodeClass(null, null, 2);
const rightLeftChild = new NodeClass(null, null, 4);
const rightRightChild = new NodeClass(null, null, 2);
const left = new NodeClass(leftLeftChild, leftRightChild, 3);
const right = new NodeClass(rightLeftChild, rightRightChild, 5);
const root = new NodeClass(left, right, 2);

module.exports = root;

// tree-sum.js

const root = require("./tree");

function sum(node) {
  if (node === null) {
    return 0;
  }
  return node.value + sum(node.left) + sum(node.right);
}

console.log("sum", sum(root));
```

Count

Implementing a function that counts all the nodes in the trees is quite trivial now that we are beginning to grasp the nature of recursion. We can reuse our summary function from before and simply count every non-null node as 1 and null as 0. So, we simply take the existing summary function and modify it to this:

```
//tree-count.js

const root = require("./tree");

function count(node) {
  if (node === null) {
    return 0;
  } else {
    return 1 + count(node.left) + count(node.right);
  }
}

console.log("count", count(root));
```

The preceding code ensures we traverse each and every node successfully. Our exit condition happens when we reach null. That is, we are trying to go from a node to one of its non-existing children.

Width

To create a width function, we first need to define what we mean by width. Let's have a look at our tree again:

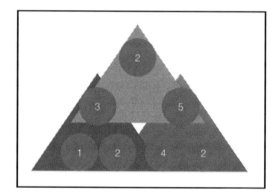

This tree has a width of **4**. How is that? For every step down in the tree, our nodes expand one step to the left and one step to the right. This means that to calculate the width correctly, we need to traverse the edges of our tree. Every time we have to traverse a node to the left or to the right, we increment the width. What we are interested in doing from a calculation standpoint is to traverse the tree like this:

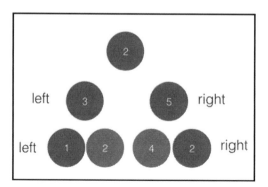

The code should therefore reflect this fact. We can implement this like this:

```
// tree-width.js

const root = require("./tree");

function calc(node, direction) {
  if (node === null) {
    return 0;
  } else {
    return (
      1 + (direction === "left" ?
      calc(node.left, direction) :
      calc(node.right, direction))
    );
  }
}

function calcWidth(node) {
  return calc(node.left, "left") + calc(node.right, "right");
}

console.log("width", calcWidth(root));
```

Note especially how, in the `calcWidth()` function, we call
`calc()` with `node.left` and `node.right`, respectively, as arguments. We also add a `left`
and `right` argument which, in the method `calc()`, means that we will keep going in that
direction. Our exit condition is when we eventually hit null.

Asynchronous data streams

An asynchronous data stream is a stream of data where values are emitted, one after
another, with a delay between them. The word asynchronous means that the data emitted
can appear anywhere in time, after one second or even after two minutes, for example. A
way to model asynchronous streams is to place the emitted values on a time axis, like so:

There are a lot of things that can be considered asynchronous. One such thing is fetching data through AJAX. When the data arrives depends on a number of factors, such as:

- The speed of your connection
- The responsiveness of the backend API
- The size of the data, and many more factors.

The point is the data isn't arriving right at this very second.

Other things that can be considered asynchronous are user initiated events, such as scrolling or mouse clicks. These are events that can happen at any point in time, depending on the user's interaction. As such, we can consider these UI events as a continuous stream of data on a time axis. The following diagram depicts a stream of data representing a user clicking several times. Each click leads to a click event, **c**, which we place on a time axis:

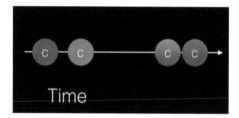

At first glance, our diagram depicts four click events. Taking a closer look, we see that the click events seem grouped. The preceding diagram contains two pieces of information:

- That a number of click events have occurred
- That the click events have occurred with a certain delay in between events

Here, we can see that the two first clicks seem to happen very close together in time; when two events happen very close in time, this will be interpreted as a double-click. Therefore, our image above thus tells us about the events that occurred; it also tells us when and how often they occurred. Looking at the previous diagram, it is quite easy to distinguish between a single-click and a double-click.

We can assign different actions to each click behavior. A double-click might mean that we want to zoom-in, whereas a single-click might mean we want to select something; exactly what is up to the application you are writing.

A third example is that of input. What if we have a situation where the user is typing and stops typing after a while? After a certain amount of time has passed, the user expects the UI to react. This is the case with a search field. In that case, the user might enter something in a search field and press a search button when done. Another way to model that situation in a UI is to just provide a search field and wait for the user to stop typing as a sign of when to start searching for what the user wants. The final example is known as **autocomplete** behavior. It can be modeled in the following way:

The first three characters entered seem to belong to the same search query, whereas the fourth character entered occurs a lot later and probably belongs to another query.

The point of this section has been to highlight that different things lend themselves to being modeled as streams, and that the time axis and the placement of the emitted values on it can come to mean something.

Comparing lists to async streams – preparing for RxJS

We have discussed so far how we can model asynchronous events as a continuous stream of data on a time axis, or stream modeling. Events can be AJAX data, mouse clicks, or some other type of event. Modeling things this way makes for an interesting perspective on things but, looking at a double-click situation for example, doesn't mean much unless we are able to dig out the data. There might be another case where there is data that we need to filter out. What we are discussing here is how to manipulate streams. Without that ability, stream modeling itself has no practical value.

There are different ways to manipulate data: sometimes we want to change the data emitted to some other data and sometimes we might want to change how often the data is being emitted to a listener. Sometimes, we want our stream of data to become a totally different stream. We will try to model the following situations:

- **Projection**: Changing the data of the value being emitted
- **Filtering**: Changing what gets emitted

Combining the functional programming paradigm with streams

This chapter has covered functional programming and asynchronous data streams. Working with RxJS doesn't require a deep understanding of functional programming, but you do need to understand what declarative means, in order to focus on the right things. Your focus should be on what you want done, not how you want it done. RxJS, as a library, will take care of the how. More on that in the upcoming chapter.

These might seem like two different topics. Combining the two, however, gives us the ability to manipulate streams. A stream can be seen as a list of data, where the data is available at a certain point in time. If we start treating our streams as lists, especially immutable lists, then there are operations that go with lists that manipulate lists by applying operators to them. The result of the manipulation is a new list, not a mutated list. So let's start applying our list philosophy and its operators to the following situations.

Projection

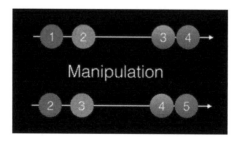

Here, we can see that our stream is emitting the values **1**, **2**, **3**, and **4**, and then a manipulation happens that changes every value by incrementing it by one. This is quite a simple situation. If we consider this as a list, we can see that what we do here is simply a projection, which we would code like this:

```
let newList = list.map(value => value + 1)
```

Filtering

There might be some items in a list, as well as in a stream, that you do not want. What you do to fix that is to create a filter that filters out the unwanted data. Modeling our initial array, the manipulation, and the resulting array, we get the following:

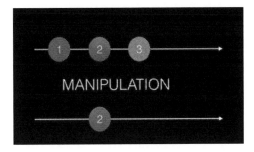

In JavaScript, we can accomplish this by writing the following code:

```
let array = [1,2,3];
let filtered = array.filter(data => data % 2 === 0);
```

Combining mindsets

So, what are we trying to say with this section. Clearly, we have shown examples of how to manipulate lists. Well, what we have done is shown how we can display items on an axis. In that sense, we can see how it is easy to think of asynchronous events and lists of values in the same way, as we are graphically picturing them in the same way. The question is, why do we want to do that? The reason is that this is the mindset the RxJS library wants you to have when you start manipulating and crafting streams in the upcoming chapter.

Summary

This chapter has established that we can model asynchronous events as values on a time axis. We introduced the idea of comparing these streams to lists and thereby applying functional methods to them that would not change the lists themselves but merely create a new list. The benefit of applying the functional paradigm is that we can focus on *what* to achieve rather than *how* to achieve it, thereby having a declarative approach. We realize it's not easy to combine async and lists and create readable code from it. Fortunately, this is what the RxJS library does for us. It is this realization that prepares us for the coming chapter, Chapter 5, *RxJS Basics*, where we introduce RxJS as a library just that: create order in the async mess while modeling everything as a stream. With RxJS, we can truly focus on *what* rather than *how*, as it comes with a bunch of stream manipulation functions. After having read the next chapter, you will understand how RxJS works on a fundamental level, but also how it addresses the problems mentioned in this chapter.

5
RxJS Basics

Reactive Extensions for JavaScript (RxJS) is a set of libraries created by Matt Podwysocky. Version 4 of the library is maintained and developed by Microsoft. Version 4 can be found at the following link: `https://github.com/Reactive-Extensions/RxJS`.

Version 5 is a complete rewrite of version 4 and can be found at the following address: `https://github.com/ReactiveX/rxjs`. Its largest contributor is *Ben Lesh*, with other notable contributors including *Andre Staltz*. Version 5 is also Angular's choice of library for handling HTTP, among other things.

In this chapter, you will learn:

- Which patterns make up RxJS
- The core concepts of RxJS
- How to manually create your own Observables and subscribe to them
- The many ways you can create an Observable
- The importance of managing cleanup
- Understanding what lies beneath by learning to implement the core part of the RxJS library

Observer pattern

The Observer pattern is a Gang of Four pattern. It is a pattern made famous by being included in the book *Design Patterns: Elements of Reusable Object-Oriented Software* by *Erich Gamma, Richard Helm, Ralph Johnson*, and *John Vlissides*. The pattern has two key players involved: a **Subject** and an **Observer**. A Subject is observed by an Observer. Typically, a Subject holds an internal list of Observers that should be notified when a change happens on the Subject. It is quite common that the Subject is a model and the Observers are some kind of UI component. In short, Subjects should be able to:

- Hold a list of Observers
- Add an Observer
- Remove an Observer
- Notify all Observers when a change happens

The Observer, on the other hand, should only hold one property, and that is an `update()` method that can be called by a Subject when an update has occurred. The idea behind this pattern is to create a loose coupling between different layers. Neither Subjects nor Observers should know about each other directly by name, but rather by abstractions. A class diagram for a Subject might therefore look like the following:

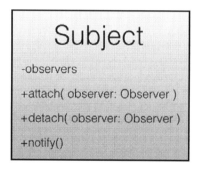

Here, we are including all the required methods: `attach()`, `detach()` and `notify()`, and we clearly specify that we are dealing with the abstraction Observer and not a concrete type. As for the Observer, this is usually an interface with just one method, `update()`, and can be represented by the following class diagram:

Given these class diagrams, let's write down some code to demonstrate what an implementation might look like, and let's start with the Subject. For this example, we will be using TypeScript, as TypeScript knows what an interface is:

```typescript
// observer-subject/subject.ts

import { Observer } from "./observer";

export class Subject {
  observers: Array<Observer>;
  constructor() {
    this.observers = new Array<Observer>();
  }

  attach(observer: Observer) {
    if (this.observers.indexOf(observer) === -1) {
      this.observers.push(observer);
    }
  }

  detach(observer) {
    let index = this.observers.indexOf(observer);
    if (index !== -1) {
      this.observers = this.observers.slice(index, 1);
    }
  }

  notify() {
    this.observers.forEach(observer => observer.update());
  }
}
```

As you can see, the basic implementation is very short but it is a powerful construct. As for the `Observer`, it is even shorter:

```
// observer-subject/observer.ts
export interface Observer {
  update();
}
```

We can try this out by creating a file, `app.ts`, like so:

```
// observer-subject/app.ts

import { Subject } from "./subject";
import { Observer } from "./observer";

const subject = new Subject();
const observer = <Observer>{
  update: () => console.log("First Observer Updated")
};

const observer2 = <Observer>{
  update: () => console.log("Second Observer updated")
};

subject.attach(observer);
subject.attach(observer2);
subject.notify();

// should emit:
// First Observer Updated
// Second Observer updated
```

By running the preceding code, we see that the `Subject` instance allows us to attach `Observer` instances to it by calling the `attach()` method. We then call `notify()` on the `Subject` instance to ensure that all subscribing `Observer` instances gets notified.

OK, so now we have some core implementation in place, what does an actual use case look like? Imagine that we have a `ProductModel` class playing the role of a `Subject` and a `ProductUI` class playing the role of an `Observer`. A simple implementation of the `ProductModel` class might look like the following:

```
// product-model/product.model.ts

import { Subject } from "./subject";

export class ProductModel extends Subject {
```

```
    private titleValue = "";
    private makeValue = "";

    get title(){
      return this.titleValue;
    }

    set title(value) {
      this.titleValue = value;
      this.notify();
    }

    get make() {
      return this.makeValue;
    }

    set make(value) {
      this.makeValue = value;
      this.notify();
    }
  }
```

Here, we can see that we have two properties, title and make, and when both of them change, we call the notify() method that we inherit from the base class, Subject. Let's have a look at what a ProductUI class can look like:

```
// product-model/product.ui.ts

import { Observer } from "./observer";
import { ProductModel } from "./product.model";

export class ProductUI implements Observer {
  constructor(private model: ProductModel) {
    this.model.attach(this); // add ProductUI to the observer list
    this.renderUI();
  }

  renderUI() {
    console.log("calling renderUI");
    this.draw();
  }

  draw() {
    // implement
    console.log("calling draw");
  }
```

```
    update() {
      console.log("calling update");
      this.renderUI(); // rerender the UI when update() is called
    }
  }
```

In the preceding code, we see that we receive a `ProductModel` instance in the constructor and that we also call `attach()` on said instance so that it is registered as an `Observer`. We also define an `update()` method, in which we decide that we will rerender the UI, should it be invoked.

This is a typical example of using the Observer pattern and using it for model-to-UI communication is just one of many usage possibilities. The general principle is to communicate between `Subject` and `Observer` instances in a loosely coupled way. The true benefit is to be able to have multiple `Observer` instances on one `Subject` so that if the `Subject` changes, all its `Observer` instances can change with it. This is also called Publish/Subscribe, which is usually shortened to Pub/Sub.

RxJS core concepts

RxJS consists of some core concepts that are important for you to understand early on. Those are:

- **Observable**: This is a class representing a stream of data.
- **Observer**: This is a class able to emit data.
- **Producer**: This is what internally produces data, which the Observer ultimately emits.
- **Operator**: This is a method on an Observable, which allows us to manipulate the stream itself or the data it emits.
- **Stream**: This is synonymous with an instance of an Observable. The reason for it being called a stream is that you should think of the data as continuous and not really having an end, unless you explicitly define an end.

Observable and Observer

Having defined all the concepts we need to know initially, it is now time to put it all in context to further our understanding. Let's start off by defining an `Observable` and work ourselves into each previously mentioned concept. An `Observable` can be created with the following code:

```
let stream$ = Rx.Observable.create(observer => observer.next(1));
```

This is the least amount of code needed to create an `Observable`. At this point nothing is written to the screen because we need to subscribe to the stream. Let's add a Subscriber to our `Observable`. We do that by calling the method `subscribe()` on our stream instance:

```
let stream$ = Rx.Observable.create(observer => observer.next(1));
stream$.subscribe(data => console.log('data',data) ) // write data, 1 to
the console
```

Looking at this code, we see that the `Observable` calls the method `create()`, which in turn creates an instance of an `Observable`. What is interesting is how the `create()` method takes a function as a parameter; a function that itself takes an Observer instance. So, we have an API that looks like this: `Observer.create(fn(observerInstance))`. What happens inside said function is that we call `observer.next(1)`. At a higher level, we have an `Observable` that is created by us using a `factory` function `create()`. The `create` function takes a function as a parameter which defines the behavior of the `Observable`. Our `Observable` behavior in this case is very simple, which is to emit the value 1. When we call `observer.next(1)`, we emit data. To get hold of what is emitted, we need to call the `subscribe()` method.

Producer

If we try to compare this to the Observer pattern, we will see that some concepts reoccur, such as Observer. In this pattern, the Observer was notified when something happened and the Subject took the initiative to change. Looking at the previous code, it looks like the Observer is the one that takes the initiative to change. This isn't strictly true though; it is more of a mediator, which brings us to our next concept in RxJS, the `Producer`. The `Producer` is responsible for generating the values we need. By involving a `Producer` in our code, we see that the Observer is more of a mediator:

```
// rxjs-example/producer.js

const Rx = require("rxjs/Rx");
```

```
class Producer {
  constructor() {
    this.counterMax = 5;
    this.current = 0;
  }

  hasValues() {
    return this.current < this.counterMax;
  }

  next() {
    return this.current++;
  }
}

let stream$ = Rx.Observable.create(observer => {
  let producer = new Producer();

  while (producer.hasValues()) {
    observer.next(producer.next());
  }
});

stream$.subscribe(data => console.log("data", data));
// data 0, data 1, data 2, data 3, data 4
```

As we can see here, the producer is the one responsible for generating the data, while the Observer is responsible for passing on that data to a subscriber.

Observable error and completion

There is more to a stream than just generating data; a stream can generate errors as well as reaching its completion. If an error or a completion happens, the stream will not generate any more values. To signal that we have an error, we call the `error()` method on the Observer, like so:

```
let stream$ = Rx.Observable.create(observer => {
  observer.error('we have an error');
});
```

To capture the emitted error, we need to introduce a second callback in our call to `subscribe()`, like so:

```
// rxjs-example/error.js

const Rx = require("rxjs/Rx");

let stream$ = Rx.Observable.create(observer => {
  observer.error("we have an error");
});

stream$.subscribe(
  data => console.log("data", data),
  error => console.error("err", error)
)
```

So far, we have learned how to emit data but also how to signal an error. The last thing we can do is to close the stream, or complete it, as closing is also known. We do that by calling `complete()` on the Observer. This will ensure that no more values are emitted. To capture a completion signal, we need to add another callback in our `subscribe()` call. You use it in the following way:

```
// rxjs-example/completion.js

const Rx = require("rxjs/Rx");

let stream$ = Rx.Observable.create(observer => {
  observer.next(1);
  observer.complete();
});

stream$.subscribe(
  data => console.log("data", data), // 1
  error => console.error("err", error), // never hit
  () => console.log("complete")
); // will be hit
```

Operator

Our last concept to cover is the operator. An operator is simply a method that acts on an Observable and changes the stream in some way. Operators are by nature immutable. This immutability makes the code easier to test and reason about. RxJS comes with over 60 operators to help in most situations where you define your streams and their behavior.

There might be a case where you need to create your own operator, but most likely there is an operator out there that already does what you want.

When you define your stream and its behavior, you will use one or more operators. It might look like the following:

```
let stream$ = Rx.Observable.of(1,2)
  .map( x => x +1 )
  .filter( x > 2 );

stream$.subscribe( data => console.log('data', data))
// data 3
```

Here, we can see that we are using the `.map()` operator and `.filter()` to change our stream's data. `.map()` operates on each value in the stream by incrementing each value by one. `.filter()` operates on the changed stream; a change brought about by calling `.map()`. It also operates on each value in the stream but conditionally decides what should be emitted. The end result is only one value being emitted, 3. There are a ton more operators, but this should give you an idea of what operators are and how they can be used.

Creating Observables

Most of the time, when creating Observables, you won't use the `create()` method to do so. You will use other methods instead. Why is that? Well, an Observable instance usually originates from some asynchronous concept. In the context of using RxJS for creating Angular applications, an Observable instance will be created by doing one of the following things:

- Creating or fetching data over HTTP with AJAX
- Listening to input changes with reactive forms
- Listening to routing changes
- Listening to UI events
- Wrapping an asynchronous concept

In RxJS, there are different creation operators that will help you solve these tasks, but the Angular framework might actually create Observables internally. Let's look at some creation operators other than the `create()` method:

Creation operators

An Observable is, as we stated before, a representation of data being emitted over time. Sometimes, the data arrives straight away and sometimes it takes time. Regardless of which, it is really powerful to be able to model that data in the same way.

of()

Let's look at a very simple creation operator, `of()`. This takes a variable number of arguments, which will be emitted as values, like so:

```
let stream$ = Rx.Observable.of(1, 2, 3, 4);
stream$.subscribe( data => console.log(data)) // 1, 2, 3 ,4
```

The values are fired off immediately. This is very useful when you just want to test things out.

interval()

Another interesting operator is the `interval()` operator, which takes a number of milliseconds as a parameter. This defines the number of milliseconds delay there should be between every piece of emitted data. This will start from the number 0. One thing to keep in mind is that it will generate values forever unless, for example, a `take()` operator is applied to it. A `take()` operator will limit the number of emitted values and close the stream. A typical usage of the operator is the following:

```
let stream$ = Rx.Observable.interval(1000)
  .take(3); // 1s delay between values, starting at 0

stream$.subscribe(data => console.log(data))
// 0, 1, 2
```

from()

The `from()` operator allows us to create an `Observable` from some other asynchronous/synchronous concept. It's really powerful when almost anything can be made into an `Observable`, as this allows for rich composition. Here is what a typical snippet can look like:

```
let stream$ = Rx.Observable.from(new Promise((resolve, reject) => {
  resolve('some data');
```

```
});

stream$.subscribe( data => console.log(data)); // some data

let stream2$ = Rx.Observable.from([1,2,3,4]);
stream2$.subscribe( data => console.log(data)); // 1,2,3,4
```

fromEvent()

We have mentioned rich composition a few times already and the power of making everything into an Observable. We have turned promises and into Observables, which have made everything into streams of data, making the whole situation more easy to reason about. What we mean by that is, when every async concept is being turned into an Observable, we are suddenly able to think about them in the same way. Operators that can be applied to mouse-clicks can also be applied to AJAX requests and so on.

To add to this, we can even make UI events into Observables. By using the .fromEvent() operator, we are able to take an element and its corresponding event and make that an Observable. This is true power at our fingertips, which allows us to turn scenarios such as autocomplete into a matter of 3-4 lines of code. A typical usage of this operator looks like this:

```
let elem = document.getElementById('input');
// we assume we have a <input id="input"> in our markup

let keyStream$ = Rx.Observable.fromEvent(elem, 'keyUp');
// listens to the keyUp event
```

bindCallback()

So far, we have listed a lot of ways, synchronous as well as asynchronous, in which a construct could be turned into an Observable. Callbacks is the first pattern to try to resolve the whole asynchronous matter and it should be said that a callback is probably the worst way to solve asynchronous code because of its poor readability. Luckily, there is an operator that takes a callback and turns it into an Observable called bindCallback(). It can be used in the following way:

```
function fnWithCallback(cb) {
  setTimeout(() => cb('data'), 3000);
}
```

```
let fnWithCallbackBinded = Rx.Observable.bindCallback(fnWithCallback);
let source$ = fnWithCallbackBinded();

source$.subscribe(data => console.log('callback', data));
```

We can see that we start off by defining a function called `fnWithCallback()`. We pass this as an argument to the `bindCallback()` method. This produces a `fnWithCallbbackBinded()` function. Invoking said function will produce an `Observable` that we can subscribe to. So, every time `cb('data')` in the `fnWithCallback()` function is invoked because of the `setTimeout()`, this will lead to the data callback for our `source$` being invoked. How does this work in practice? It's really quite simple. Let's try to implement our own `Observable` for this. We have learned the following:

- A `bindCallback()` method takes a function as a parameter
- Invoking `bindCallback()` should produce a function
- Invoking the result of calling `bindCallback()` should produce an `Observable`
- Calling `subscribe()` should mean that our data callback should be the `cb` parameter in `fnWithCallback()`

The resulting implementation should therefore look like this:

```
// rxjs-creation-operators/bind-callback.ts

class Observable {
  behaviorFn;
  constructor(behaviorFn) {
    this.behaviorFn = behaviorFn;
  }

  static bindCallback(behaviorFn): Function {
    return (): Observable => {
      return new Observable(behaviorFn);
    };
  }

  subscribe(dataCb) {
    this.behaviorFn(dataCb);
  }
}

let fn = Observable.bindCallback(cb => {
  setTimeout(() => cb("data"), 3000);
});
```

```
const stream$ = fn();
stream$.subscribe(data => console.log("data", data));
// outputs: data data
```

Cleanup

We have now covered core concepts such as Observable, Observer, Producer, and operators. We have also looked into how we can manually create an Observable, but realized that there are different creation operators that will help you create Observables from other constructs, and sometimes the Angular framework itself will create the Observable for you. We have failed to mention one important thing though, cleanup. There will be situations where an Observable will allocate resources or simply go on forever, as with the `interval()` operator. There is one clear remedy to that—define and run a cleanup function when we are done with the Observable. Defining such a function forces us to return to the `create` operator and amend some code in its behavior function, like so:

```
let stream$ = Rx.Observable.create(observer => {
  let counter = 0;
  let id = setInterval(() => observer.next(counter++), 1000);

  return function cleanUpFn() { clearInterval(id); }
});
```

Subscriptions

The preceding code describes a situation where there is a need for a cleanup to happen. We have defined a `setInterval()` construct that seemingly emits values forever. `cleanUpFn()` has the ability to cancel that behavior, providing it is being invoked. We return `cleanUpFn()` at the end of our behavior function.

The question is, how do we get hold of it? The answer is that we need to talk about a new concept: subscription. A subscription is something that we get back when calling `subscribe()` on a stream. Let's amend the preceding code with just that:

```
let stream$ = Rx.Observable.create(observer => {
  let counter = 0;
  let id = setInterval(() => observer.next(counter++), 1000);
  return function cleanUpFn() { clearInterval(id); }
});

let subscription = stream$.subscribe((data) => console.log('data'));
```

```
setTimeout(() => subscription.unsubscribe(), 2000);
```

In the preceding code, we have created the variable `subscription` by calling `subscribe()`, but the really interesting part happens in the last line: we define a timeout that calls `unsubscribe()` on our `subscription`. This will call our `cleanUpFn()` so that the interval is cancelled.

Not many streams that you deal with will need to be unsubscribed from, but the ones that allocate resources or start off some construct that goes on forever, without us intercepting, will need to have a cleanup behavior which we need to invoke once we are done with our stream.

Creating a core implementation of RxJS

There are different phases to understanding something. Understanding a library is about learning its concepts and utilizing its methods in the correct way. Then comes deeper understanding, such as knowing what methods to use, based on some best practice guide you found in a blog. Finally, you come to a really deep stage of understanding where you want to understand what is going for relay and starts mucking about in the source code itself and maybe try to enhance it by submitting **Pull Request** to a project, most likely based on GitHub.

This section aims to give you part of that deeper knowledge straight away. We are aware that your head might be spinning a little at this point, with all the new concepts you have learned, together with some nifty operators. Let's start from scratch with the concepts first introduced and attempt to reverse engineer what is going on.

Implementing create()

At the beginning of this chapter, we were taught how to create an Observable. The code looked like this:

```
let stream$ = Rx.Observable.create( observer => observer.next(1));
stream$.subscribe( data => console.log(data));
```

Just by looking at the code, we can make educated guesses as to what's going on underneath. It's clear we need an `Observable` class.

The class needs a `create()` method that takes a function as a parameter. The `create()` method should return an `Observable`. Furthermore, our `Observable` class needs a `subscribe()` method that takes a function as a parameter. Let's start off there and see where we land.

First, let's define our `Observable` class with the aforementioned methods:

```
class MyObservable {
  static create(behaviourFn): MyObservable {}
  constructor() {}
  subscribe(dataFn) {}
}
```

OK, so we have a class with three methods in it; let's attempt to implement the methods. Let's take what we know about the `create()` method and start from there:

```
class MyObservable {
  static create(behaviourFn): MyObservable {
    return new Observable(behaviourFn);
  }
  constructor(private behaviourFn) {}
  subscribe(dataFn) {}
}
```

We highlighted the required changes in bold and introduced a field on the class called `behaviourFn()`. Furthermore, our `create()` method instantiated an `Observable` by passing in `behaviourFn` from the `create()` method parameter. This means the constructor needs to take a function as a parameter and save that for later use. What do we know about the `behaviourFn()` that was passed into the create method? We know it takes an Observer instance as a parameter and it also lays out what values the Observer instance should emit. For anything to be able to capture those emitted values, we need to implement our last method, `subscribe()`. We know that `subscribe()` takes `dataFn()` as a parameter and needs to somehow invoke our `behaviourFn` when the `subscribe()` method is being invoked to trigger the behavior. Let's therefore amend that in our existing code:

```
class MyObservable {
  static create(private behaviourFn): MyObservable {
    return new MyObservable(behaviourFn);
  }
  constructor(behaviourFn) { this.behaviourFn = behaviourFn; }
  subscribe(dataFn) {
    this.behaviourFn(observer);
  }
}
```

At this point, we realize that we need an `Observer` class so that we actually have something to pass to our `behaviourFn()`. Another thing we need to figure out is how to invoke `dataFn()` and when. After a thinking for a minute, we realize the Observer must be the one responsible for invoking `dataFn()` so it seems only reasonable that `dataFn()` is passed into the constructor of our `Observer` class for later use, like so:

```
class Observer {
  constructor(private dataFn) {}
  next(value) { this.dataFn(val) }
}
```

By implementing this `Observer` class, we have done three things: one is to pass the `dataFn()` through the constructor and make it into a field on the `Observer` class; another is to create a `next()` method on the `Observer`, which had to be done as we learned that an Observer instance should call `next()` to generate values; the third and final thing we did was to ensure that we invoked `dataFn()` inside of the `next()` method to be sure that the subscriber is being told every time we generate a value by calling the `next()` method. Putting all of this code together, we have created a very bare implementation of RxJS, which actually works! To better understand what we have so far, let's display all the code used so far:

```
// rxjs-core/Observable.ts

class Observer {
  constructor(private dataFn) {}
  next(value) { this.dataFn(value) }
}

class MyObservable {
  behaviourFn;
  static create(behaviourFn): MyObservable {
    return new Observable(behaviourFn);
  }
  constructor(behaviourFn) { this.behaviourFn = behaviourFn; }
  subscribe(dataFn) {
    let observer = new Observer(dataFn);
    this.behaviourFn( observer );
  }
}

let stream$ = MyObservable.create( observer => observer.next(1)); // 1
```

Handling subscriptions

We learned how to implement a very basic core in the last section. Earlier in the chapter, however, it was mentioned that sometimes your Observable will allocate resources or will display a behavior where it clearly won't be able to stop generating values. It is our responsibility to handle such situations in a graceful manner. RxJS has clearly laid out a path here, which is to define a cleanup function and ensure it is invoked upon calling `unsubscribe()`. Let's show such a scenario, where we clearly need to care about cleaning up:

```
// rxjs-core/Observer-with-subscription.ts

interface Subscription {
  unsubscribe();
}

class MyObservableWithSubscription {
  static create(behaviourFn): MyObservableWithSubscription {
    return new MyObservableWithSubscription(behaviourFn);
  }

  constructor(private behaviourFn) {}

  subscribe(dataFn): Subscription {
    let observer = new MyObserver(dataFn);
    let cleanUpFn = this.behaviourFn(observer);
    return {
      unsubscribe: cleanUpFn
    };
  }
}

let streamWithSubscription$ = MyObservableWithSubscription.create(observer
=> {
  let counter = 0;
  let id = setInterval(() => observer.next(counter++), 1000);
  return function cleanUpFn() {
    clearInterval(id);
  };
});

const subscription = streamWithSubscription$.subscribe(data =>
  console.log("data", data)
);

subscription.unsubscribe();
```

Looking at the code, we see that when we define the behavior function (at the bottom of the code snippet), we set up a `setInterval()` construct that calls `observer.next()` periodically. We ensure we save the reference in a variable ID. This need to be sure that we can cancel the `setInterval()` behavior when we choose to. We do that by defining a `cleanUpFn()` in the last row of the `behaviourFn` function. This brings us to the top half of our snippet. Here, we see that we amend the `subscribe()` method by ensuring we save the result of calling `this.behaviourFn()` into a variable called `cleanUpFn`. This is indeed the `cleanUpFn()` we defined in `behaviourFn()`. Lastly, we expose the `cleanUpFn()` property by returning it as part of an object and assigning it to the `unsubscribe()` property. The last thing we need to do is to call the `unsubscribe()` method to ensure our allocated resources are released or, as in this specific example, that the `setInterval()` construct is cancelled. Calling unsubscribe will call `cleanUpFn()` which in turn calls `clearInterval()`, which will cancel the interval.

Adding operators

We have come a long way in defining our own core implementation of RxJS, but we are missing an important piece of the puzzle—operators. Operators are the real power of RxJS and can be seen as a utility method that allows us to manipulate our stream with ease. Let's select `filter()` as the target of our example. A filter operator is a method that you can call on the stream. The idea is to provide it with a function that is able to determine, value for value, whether the specific value in question should be emitted. A typical use case looks like the following:

```
let stream$ = Observable.of(1,2,3)
  .filter( x => x > 1 );

stream$.subscribe( data => console.log(data))
// will emit 2,3
```

In the preceding code, we can see that the function we provide as a parameter to the filter function effectively sorts out any values not meeting the condition. In this case, all values above 1 will be emitted, thereby sorting the value 1. Let's add the `filter()` method to our previously defined `MyObservable` class, like so:

```
// rxjs-core/operator/Observable.ts, starting off with MyObservable, more
to come

import { MyObserver } from "./Observer";

class MyObservable {
  behaviorFn;
```

```
    static create(behaviourFn): MyObservable {
      return new MyObservable(behaviourFn);
    }

  constructor(behaviorFn) {
    this.behaviorFn = behaviorFn;
  }

  filter(filterFn): FilterableObservable {
    /* implement */
  }

  subscribe(dataFn) {
    let observer = new MyObserver(dataFn);
    let cleanUpFn = this.behaviorFn(observer);

    return {
      unsubscribe: cleanUpFn
    };
  }
}
```

We can see from the preceding snippet that the `filter()` method is added to the `MyObservable` and we see that it itself returns an Observable, while also taking a `filterFn()` as a parameter. The question you need to ask yourself is whether our existing `MyObservable` constructor will do. Our existing constructor takes a `behaviourFn()` and we most likely need to store the incoming `filterFn` parameter, so we need to extend the constructor or opt for a new implementation of an `MyObservable`. We ponder this for a second and realize its probably better to go for a new, more dedicated `MyObservable` as we want to avoid a lot of branching logic. Therefore, the implementation of said method should be amended to look something like this:

```
// rxjs-core/operator/Observable.ts, starting off with MyObservable, more
to come

import { MyObserver } from "./Observer";

class MyObservable {
  behaviorFn;
  static create(behaviourFn): MyObservable {
    return new MyObservable(behaviourFn);
  }

  constructor(behaviorFn) {
    this.behaviorFn = behaviorFn;
  }
```

```
filter(filterFn): FilterableObservable {
  return new FilterableObservable(filterFn, this.behaviorFn);
}

subscribe(dataFn) {
  let observer = new MyObserver(dataFn);
  let cleanUpFn = this.behaviorFn(observer);

  return {
    unsubscribe: cleanUpFn
  };
}
}
```

OK, so now we have a new class to implement, `FilterableObservable`. This class should share most of the behavior of the `MyObservable`, but instead show how we emit data. So, we are talking about inheriting from `MyObservable` but with our own special twist. Let's attempt an implementation:

```
// rxjs-core/operator/Observable.ts

import { MyObserver } from "./Observer";

class MyObservable {
  behaviorFn;
  static create(behaviourFn): MyObservable {
    return new MyObservable(behaviourFn);
  }

  constructor(behaviorFn) {
    this.behaviorFn = behaviorFn;
  }

  filter(filterFn): FilterableObservable {
    return new FilterableObservable(filterFn, this.behaviorFn);
  }

  subscribe(dataFn) {
    let observer = new MyObserver(dataFn);
    let cleanUpFn = this.behaviorFn(observer);
    return {
      unsubscribe: cleanUpFn
    };
  }
}

export class FilterableObservable extends MyObservable {
```

```
  constructor(private filterFn, behaviourFn) {
    super(behaviourFn);
  }

  subscribe(dataFn) {
    let observer = new MyObserver(dataFn);
    observer.next = value => {
      if (this.filterFn(value)) {
        dataFn(value);
      }
    };

    let cleanUpFn = this.behaviorFn(observer);
    return {
      unsubscribe: cleanUpFn
    };
  }
}

const stream$ = new MyObservable(observer => {
  observer.next(1);
  observer.next(2);
  observer.next(3);
}).filter(x => x > 2);

stream$.subscribe(data => console.log("data", data));

// prints 3
```

We can see in the preceding code snippet that we override the `subscribe()` implementation, or more specifically, we override the `next()` method on the `Observer` instance. We use `filterFn()` for what it was made for, to assess whether something should be generated or not. We have now successfully implemented the `filter()` operator.

Revisiting the basics, adding errors, and complete

After having taken on the heroic feat of implementing the basics of RxJS, we hopefully feel pretty good about understanding its inner workings. So far, we have only implemented `dataFn` in `subscribe()`; there are two more callbacks in the `subscribe()` method that we need to implement. Let's look at a code snippet and highlight what is missing:

```
let stream$ = Rx.Observable.of(1,2,3);
stream$.subscribe(
  data => console.log(data),
  err => console.error(err),
  () => console.log('complete');
)
```

We have highlighted the two last callbacks as the missing functionality. We know from before that to trigger the error callback, we need to call `observer.error('some message')`. We also know that no values should be emitted after an error is raised. Let's provide an example of such a case:

```
let stream$ = Rx.Observable.create( observer => {
  observer.next(1);
  observer.error('err');
  observer.next(2);
});

stream$.subscribe(
  data => console.log(data),
  err => console.error(err)
);
// should emit 1, err
```

At this point, we realize that our `Observer` class is the one that needs amending to support the `error()` method call. We also need to be wary of the condition we just described, as no more values should be emitted after an error has occurred. Let's jump into an implementation:

```
class Observer {
  hasError: boolean;
  constructor(private dataFn, private errorFn) {}
  next(value) {
    if (!this.hasError) {
      this.dataFn(value);
    }
  }

  error(err) {
    this.errorFn(err);
    this.hasError = true;
  }
}
```

We can see in the preceding snippet that we pass another parameter into the errorFn constructor. The next() method needed updating, so we needed to envelope it with a conditional that says whether to generate a value or not. Lastly, we needed to define the error() method as calling the passed-in errorFn and setting the hasError field to true.

We need to do one more thing and that is to update our subscribe() method in the Observable class:

```
class Observable {
  behaviourFn;
  static create(behaviourFn): Observable {
    return new Observable(behaviourFn);
  }

  constructor(behaviourFn) {
    this.behaviourFn = behaviourFn;
  }

  subscribe(dataFn, errorFn) {
    let observer = new Observer(dataFn, errorFn);
    let cleanUpFn = this.behaviourFn(observer);

    return {
      unsubscribe: cleanUpFn
    };
  }
}
```

A little heads up is that when we define the filter() operator to override the next() method, we need to ensure this one takes hasError into consideration when determining whether to generate a value. We'll leave this to you, dear reader, to implement.

The last order of business is to support completion. Completion has many similarities with raising an error, in the sense that no more values should be emitted. The difference is that we should hit the last callback instead. As with the error() method implementation, we start with the Observer implementation:

```
// rxjs-core/error-complete/Observer.ts

class Observer {
  hasError: boolean;
  isCompleted: boolean;

  constructor(
    private dataFn,
    private errorFn,
    private completeFn
  ) {}

  next(value) {
    if(!this.hasError && !this.isCompleted) {
      this.dataFn(value);
    }
  }

  error(err) {
    this.errorFn(err);
    this.hasError = true;
  }

  complete() {
    this.completeFn();
    this.isCompleted = true;
  }
}
```

Given the preceding code, we see that our changes entail adding an isCompleted field. We also pass a completeFn() in the constructor. Logic needs to be added in the next() value, as completion is now another state we need to look for besides error. Lastly, we added the complete() method, which just invokes the passed-in function and sets the isComplete field to true.

As before, we need to update the `Observable` class to pass the complete function:

```
// rxjs-core/error-complete/Observable.ts

import { Observer } from './Observer';

class Observable {
  behaviourFn;

  static create(behaviourFn): Observable {
    return new Observable(behaviourFn);
  }

  constructor(behaviourFn) {
    this.behaviourFn = behaviourFn;
  }

  filter(filterFn):Observable {
    return new FilterableObservable(
      filterFn,
      this.behaviourFn
    );
  }

  subscribe(dataFn, errorFn, completeFn) {
    let observer = new Observer(dataFn, errorFn, completeFn);
    let cleanUpFn = this.behaviourFn( observer );

    return {
      unsubscribe: cleanUpFn
    };
  }
}

const stream$ = new Observable(observer => {
  observer.next(1);
  observer.error("error");
  observer.next(2);
});

stream$.subscribe(
  data => console.log("data", data),
  err => console.log("error", err),
  () => console.log("completed")
);

// prints 1, error, no more is emitted after that
```

A quick reality check here: we have actually implemented the core functionality of RxJS—Observer, Observable, and one operator. We are much closer to understanding what is going on. We realize that implementing the other 59 operators is quite a feat, and it is probably not a good idea when there is a team maintaining the existing RxJS repository. Our newfound knowledge is not for nothing; understanding what is going on can never be wrong. Who knows? Maybe one of you readers will become a contributor; you have certainly been given the tools.

Summary

We started off by talking about the patterns that make up RxJS. We continued by describing its core concepts. This was followed by describing how and when it was necessary to create your own Observable, opt for one of RxJS many creation operators, or rely on the Angular framework to do this job for you. We briefly discussed the importance of cleaning up after your Observable and when it was a good idea to do so.

Lastly, we took on the task of implementing part of the RxJS core to gain a deeper understanding of its core concepts and how it all came together. This has hopefully given you a pretty solid foundation and in-depth understanding of RxJS as we venture into the next chapter, which will cover more operators, and some more advanced concepts.

6

Manipulating Streams and Their Values

Let's start with a recap of the previous chapter and remind ourselves how far we have come already in understanding RxJS. We learned about concepts such as `Observable`, `Observer`, and `Producer`, and how they interplay. Furthermore, we got insight into the subscription process so we could actually receive our coveted values. We also looked at how unsubscribing from streams works and in which cases it is necessary to define such a behavior. Lastly, we got our hands dirty by learning how to build a core implementation of RxJS and thereby got to see all those concepts in action. Armed with all that knowledge, we should feel quite confident about the foundation of RxJS, but as was mentioned in the last chapter, we need help from operators to actually do something meaningful with our streams.

Let's not delay any further and start talking about this chapter. Operators are functions we can call on our streams to perform manipulation in many different ways. Operators are immutable, which makes the stream easy to reason about and will also make it quite easy to test. As you will see throughout this chapter, we will seldom deal with just one stream, but many streams, and it is understanding how to forge and control these streams that allows you to go from thinking it's *dark magic* to actually being able to apply RxJS when and where you need it.

In this chapter, we will cover:

- How to use basic operators
- Debugging streams with operators as well as with existing tools
- Digging deeper into different operator categories
- Developing the mindset to solve a problem the Rx way

Starting out

You almost always start out coding with RxJS by creating a stream of static values. Why static values? Well, there is no need to make it unnecessarily complex, and all you really need to start reasoning is an `Observable`. As you gradually progress in your problem solving, you might replace the static values with a more appropriate call to an AJAX call, or from another asynchronous source that your values originate from.

You then start thinking about what you want to achieve. This leads you to consider which operators you might need and in which order you need to apply them. You might also think about how to divide your problem up; this usually means creating more than one stream, where each stream solves a specific problem that connects to the larger problem you are trying to solve.

Let's start with stream creation and see how we can take our first steps working with streams.

The following code creates a stream of static values:

```
const staticValuesStream$ = Rx.Observable.of(1, 2, 3, 4);

staticValuesStream$.subscribe(data => console.log(data));
// emits 1, 2, 3, 4
```

That is a very basic example of how we can create a stream. We use the `of()` creation operator, which takes any number of arguments. All the arguments are emitted, one by one, as soon as there is a subscriber. In the preceding code, we also subscribe to `staticValuesStream$` by calling the `subscribe()` method and passing a function that takes the emitted value as a parameter.

Let's introduce an operator, `map()`, which acts like a projection and allows you to change what is being emitted. The `map()` operator gets called on each value in the stream before it is emitted.

You use the `map()` operator by supplying it with a function and carrying out a projection, like so:

```
const staticValuesStream$ =
Rx.Observable
  .of(1, 2, 3, 4)
  .map(data => data + 1);

staticValuesStream$.subscribe(data => console.log(data))
// emits 2, 3, 4, 5
```

In the preceding code, we have appended the `map()` operator to `staticValuesStream$` and we apply it to each value before emitting it and incrementing it by one. The resulting data is therefore changed. This is how you append operators to a stream: simply create the stream, or take an existing one, and append the operators one by one.

Let's add another operator, `filter()`, to ensure that we really understand how to work with operators. What does `filter()` do. Well, just like the `map()` operator, it is applied to each value, but instead of creating a projection, it decides which values will be emitted. `filter()` takes a Boolean. Any expression evaluated to `true` means the value will be emitted; if `false`, the expression will not be emitted.

You use the `filter()` operator in the following way:

```
const staticValuesStream$ =
Rx.Observable
  .of(1, 2, 3, 4)
  .map(data => data + 1)
  .filter(data => data % 2 === 0 );

staticValuesStream$.subscribe(data => console.log(data));
// emits 2, 4
```

We add the `filter()` operator by chaining it to the existing `map()` operator. The condition we give our `filter()` operator says to only return `true` for values that are divisible by 2, that's what the modulus operator does. We know from before that the `map()` operator alone ensures that the values 2, 3 , 4, and 5 are emitted. These are the values that are now being evaluated by the `filter()` operator. Out of those four values, only 2 and 4 fulfill the condition set out by the `filter()` operator.

Of course, when working on a stream and applying operators, things might not always be as simple as the preceding code. It might not be possible to anticipate exactly what gets emitted. For those occasions, we have a few tricks we can use. One such trick is to use the do() operator, which will allow us to inspect each value without changing it. This gives us ample opportunity to use it for debugging purposes. Depending on where we are in the stream, the do() operator will output different values. Let's look at different situations where it matters where the do() operator is applied:

```
const staticValuesStream$ =
Rx.Observable.of(1, 2, 3, 4)
  .do(data => console.log(data)) // 1, 2, 3, 4
  .map(data => data + 1)
  .do(data => console.log(data)) // 2, 3, 4, 5
  .filter(data => data % 2 === 0 )
  .do(data => console.log(data)); // 2, 4

// emits 2, 4
staticValuesStream$.subscribe(data => console.log(data))
```

As you can see, just by using the do() operator, we have a nice way to debug our streams, which becomes necessary as our streams grow in complexity.

Understanding operators

So far, we have shown how to create a stream and use some very basic operators on it to change what values get emitted. We also introduced how to inspect your stream without changing it by using the do() operator. Not all operators are as easy to understand as the map(), filter(), and do() operators. There are different tactics you can use to try to understand what each operator does so you know when to use them. Using the do() operator is one way, but there is a graphical approach you can take. This approach is known as a marble diagram. It consists of an arrow that represents time passing from left to right. There are circles, or marbles, on this arrow that represent emitted values. The marbles have a value in them, but the distance between the marbles might also describe what is happening over time. A marble diagram usually consists of at least two arrows with marbles on them, as well as an operator. The idea is to represent what happens to a stream when an operator is applied. The second arrow usually represents the resulting stream.

Here's an example of a marble diagram:

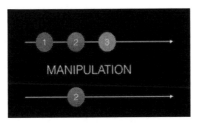

Most operators in RxJS are depicted by a marble diagram on the site RxMarbles: `http://rxmarbles.com/`. This is a truly great resource to quickly gain an understanding of what operators do. However, to truly understand RxJS you need to code; there is no getting around it. There are different ways of doing that of course. You can easily set up your own project and install RxJS from NPM, refer to it through a CDN link, or you can use a page such as JS Bin (`www.jsbin.com`), which gives you the ability to easily add RxJS as a library and allows you to start coding straight away. It looks something like this:

JS Bin makes it easy to start, but wouldn't it be great if we could combine marble diagrams and JS Bin, and get a graphical representation of what you code, when you code? You can get just that with RxFiddle: `http://rxfiddle.net/`. You can enter your code, click **Run**, and you are shown a marble diagram of what you just coded, which will look like this:

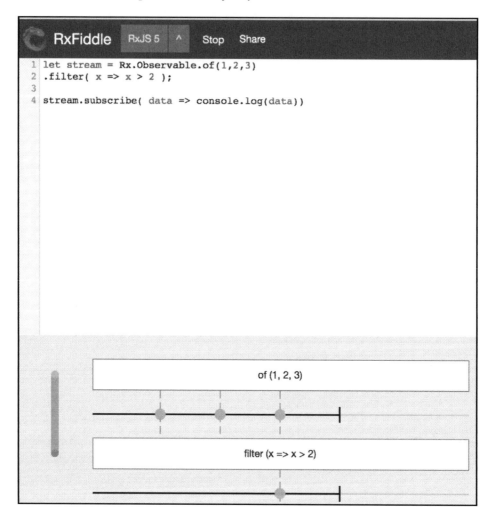

Stream in a stream

We have been looking at different operators that change the values being emitted. There is another different aspect to streams: what if you need to create a new stream from an existing stream? Another good question is: when does such a situation usually occur? There are plenty of situations, such as:

- Based on a stream of keyUp events, do an AJAX call.
- Count the number of clicks and determine whether the user single, double, or triple-clicked.

You get the idea; we are starting with one type of stream that needs to turn into another type of stream.

Let's first have a look at creating a stream and see what happens when we try to create a stream as the result of using an operator:

```
let stream$ = Rx.Observable.of(1,2,3)
   .map(data => Rx.Observable.of(data));

// Observable, Observable, Observable
stream$.subscribe(data => console.log(data));
```

At this point, every value that passes through the `map()` operator produces a new `Observable`. When you subscribe to `stream$`, each value that is emitted will be a stream. Your first instinct might be to attach a `subscribe()` to each of those values, like this:

```
let stream$ = Rx.Observable
   .of(1,2,3)
   .map(data => Rx.Observable.of(data))


stream$.subscribe(data => {
   data.subscribe(val => console.log(val))
});

// 1, 2, 3
```

Fight this urge. This will only create code that is hard to maintain. What you want to do is merge all these streams into one so, that you just need one `subscribe()`. There is an operator just for that, called `flatMap()`. What `flatMap()` does is to take your array of streams and turn them into one stream, a metastream.

It is used in the following way:

```
let stream$ = Rx.Observable.of(1,2,3)
  .flatMap(data => Rx.Observable.of(data))

stream$.subscribe(data => {
  console.log(val);
});

// 1, 2, 3
```

OK, we get it, we don't want a stream of Observables, but rather a stream of values. This operator seems really great. We still aren't quite certain when to use though. Let's make this a bit more realistic. Imagine you have a UI that consists of an input field. The user enters characters into that input field. Imagine that you want to react to one or more characters being entered and, for example, perform an AJAX request as the result of characters being entered. We focus on two things here: how to collect characters being entered and how to perform an AJAX request.

Let' start with the first thing, capturing characters entered into an input field. For this, we need an HTML page and a JavaScript page. Let's start with the HTML page:

```
<html>
  <body>
    <input id="input" type="text">
    <script src="https://unpkg.com/rxjs/bundles/Rx.min.js"></script>
    <script src="app.js"></script>
  </body>
</html>
```

This depicts our input element and a script reference to RxJS, as well as a reference to the app.js file. Then we have app.js file, where we get a reference to the input element and start listening to keystrokes as soon as they are entered:

```
let elem = document.getElementById('input');
let keyStream$ = Rx.Observable
  .fromEvent(elem, 'keyup')
  .map( ev => ev.key);

keyStream$.subscribe( key => console.log(key));

// emits entered key chars
```

Worth highlighting is the fact that we start listening to keyup events being emitted by calling the fromEvent() creation operator. Thereafter, we apply the map() operator to dig out the character value store on ev.key. Lastly, we subscribe to the stream. As expected, running this code will lead to characters being typed in the console as soon as you input values in the HTML page.

Let's make this more tangible by doing an AJAX request based on what we type. For this, we will be using the fetch() API and an online API called swapi (swapi.com), which contains a collection of APIs containing information on the Star Wars movies. Let's first define our AJAX call and then see how it fits into our existing stream of keys.

We said we would use fetch(). It lets us formulate a GET request as simple as this:

```
fetch('https://swapi.co/api/people/1')
  .then(data => data.json())
  .then(data => console.log('data', data));
```

Of course, we want to turn this request into an Observable so that it can play well with our keyStream$. Fortunately for us, this is easily accomplished through the use of the from() operator. Let's, however, first rewrite our fetch() call into a method that's easy to work with. The result of the rewrite looks like this:

```
function getStarwarsCharacterStream(id) {
  return fetch('https://swapi.co/api/people/' + id)
    .then(data => data.json());
}
```

This code allows us to provide an argument used to construct a URL which we use to fetch some data with AJAX. At this point, we are ready to connect our function to our existing stream. We do that by typing the following:

```
let keyStream$ = Rx.Observable.fromEvent(elem, 'keyup')
  .map(ev => ev.key)
  .filter(key => key !== 'Backspace')
  .flatMap( key =>
    Rx.Observable
      .from(getStarwarsCharacterStream(key))
  );
```

We highlight the usage of the flatmap() operator in bold using our from() conversion operator. The operator mentioned last takes our getStarwarsCharacterStream() function as a parameter. The from() operator converts said function into a stream.

Here, we have learned how to connect two different streams, but also how to convert a `Promise` into a stream. As good as this approach seems on paper, using `flatMap()` has its limitations and it is important to understand what they are. For that reason, let's talk about the `switchMap()` operator next. The benefits of using a `switchMap()` operator will become clearer when we execute long-running tasks. For argument's sake, let's define such a task, like so:

```
function longRunningTask(input) {
  return new Promise(resolve => {
    setTimeout(() => {
      resolve('response based on ' + input);
    }, 5000);
  });
}
```

In this code, we have a function that takes 5 seconds to execute; enough time to show the point we are trying to make. Next, let's show what the effect is if we keep using the `flatMap()` operator in the following code:

```
let longRunningStream$ = keyStream$
  .map(ev => ev.key)
  .filter(key => elem.value.length >3)
  .filter( key => key !== 'Backspace')
  .flatMap( key =>
    Rx.Observable
      .from(longRunningTask(elem.value))
  );

longRunningStream$.subscribe(data => console.log(data));
```

The preceding code works in the following way: every time we hit a key, it generates an event. However, we have a `.filter()` operator in place that ensures an event is only generated when at least four keys are entered, `filter(key => elem.value.length >3)`. Let's talk about the user's expectation at this point. If a user enters keys in an input control, they most likely expect a request to be made when they are done typing. A user defines being done as entering a few characters and also that they should be able to remove characters if they were mistyped. So, therefore, we can assume the following input sequence:

```
// enters abcde
abcde
// removes 'e'
```

At this point, they have entered characters and, within a reasonable amount of time, edited their answer. The user expects to receive an answer based on abcd. Using the flatMap() operator, however, means the user will get two answers back because, in reality, they typed abcde and abcd. Imagine we get a results list based on these two inputs; it would most likely be two lists that looked somewhat different. The response based on our code would look like this:

```
response based on 1234
response based on 12345
```

Our code most likely would be able to handle the situation described by rerendering the results list as soon as a new response arrives. There are two problems with this though: firstly, we do an unnecessary network request for abcde, and secondly, if the backend is fast enough in responding, we will see a flickering in the UI as the result list is rendered once and then, shortly after, is rendered again, based on the second response. This is not good, and we want to have a situation where the first request will be abandoned if we keep on typing. This is where the switchMap() operator comes in. It does exactly that. Let's therefore alter the preceding code to the following:

```
let longRunningStream$ = keyStream$
  .map(ev => ev.key)
  .filter(key => elem.value.length >3)
  .filter( key => key !== 'Backspace')
  .switchMap( key =>
    Rx.Observable
    .from(longRunningTask(elem.value))
  );
```

In this code, we simply switched our flatMap() to a switchMap(). When we now execute the code in the exact same way, that is, the user firstly typing 12345 and shortly altering that to 1234, the end result is:

```
response based on abcde
```

As we can see, we get one request only. The reason for this is that the previous event is aborted when a new event happens—switchMap() is doing its magic. The user is happy and we are happy.

AJAX

We have already touched upon the topic of making AJAX requests. There are many ways to make AJAX requests; the two most common approaches are:

- Using the fetch API; the fetch API is a web standard and is thus built into most browsers
- Using the `ajax()` method, nowadays built into the RxJS library; it used to exist in a library called Rx.Dom

fetch()

The `fetch()` API is a web standard. You can find the official documentation at the following link: `https://developer.mozilla.org/en-US/docs/Web/API/Fetch_API`. The `fetch()` API is `Promise`-based, which means we need to convert it to an `Observable` before use. The API exposes a `fetch()` method, which takes a mandatory URL parameter as the first argument, with the second argument being an optional object that allows you to control which body to send, if any, which HTTP verb to use, and so on.

We have already mentioned how to best deal with it in the context of RxJS. It is worth repeating though. It is not as simple as just taking our fetch and sticking it into the `from()` operator though. Let's write some code and see why:

```
let convertedStream$ =
Rx.Observable.from(fetch('some url'));

convertedStream$.subscribe(data => 'my data?', data);
```

We get our data right? Sorry, no, we get a `Response` object back. But that's easy, just call a `json()` method in the `map()` operator and surely then we have our data? Again, sorry no, the `json()` method returns a `Promise` when you type the following:

```
let convertedStream$ = Rx.Observable.from(fetch('some url'))
  .map( r=> r.json());

// returns PromiseObservable
convertedStream$.subscribe(data => 'my data?', data);
```

We have already shown a possible solution to this in the previous section, and that is the following construct:

```
getData() {
  return fetch('some url')
    .then(r => r.json());
}

let convertedStream$ = Rx.Observable.from(getData());
convertedStream$.subscribe(data => console.log('data', data));
```

What we did in this code was to simply take care of digging out our data before handing it over to the `from()` operator. It doesn't feel quite RxJS to play around with Promises. There is a more stream-based approach you can take; we were almost there before, we just needed to make a minor adjustment:

```
let convertedStream$ = Rx.Observable.from(fetch('some url'))
  .flatMap( r => Rx.Observable.from(r.json()));

// returns data
convertedStream$.subscribe(data => console.log('data'), data);
```

And there it is: our `fetch()` call is now providing us data like a stream. So what did we do? Well, we changed our `map()` call to a `flatMap()` call. The reason for that was that when we called `r.json()`, we got a `Promise`. We fixed that by wrapping it in a `from()` call, `Rx.Observable.from(r.json())`. That would make the stream emit a `PromiseObservable` unless we changed from `map()` to `flatMap()`. As we learned in the previous section, if we risk creating a stream within a stream, we need `flatMap()` to come to our rescue, which it did.

ajax() operator

Unlike the `fetch()` API, which is `Promise`-based, the `ajax()` method is actually `Observable`-based, which makes our job a little easier. Using it is quite straightforward, like so:

```
Rx.Observable
  .ajax('https://swapi.co/api/people/1')
  .map(r => r.response)
  .subscribe(data => console.log('from ajax()', data));
```

As we can see, the preceding code calls the `ajax()` operator with a URL as an argument. The second thing worthy of mentioning is the call to the `map()` operator, which digs out our data from the `response` property. Because it is an `Observable`, we just have to subscribe to it as usual by calling the `subscribe()` method and providing it with a listener function as an argument.

This covers a simple case when you want to fetch data using the HTTP verb `GET`. Fortunately for us, it is quite easy to create, update, or delete by using an overloaded version of the `ajax()` operator which takes an `AjaxRequest` object instance which has the following fields:

```
url?: string;
body?: any;
user?: string;
async?: boolean;
method?: string;
headers?: Object;
timeout?: number;
password?: string;
hasContent?: boolean;
crossDomain?: boolean;
withCredentials?: boolean;
createXHR?: () => XMLHttpRequest;
progressSubscriber?: Subscriber<any>;
responseType?: string;
```

As we can see from this object specification, all the fields are optional and there are also quite a few things we can configure with our request, such as `headers`, `timeout`, `user`, `crossDomain`, and so on; pretty much what we would expect from a nice AJAX wrapping functionality. Except for the overload of the `ajax()` operator, a few shorthand options also exist:

- `get()`: Fetches data using the `GET` verb
- `put()`: Updates data using the `PUT` verb
- `post()`: Creates data using the `POST` verb
- `patch()`: The idea with using the `PATCH` verb is to update a partial resource
- `delete()`: Removes data using the `DELETE` verb
- `getJSON()`: Fetches data using the `GET` verb and sets the response type to `application/json`

Cascading calls

So far, we have covered the two main ways you will use AJAX to send or receive data. When it comes to receiving data, it's usually not as simple as fetching the data and rendering it. In fact, you will most likely have a dependency on when you can fetch which data. A typical example of this is needing to perform a login call before you can fetch the remaining data. In some cases, it might be that you need to first log in, then fetch the data of the logged in user, and once you have that you can fetch messages, orders, or whichever kind of data you need that might be specific to a certain user. This whole phenomenon of fetching data in this way is called cascading calls.

Let's have a look at how we use cascading calls with Promises and gradually learn how to do the same with RxJS. We are taking this little detour as we assume that most of you reading this book are familiar with Promises.

Let's look at the dependent case we first mentioned, where we need to perform the following steps in this order:

1. The user first logs in to the system
2. Then we fetch information about the user
3. Then we fetch information about the user's orders

Using promises, it would look something like this in code:

```
// cascading/cascading-promises.js

login()
  .then(getUser)
  .then(getOrders);

// we collect username and password from a form
const login = (username, password) => {
  return fetch("/login", {
    method: "POST",
    body: { username, password }
  })
  .then(r => r.json())
  .then(token => {
    localStorage.setItem("auth", token);
  });
};

const getUser = () => {
  return fetch("/users", {
    headers: {
```

```
      Authorization: "Bearer " + localStorage.getToken("auth")
    }
  }).then(r => r.json());
};

const getOrders = user => {
  return fetch(`/orders/user/${user.id}`, {
    headers: {
      Authorization: "Bearer " + localStorage.getToken("auth")
    }
  }).then(r => r.json());
};
```

This code describes how we first log in to the system, using the `login()` method, and obtain a token. We use this token in any future calls to ensure we make authenticated calls. We also see how we perform the `getUser()` call and obtain a user instance. We use that same user instance to perform our last call, `getOrders()`, whereby the user ID is used as a routing parameter: `` `/orders/user/${user.id}` ``.

We have shown how to perform cascading calls using promises; we did this to establish a common ground for the problem we are trying to solve. The RxJS approach is very similar: we have shown that the `ajax()` operator exists and makes our lives easier when dealing with AJAX calls. To achieve the cascading calls effect with RxJS, we simply need to use the `switchMap()` operator. This will lead to our code looking like this:

```
// cascading/cascading-rxjs.js

let user = "user";
let password = "password";

login(user, password)
  .switchMap(getUser)
  .switchMap(getOrders);

// we collect username and password from a form
const login = (username, password) => {
  return Rx.Observable.ajax("/login", {
    method: "POST",
    body: { username, password }
  })
  .map(r => r.response)
  .do(token => {
    localStorage.setItem("auth", token);
  });
};
```

```
const getUser = () => {
  return Rx.Observable.ajax("/users", {
    headers: {
      Authorization: "Bearer " + localStorage.getToken("auth")
    }
  }).map(r => r.response);
};

const getOrders = user => {
  return Rx.Observable.json(`/orders/user/${user.id}`, {
    headers: {
      Authorization: "Bearer " + localStorage.getToken("auth")
    }
  }).map(r => r.response);
};
```

We have highlighted the parts that need changing in the preceding code. In short, the changes are:

- `fetch()` is replaced by the `ajax()` operator
- We call `.map(r => r.response)` instead of `.then(r => r.json())`
- We do `.switchMap()` calls for each cascading call instead of `.then(getOrders)`

There is one more interesting aspect that we need to cover, namely that of parallel calls. When we fetched the user and the order, we waited for a previous call to fully complete before we initiated the next call. In a lot of cases, this might not be strictly necessary. Imagine that we have a similar case to the previous one, but there is a lot of interesting information surrounding the user that we want to fetch. Instead of just fetching orders, the user might have a friends collection or a collection of messages. The precondition for fetching that data is only that we fetched the user, so we know which collection of friends we should query for and which collection of messages we need. In the world of promises, we would use the `Promise.all()` construct to achieve parallelization. With that in mind, we update our `Promise` code to look like this:

```
// parallell/parallell-promise.js

// we collect username and password from a form
login(username, password) {
  return new Promise(resolve => {
    resolve('logged in');
  });
}

getUsersData(user) {
```

```
    return Promise.all([
      getOrders(user),
      getMessages(user),
      getFriends(user)
      // not implemented but you get the idea, another call in parallell
    ])
  }

  getUser() {
    // same as before
  }

  getOrders(user) {
    // same as before
  }

  login()
    .then(getUser)
    .then(getUsersData);
```

As we can see from the preceding code, we introduce the new
getUsersData() method, which fetches orders, messages, and friends collections in
parallel, making our app responsive sooner, as the data will arrive sooner than if we just
fetched it one after another.

We can easily achieve the same thing with RxJS by introducing the forkJoin() operator. It
takes a list of streams and fetches everything in parallel. We therefore update our RxJS code
to look like the following:

```
// parallell/parallell-rxjs.js

import Rx from 'rxjs/Rx';
// imagine we collected these from a form
let user = 'user';
let password = 'password';

login(user, password)
  .switchMap(getUser)
  .switchMap(getUsersData)

// we collect username and password from a form
login(username, password) {
  // same as before
}

getUsersData(user) {
  return Rx.Observable.forkJoin([
```

```
      getOrders(),
      getMessages(),
      getFriends()
   ])
}

getUser() {
   // same as before
}

getOrders(user) {
   // same as before
}

login()
   .then(getUser)
   .then(getUsersData);
```

A deeper look

So far, we have had a look at some operators that will let you create streams or change streams with the `map()` and `filter()` operators, we have learned how to manage different AJAX scenarios, and so on. The basics are there, but we haven't really approached the topic of operators in a structured way. What do we mean by that? Well, operators can be thought of as belonging to different categories. The number of operators at our disposal is a staggering 60 plus. It's going to take us time to learn all that, if we ever do. Here is the thing though: we just need to know which different types of operators exist so that we can apply them where appropriate. This reduces our cognitive load and our memory. Once we know which categories we have, we just have to drill down, and most likely we will end up knowing 10-15 operators in total and the rest we can just look up when we need them.

Currently, we have the following categories:

- **Creation operators**: These operators help us create streams in the first place. Almost anything can be converted into a stream with the help of these operators.
- **Combination operators**: These operators help us combine values as well as streams.
- **Mathematical operators**: These operators perform mathematical evaluations on the values being emitted.

- **Time-based operators**: These operators change at which speed values are emitted.
- **Grouping operators**: The idea with these operators is to operate on a group of values rather than individual ones.

Creation operators

We use creation operators to create the streams themselves, because let's face it: what we need to turn into a stream isn't always going to be a stream, but by making it into a stream, it will have to play nicely with other streams and, best of all, will get to leverage the full power of using operators.

So, what do these other non-streams consist of? Well, it could be anything asynchronous or synchronous. The important thing is that it is data that needs to be emitted at some point. Therefore, a range of creation operators exist. In the coming subsections, we will present a subset of all those that exist, enough for you to realize the power of turning anything into a stream.

of() operator

We have already had the chance to use this operator a few times. It takes an unknown number of comma-separated arguments, which can be integers, strings, or objects. This is an operator you want to use if you just want to emit a limited set of values. To use it, simply type:

```
// creation-operators/of.js

const numberStream$ = Rx.Observable.of(1,2, 3);
const objectStream$ = Rx.Observable.of({ age: 37 }, { name: "chris" });

// emits 1 2 3
numberStream$.subscribe(data => console.log(data));

// emits { age: 37 }, { name: 'chris' }
objectStream$.subscribe(data => console.log(data));
```

As can be seen from the code, it really doesn't matter what we place in our `of()` operator, it is able to emit it anyway.

from() operator

This operator can take arrays or a `Promise` as input and turn them into a stream. To use it, simply call it like this:

```
// creation-operators/from.js

const promiseStream$ = Rx.Observable.from(
  new Promise(resolve => setTimeout(() => resolve("data"),3000))
);

const arrayStream$ = Rx.Observable.from([1, 2, 3, 4]);

promiseStream$.subscribe(data => console.log("data", data));
// emits data after 3 seconds

arrayStream$.subscribe(data => console.log(data));
// emits 1, 2, 3, 4
```

This saves us a lot of headache by not having to deal with different types of asynchronous calls.

range() operator

This operator lets you specify a range, a number to start from and a number to end on. This is a nice shorthand that quickly lets you create a stream with a range of numbers. To use it, simply type:

```
// creation-operators/range.js

const stream$ = Rx.Observable.range(1,99);

stream$.subscribe(data => console.log(data));
// emits 1... 99
```

fromEvent() operator

Now it gets really interesting. The `fromEvent()` operator allows us to mix a UI event such as a `click` or a `scroll` event and turn it into a stream. So far, we have operated under the assumption that asynchronous calls is something that only has to do with AJAX calls. This is far from true. The fact that we can mix UI events with any type of asynchronous calls creates a really interesting situation that allows us to compose really powerful, expressive code. We will touch on this topic further in the coming section, *Thinking in streams*.

To use this operator, you need to provide it with two arguments: a DOM element and the name of an event, like so:

```
// creation-operators/fromEvent.js

// we imagine we have an element in our DOM looking like this <input
id="id" />
const elem = document.getElementById("input");
const eventStream$ = Rx.Observable
  .fromEvent(elem, "click")
  .map(ev => ev.key);

// outputs the typed key
eventStream$.subscribe(data => console.log(data));
```

Combination

Combination operators are about combining values from different streams. We have a few operators at our disposal that can help us out. This kind of operator makes sense when we, for some reason, don't have all the data in one place but need to acquire it from more than one place. Combining data structures from different sources could be tedious and error-prone work if it weren't for the powerful operators we are about to describe.

merge() operator

The `merge()` operator takes data from different streams and combines it. Here is the thing though: these streams can be of any kind as long as they are of type `Observable`. This means we can combine data from a timing operation, a promise, static data from an `of()` operator, and so on. What merging does is to interleave the emitted data. This means that it will emit from both streams at the same time in the following example. Using the operator comes in two flavors, as a static method but also as an instance method:

```
// combination/merge.js

let promiseStream = Rx.Observable
.from(new Promise(resolve => resolve("data")))

let stream = Rx.Observable.interval(500).take(3);
let stream2 = Rx.Observable.interval(500).take(5);

// instance method version of merge(), emits 0,0, 1,1 2,2 3, 4
stream.merge(stream2)
  .subscribe(data => console.log("merged", data));
```

```
// static version of merge(), emits 0,0, 1,1, 2, 2, 3, 4 and 'data'
Rx.Observable.merge(
  stream,
  stream2,
  promiseStream
)
.subscribe(data => console.log("merged static", data));
```

The takeaway here is that if you just need to combine one stream with another, then use the instance method version of this operator, but if you have several streams, then use the static version. Furthermore, the order in which the streams are specified matters.

combineLatest()

Imagine you have a situation where you have set up connections with several endpoints that serve you with data. What you care about is the latest data that was emitted from each endpoint. You might be in a situation where one or several endpoints stop sending data after a while and you want to know what the last thing that happened was. In this situation, we want the ability to combine all the latest values from all of the involved endpoints. That's where the combineLatest() operator comes in. You use it in the following way:

```
// combination/combineLatest.js

let firstStream$ = Rx.Observable
  .interval(500)
  .take(3);

let secondStream$ = Rx.Observable
  .interval(500)
  .take(5);

let combinedStream$ = Rx.Observable.combineLatest(
  firstStream$,
  secondStream$
)

// emits [0, 0] [1,1] [2,2] [2,3] [2,4] [2,5]
combinedStream$.subscribe(data => console.log(data));
```

What we can see here is that firstStream$ stops emitting values after a while thanks to the take() operator, which limits the number of items. However, the combineLatest() operator ensures we are still given the very last value firstStream$ emitted.

zip()

The point of this operator is to stitch as many values together as possible. We may be dealing with continuous streams, but also with streams that have a limit to the number of values they emit. You use this operator in the following way:

```
// combination/zip.js

let stream$ = Rx.Observable.of(1, 2, 3, 4);
let secondStream$ = Rx.Observable.of(5, 6, 7, 8);
let thirdStream$ = Rx.Observable.of(9, 10);

let zippedStream$ = Rx.Observable.zip(
  stream$,
  secondStream$,
  thirdStream$
)

// [1, 5, 9] [2, 6, 10]
zippedStream$.subscribe(data => console.log(data))
```

As we can see, here, we stitch values together vertically, and by the least common denominator, `thirdStream$` is the shortest, calculating the number of emitted values. This means we will take values from left to right and zip them together. As `thirdStream$` only has two values, we end up with only two emits.

concat()

At first look, the `concat()` operator looks like another `merge()` operator, but this is not entirely true. The difference is that a `concat()` waits for other streams to be completed first before emitting a stream from the next stream in order. How you arrange your stream in your call to `concat()` matters. The operator is used in the following way:

```
// combination/concat.js

let firstStream$ = Rx.Observable.of(1,2,3,4);
let secondStream$ = Rx.Observable.of(5,6,7,8);

let concatStream$ = Rx.Observable.concat(
  firstStream$,
  secondStream$
);

concatStream$.subscribe(data => console.log(data));
```

Mathematical

Mathematical operators are simply operators that carry out mathematical operations on values, such as finding the largest or smallest value, summarizing all values, and so on.

max

The `max()` operator finds the largest value. This comes in two flavors: we either just call the `max()` operator with no arguments, or we give it a `compare` function. The `compare` function then decides whether something is larger than, smaller than, or equal to an emitted value. Let's have a look at the two different versions:

```
// mathematical/max.js

let streamWithNumbers$ = Rx.Observable
  .of(1,2,3,4)
  .max();

// 4
streamWithNumbers$.subscribe(data => console.log(data));

function comparePeople(firstPerson, secondPerson) {
  if (firstPerson.age > secondPerson.age) {
    return 1;
  } else if (firstPerson.age < secondPerson.age) {
    return -1;
  }
  return 0;
}

let streamOfObjects$ = Rx.Observable
  .of({
    name : "Yoda",
    age: 999
  }, {
    name : "Chris",
    age: 38
  })
  .max(comparePeople);

// { name: 'Yoda', age : 999 }
streamOfObjects$.subscribe(data => console.log(data));
```

We can see in the preceding code that we get one result back and it is the largest one.

min

The `min()` operator is pretty much the opposite of the `max()` operator; it comes in two flavors: with parameter and without parameter. Its task is to find the smallest value. To use it, type:

```
// mathematical/min.js

let streamOfValues$ = Rx.Observable
  .of(1, 2, 3, 4)
  .min();

// emits 1
streamOfValues$.subscribe(data => console.log(data));
```

sum

There used to be an operator called `sum()`, but it hasn't existed for several versions. What there is instead is `.reduce()`. With the `reduce()` operator, we can easily achieve the same thing. The following is how you would write a `sum()` operator using `reduce()`:

```
// mathematical/sum.js

let stream = Rx.Observable.of(1, 2, 3, 4)
  .reduce((acc, curr) => acc + curr);

// emits 10
stream.subscribe(data => console.log(data));
```

What this does is to loop through all the emitted values and sum up the results. So, in essence, it sums up everything. Of course, this kind of operator can not only be applied to numbers, but to objects as well. The difference lies in how you carry out the `reduce()` operation. The following example covers such a scenario:

```
let stream = Rx.Observable.of({ name : "chris" }, { age: 38 })
  .reduce((acc, curr) => Object.assign({},acc, curr));

// { name: 'chris', age: 38 }
stream.subscribe(data => console.log(data));
```

As you can see from the preceding code, the `reduce()` operator ensures that all the object's properties get merged together into one object.

Time

Time is a very important concept when talking about streams. Imagine you have multiple streams that have different bandwidths, or one stream is just faster than the other, or you have a scenario where you want to retry an AJAX call within a certain time interval. In all of these situations, we need to control how fast the data is being emitted, and time plays an important role in all these scenarios. At our disposal, we have a ton of operators that, like a magician, enable us to craft and control our values as we see fit.

interval() operator

In JavaScript, there is a `setInterval()` function that enables you to execute code at regular intervals, up until the point that you choose to stop it. RxJS has an operator that behaves just like that, the `interval()` operator. It takes one parameter: normally, the number of milliseconds between emitted values. You use it in the following way:

```
// time/interval.js

let stream$ = Rx.Observable.interval(1000);

// emits 0, 1, 2, 3 ... n with 1 second in between emits, till the end of
time
stream$.subscribe(data => console.log(data));
```

A word of caution is that this operator will continue emitting until you stop it. The best way to stop it is to combine it with a `take()` operator. A `take()` operator takes a parameter that specifies how many emitted values it wants before stopping. The updated code looks like this:

```
// time/interval-take.js

let stream$ = Rx.Observable.interval(1000)
  .take(2);

// emits 0, 1, stops emitting thanks to take() operator
stream$.subscribe(data => console.log(data));
```

timer() operator

The `timer()` operator has the job of emitting values after a certain amount of time. It comes in two flavors: you either emit just one value after a number of milliseconds, or you keep on emitting values with a certain amount of delay between them. Let's look at the two different flavors available:

```
// time/timer.js

let stream$ = Rx.Observable.timer(1000);

// delay with 500 milliseconds
let streamWithDelay$ = Rx.Observable.timer(1000, 500)

// emits 0 after 1000 milliseconds, then no more
stream$.subscribe(data => console.log(data));

streamWithDelay$.subscribe(data => console.log(data));
```

delay() operator

The `delay()` operator delays all the values being emitted and is used in the following way:

```
// time/delay.js

let stream$ = Rx.Observable
.interval(100)
.take(3)
.delay(500);

// 0 after 600 ms, 1 after 1200 ms, 2 after 1800 ms
stream.subscribe(data => console.log(data));
```

sampleTime() operator

The `sampleTime()` operator is used to only emit values after the sample period has passed. A good use case for this is when you want to have a *cooldown* functionality. Imagine you have users that press a **Save** button way too often. It might be that saving takes a few seconds to complete. A way to approach this is to disable the **Save** button while saving. Another valid approach is to simply ignore any presses of the button until the operation has had the chance to complete. The following code does just that:

```
// time/sampleTime.js
```

```
let elem = document.getElementById("btn");
let stream$ = Rx.Observable
   .fromEvent(elem, "click")
   .sampleTime(8000);

// emits values every 8th second
stream$.subscribe(data => console.log("mouse clicks",data));
```

debounceTime() operator

The `sampleTime()` operator was able to ignore the user for a certain period of time, but the `debounceTime()` operator takes a different approach. Debounce as a concept means that we wait for things to calm down before emitting a value. Imagine an input element that the user types into. The user will stop typing eventually. We want to make sure the user has actually stopped, so we wait for a while before we actually do something. This is what the `debounceTime()` operator does for us. The following example shows how we can listen to the user typing into an input element, wait for the user to stop typing, and lastly, perform an AJAX call:

```
// time/debounceTime.js
const elem = document.getElementById("input");

let stream$ = Rx.Observable.fromEvent(elem, "keyup")
   .map( ev => ev.key)
   .filter(key => key !== "Backspace")
   .debounceTime(2000)
   .switchMap( x => {
     return new
Rx.Observable.ajax(`https://swapi.co/api/people/${elem.value}`);
   })
   .map(r => r.response);

stream$.subscribe(data => console.log(data));
```

When the user then types a number in the text box, the keyup event will be triggered after 2 seconds of inactivity. After that, an AJAX call will be carried out using our text box input.

Grouping

Grouping operators allow us to operate on a group of collected events rather than one emitted event at a time.

buffer() operator

The idea with the `buffer()` operator is that we can collect a bunch of events without them being emitted straight away. The operator itself takes an argument, an `Observable` that defines when we should stop collecting events. At that point in time, we can choose what to do with those events. Here is how you can use this operator:

```
// grouping/buffer.js

const elem = document.getElementById("input");

let keyStream$ = Rx.Observable.fromEvent(elem, "keyup");
let breakStream$ = keyStream$.debounceTime(2000);
let chatStream$ = keyStream$
  .map(ev => ev.key)
  .filter(key => key !== "Backspace")
  .buffer(breakStream$)
  .switchMap(newContent => Rx.Observable.of("send text as I type",
newContent));

chatStream$.subscribe(data=> console.log(data));
```

What this does is to collect events until there has been 2 seconds of inactivity. At that point, we release all the key events we have buffered up. When we release all those events, we can, for example, send them somewhere via AJAX. This is a typical scenario in a chat application. Using the preceding code, we can always send the latest character that has been typed.

bufferTime() operator

A very similar operator to `buffer()` is `bufferTime()`. This one lets us specify how long we would like to buffer events for. It is a bit less flexible than `buffer()`, but can still be quite useful.

Thinking in streams

So far, we have gone through a bunch of scenarios that have shown us which operators are at our disposal and how they can be chained. We have also seen how operators such as `flatMap()` and `switchMap()` can really change things as we move from one type of observable to another. So, which approach should you take when working with Observables? Obviously, we need to express an algorithm using operators, but where do we start? The first thing we need to do is to think of the start and the end. Which types of events do we want to capture and what should the end result look like? That already gives us a hint as to the number of transformations we need to carry out to get there. If we want to transform the data only, then we can probably make do with a `map()` operator and a `filter()` operator. If we want to transform from one `Observable` to the next, then we need a `flatMap()` or a `switchMap()`. Do we have a specific behavior, such as waiting for the user to stop typing? If so, then we need to look at `debounceTime()` or similar. It's really the same as all problems: break it down, see which parts you have, divide, and conquer. Let's try to break this down into a list of steps though:

- What are the inputs? UI events or something else?
- What are the outputs? The end result?
- Given the second bullet, which transformations do I need to get there?
- Do I deal with more than one stream?
- Do I need to handle errors, and if so, how?

This has hopefully introduced you to how to think about streams. Remember, start small and work your way toward your goal.

Summary

We set out to learn more about basic operators. In doing so, we encountered the `map()` and `filter()` operators, which allowed us to control what was being emitted. Knowledge of the `do()` operator gave us a way to debug our streams. Furthermore, we learned about the existence of sandboxed environments, such as JS Bin and RxFiddle, and how they can help us to quickly get started with RxJS. AJAX was the next topic that we delved into, and we built an understanding of the different scenarios that might occur. Moving on deeper into RxJS, we looked at different operator categories. We barely scratched the surface on that one, but it offered us a way to approach how to learn which types of operators are in the library. Finally, we finished off this chapter by looking at how to change and develop our mindset to thinking about streams.

It is with all this acquired knowledge that we are now ready to venture into more advanced Rx topics in the next chapter. We know our basics, now the time has come to master them.

7
RxJS Advanced

We just finished our last chapter that taught us more about what operators exist and how to utilize them effectively. Armed with this knowledge, we will now go into this subject in more depth. We will go from learning about what parts exist, to actually understanding the nature of RxJS. Knowing the nature of RxJS involves understanding more about what makes it tick. To uncover this, we need to cover topics such as what the differences are between hot, warm, and cold Observables; knowing about Subjects and what they are good for; and the sometimes ignored topic of Schedulers.

There are also other aspects of working with Observables that we want to cover, namely, how to deal with errors and how to test your Observables.

In this chapter, you will learn about:

- Hot, cold, and warm Observables
- Subjects: how they differ from Observables, and when to use them
- Pipeable operators, a recent addition to the RxJS library, and how they affect how you compose Observables
- Marble testing, the testing machinery in place that helps you with testing your Observables

Hot, cold, and warm Observables

There are hot, cold, and warm Observables. What do we actually mean by that? For starters, let's say that most things you will deal with are cold Observables. Not helping? If we say that cold Observables are lazy, does that help? No? OK, let's talk about Promises for a second. Promises are hot. They are hot because when we execute their code, it happens straight away. Let's see an example of that:

```js
// hot-cold-warm/promise.js

function getData() {
  return new Promise(resolve => {
    console.log("this will be printed straight away");
    setTimeout(() => resolve("some data"), 3000);
  });
}

// emits 'some data' after 3 seconds
getData().then(data => console.log("3 seconds later", data));
```

If you come from a non-RxJS background, you will most likely, at this point, think: OK, yes, that's what I expected. This is the point we are trying to make, though:
Calling `getData()` makes your code run straight away. This differs from RxJS in the sense that similar RxJS code will actually not run until there is a listener/subscriber that cares about the result. RxJS answers the old philosophical question: Does a tree make a sound when it falls in the forest if no one is there to listen? In the case of Promises, it does. In the case of an Observable, it doesn't. Let's clarify what we just said with a similar code example using RxJS and Observables:

```js
// hot-cold-warm/observer.js

const Rx = require("rxjs/Rx");

function getData() {
  return Rx.Observable(observer => {
    console.log("this won't be printed until a subscriber exists");
    setTimeout(() => {
      observer.next("some data");
      observer.complete();
    }, 3000);
  });
}

// nothing happens
getData();
```

In RxJS, code like this is considered cold, or lazy. We need a subscriber for something to actually happen. We can add a subscriber like so:

```
// hot-cold-warm/observer-with-subscriber

const Rx = require("rxjs/Rx");

function getData() {
  return Rx.Observable.create(observer => {
    console.log("this won't be printed until a subscriber exists");
    setTimeout(() => {
      observer.next("some data");
      observer.complete();
    }, 3000);
  });
}

const stream$ = getData();
stream$.subscribe(data => console.log("data from observer", data));
```

This is a major difference in how Observables behave versus Promises, and it's important to know. This is a cold Observable; so, what is a hot Observable? It would be easy to think, at this point, that a hot Observable is something that executes straight away; there is more to it than that, however. One of the official explanations of what a hot Observable is, is that anything that subscribes to it will share the Producer with other Subscribers. The Producer is what spouts out values internally inside the Observable. This means that the data is shared. Let's look at a cold Observable subscription scenario and contrast that with a hot Observable subscription scenario. We will start with the cold scenario:

```
// hot-cold-warm/cold-observable.js
const Rx = require("rxjs/Rx");

const stream$ = Rx.Observable.interval(1000).take(3);

// subscriber 1 emits 0, 1, 2
stream$.subscribe(data => console.log(data));

// subscriber 2, emits 0, 1, 2
stream$.subscribe(data => console.log(data));

// subscriber 3, emits 0, 1, 2, after 2 seconds
setTimeout(() => {
  stream$.subscribe(data => console.log(data));
}, 3000);
```

In the preceding code, we have three different subscribers that receive their own copy of emitted values. The values start from the beginning, every time we add a new subscriber. That might be expected when looking at the two first subscribers. As for the third one, it is added as a subscriber after two seconds. Yes, even that subscriber receives its own set of values. The explanation is that each subscriber receives its own Producer upon subscription.

With hot Observables, there is just one producer, which means the scenario above will play out differently. Let's write down the code for a hot Observable scenario:

```
// hot observable scenario

// subscriber 1 emits 0, 1, 2
hotStream$.subscribe(data => console.log(data));

// subscriber 2, emits 0, 1, 2
hotStream$.subscribe(data => console.log(data));

// subscriber 3, emits 2, after 2 seconds
setTimeout(() => {
  hotStream$.subscribe(data => console.log(data));
}, 3000);
```

The reason the third subscriber is outputting only the value 2 is that the other values have been emitted already. The third subscriber wasn't around to see that happen. On the third value emit, it is around, and that is the reason it receives the value 2.

Making a stream hot

This `hotStream$`, how can it be created? You did say that most of the streams being created are cold? We have an operator for doing just that, or two operators, in reality. We can make a stream go from cold to hot by using the operators `publish()` and `connect()`. Let's start with a cold Observable and add the mentioned operators, like so:

```
// hot-cold-warm/hot-observable.js

const Rx = require("rxjs/Rx");

let start = new Date();
let stream = Rx.Observable
  .interval(1000)
  .take(5)
  .publish();
```

```
setTimeout(() => {
  stream.subscribe(data => {
    console.log(`subscriber 1 ${new Date() - start}`, data);
  });
}, 2000);

setTimeout(() => {
  stream.subscribe(data => {
    console.log(`subscriber 2 ${new Date() - start}`, data)
  });
}, 3000);

stream.connect();
stream.subscribe(
  data => console.log(
    `subscriber 0 - I was here first ${new Date() - start}`,
    data
  )
);
```

We can see from the preceding code that we create our Observable and instruct it to emit values, one value per second. Furthermore, it should stop after five emitted values. We then call the operator `publish()`. This puts us in ready mode. We then set up a few subscriptions to happen after two seconds and three seconds, respectively. This is followed by us calling `connect()` on the stream. This will make the stream go from hot to cold. Thereby, our stream starts emitting values, and any subscriber, whenever it starts subscribing, will share a producer with any future subscriber. Lastly, we add a subscriber to happen straight after the call to `connect()`. Let's show what the output becomes with the following screenshot:

```
subscriber 0 - I was here first 1005 0
subscriber 0 - I was here first 2006 1
subscriber 1 2007 1
subscriber 0 - I was here first 3008 2
subscriber 1 3009 2
subscriber 2 3010 2
subscriber 0 - I was here first 4016 3
subscriber 1 4017 3
subscriber 2 4018 3
subscriber 0 - I was here first 5022 4
subscriber 1 5023 4
subscriber 2 5024 4
```

Our first subscriber is emitting values after one second. Our second subscriber kicks in after yet another second. This time its value is 1; it has missed out on the first value. After yet another second, the third subscriber has been attached. The first value that subscriber emits is 2; it missed out on the two first values. We clearly see how the operators `publish()` and `connect()` help to create our hot Observable, but also how it matters when you start subscribing to a hot Observable.

Why on earth would I want a hot Observable? What's the area for application? Well, imagine you have a live stream, a football game that you stream to many subscribers/viewers. They wouldn't want to see what happens from the first minute of the game when they arrive late, but, rather, where the match is right now, at the time of subscription (when they park themselves in front of the television). So, there definitely exist cases where hot Observables are the way to go.

Warm streams

So far, we have been describing and discussing cold Observables and hot Observables, but there is a third kind: the warm Observable. A warm Observable can be thought of as being created as a cold Observable, but turning into a hot Observable under certain conditions. Let's look at such a case by introducing the `refCount()` operator:

```
// hot-cold-warm/warm-observer.js

const Rx = require("rxjs/Rx");

let warmStream = Rx.Observable.interval(1000).take(3).publish().refCount();
let start = new Date();

setTimeout(() => {
  warmStream.subscribe(data => {
    console.log(`subscriber 1 - ${new Date() - start}`,data);
  });
}, 2000);
```

OK, so we started to use the operator `publish()`, and it looks like we are about to use our `connect()` operator and that we have a hot Observable, right? Well, yes, but instead of calling `connect()`, we call `refCount()`. This operator will warm our Observable up so that when the first subscriber arrives, it will act like a cold Observable. OK? That just sounds like a cold Observable, right? Let's have a look at the output first:

```
subscriber 1 - 3010 0
subscriber 1 - 4012 1
subscriber 1 - 5019 2
>
```

To answer the preceding question, yes, it's correct that it just behaves like a cold Observable; we aren't missing out on any emitted values. The interesting thing happens when we get a second subscriber. Let's add that second subscriber and see what the effects are:

```
// hot-cold-warm/warm-observable-subscribers.js

const Rx = require("rxjs/Rx");

let warmStream = Rx.Observable.interval(1000).take(3).publish().refCount();
let start = new Date();

setTimeout(() => {
  warmStream.subscribe(data => {
    console.log(`subscriber 1 - ${new Date() - start}`,data);
  });
}, 1000);

setTimeout(() => {
  warmStream.subscribe(data => {
    console.log(`subscriber 2 - ${new Date() - start}`,data);
  });
}, 3000);
```

Our second subscriber is added; now, let's have a look at what the result is:

```
subscriber 1 - 2008 0
subscriber 1 - 3009 1
subscriber 2 - 3010 1
subscriber 1 - 4014 2
subscriber 2 - 4015 2
```

What we can see from the results above is that the first subscriber is alone in receiving the number 0. When the second subscriber arrives, its first value is 1, which proves the stream has gone from acting like a cold Observable to a hot Observable.

There is another way we can do warm Observables, and that is through using the `share()` operator. The `share()` operator can be seen as more of a smart operator that allows our Observable to go from cold to hot, depending on the situation. That can be a really great idea sometimes. So, there are the following situations for Observables:

- Created as a hot Observable; the stream hasn't completed, and none of the subscribers are more than one
- Falls back into being a cold Observable; any previous subscription has had time to end before a new subscription arrives
- Created as a cold Observable; the Observable itself has had time to complete before the subscription happens

Let's try to show in code how the first bullet can happen:

```
// hot-cold-warm/warm-observable-share.js

const Rx = require("rxjs/Rx");

let stream$ = Rx.Observable.create((observer) => {
  let i = 0;
  let id = setInterval(() => {
    observer.next(i++);
  }, 400);

  return () => {
    clearInterval(id);
  };
}).share();

let sub0, sub;

// first subscription happens immediately
sub0 = stream$.subscribe(
  (data) => console.log("subscriber 0", data),
  err => console.error(err),
  () => console.log("completed"));

// second subscription happens after 1 second
setTimeout(() => {
  sub = stream$.subscribe(
  (data) => console.log("subscriber 1", data),
  err => console.error(err),
  () => console.log("completed"));
}, 1000);

// everything is unscubscribed after 2 seconds
```

```
setTimeout(() => {
  sub0.unsubscribe();
  sub.unsubscribe();
}, 2000);
```

The preceding code describes a situation where we defined a stream with a subscription that happens straight away. The second subscription happens after one second. Now, according to the definition of the share() operator, this means that the stream will be created as a cold Observable, but will, at the time of the second subscriber, be turned into a hot Observable, as there is a pre-existing subscriber and the stream has yet to complete. Let's inspect our output to verify that this is the case:

```
subscriber 0 0
subscriber 0 1
subscriber 0 2
subscriber 1 2
subscriber 0 3
subscriber 1 3
subscriber 0 4
subscriber 1 4
```

The first subscriber seems to be clearly alone in the values it gets. When the second subscriber arrives, it seems to share the producer, as it doesn't start from zero, but, rather, it starts listening where the first subscriber is.

Subjects

We are used to using Observables in a certain way. We construct them from something and we start listening to values that they emit. There is usually very little we can do to affect what is being emitted after the point of creation. Sure, we can change it and filter it, but it is next to impossible to add more to our Observable unless we merge it with another stream. Let's have a look at when we are really in control of what is being emitted when it comes to Observables, using the create() operator:

```
let stream$ = Rx.Observable.create(observer => {
  observer.next(1);
  observer.next(2);
});

stream$.subscribe(data => console.log(data));
```

We see the Observable acting as a wrapper around the thing that really emits our values, the Observer. In our Observer instance, the Observer is calling `next()`, with a parameter to emit values – values that we listen to in our `subscribe()` method.

This section is about the Subject. The Subject differs from the Observable in that it can affect the content of the stream after its creation. Let's have a look at just that with the following piece of code:

```
// subjects/subject.js

const Rx = require("rxjs/Rx");

let subject = new Rx.Subject();

// emits 1
subject.subscribe(data => console.log(data));

subject.next(1);
```

The first thing we notice is how we just call the constructor instead of using a factory method like `create()` or `from()` or similar, as we do on an Observable. The second thing we notice is how we subscribe to it on the second line, and only on the last line do we emit values by calling `next()`. Why is the code written in this order? Well, if we didn't write it this way and have the `next()` call happen as the second thing, our subscription wouldn't be there, and the value would have been emitted straight away. We know two things for sure, though: we are calling `next()`, and we are calling `subscribe()`, which makes `Subject` a double nature. We did mention another thing the `Subject` was capable of: changing the stream after creation. Our call to `next()` is literally doing that. Let's add a few more calls so we ensure we really get the idea:

```
// subjects/subjectII.js

const Rx = require("rxjs/Rx");

let subject = new Rx.Subject();

// emits 10 and 100 2 seconds after
subject.subscribe(data => console.log(data));
subject.next(10);

setTimeout(() => {
  subject.next(100);
}, 2000);
```

As we stated before, all the calls we make to the `next ()` method enable us to affect the stream; we see in our `subscribe()` method that every call to `next ()` leads to the `subscribe()` being hit, or, technically, the first function we pass into it.

Using Subject for cascading lists

So, what's the point? Why should we use Subjects over Observables? That's actually a quite deep question. There are many ways of solving most streaming-related problems; problems where it is tempting to use a Subject can often be solved through some other way. Let's have a look at what you could be using it for, though. Let's talk about cascading drop-down lists. What we mean by that is that we want to know what restaurants exist in a city. Imagine, therefore, that we have a drop-down list that allows us to select what country we are interested in. Once we select a country, we should select the city we are interested in from a drop-down list of cities. Thereafter, we get to select from a list of restaurants, and, finally, pick the restaurant that interests us. In the markup, it most likely looks like this:

```
// subjects/cascading.html

<html>
<body>
  <select id="countries"></select>
  <select id="cities"></select>
  <select id="restaurants"></select>

  <script src="https://unpkg.com/rxjs/bundles/Rx.min.js"></script>
  <script src="cascadingIV.js"></script>
</body>
</html>
```

At the start of the application, we haven't selected anything, and the only drop-down list that is selected is the first one, and it is filled with countries. Imagine that we therefore set up the following code in JavaScript:

```
// subjects/cascadingI.js

let countriesElem = document.getElementById("countries");
let citiesElem = document.getElementBtyId("cities");
let restaurantsElem = document.getElementById("restaurants");

// talk to /cities/country/:country, get us cities by selected country
let countriesStream = Rx.Observable.fromEvent(countriesElem, "select");

// talk to /restaurants/city/:city, get us restaurants by selected
restaurant
```

```
let citiesStream = Rx.Observable.fromEvent(citiesElem, "select");

// talk to /book/restaurant/:restaurant, book selected restaurant
let restaurantsElem = Rx.Observable.fromEvent(restaurantsElem, "select");
```

At this point, we have established that we want to listen to the selected events of each drop-down list, and we want, in the cases of countries or cities droplist, filter the upcoming droplist. Say we select a specific country then we want to repopulate/filter the cities droplist so that it only shows cities for the selected country. For the restaurant drop-down list, we want to perform a booking based on our restaurant selection. Sounds pretty simple, right? We need some subscribers. The cities drop-down list needs to listen to changes in the countries drop-down list. So we add that to our code:

```
// subjects/cascadingII.js

let countriesElem = document.getElementById("countries");
let citiesElem = document.getElementBtyId("cities");
let restaurantsElem = document.getElementById("restaurants");

fetchCountries();

function buildList(list, items) {
  list.innerHTML ="";
  items.forEach(item => {
    let elem = document.createElement("option");
    elem.innerHTML = item;
    list.appendChild(elem);
  });
}

function fetchCountries() {
  return Rx.Observable.ajax("countries.json")
    .map(r => r.response)
    .subscribe(countries => buildList(countriesElem, countries.data));
}

function populateCountries() {
  fetchCountries()
    .map(r => r.response)
    .subscribe(countries => buildDropList(countriesElem, countries));
}

let cities$ = new Subject();
cities$.subscribe(cities => buildList(citiesElem, cities));

Rx.Observable.fromEvent(countriesElem, "change")
  .map(ev => ev.target.value)
```

```
  .do(val => clearSelections())
  .switchMap(selectedCountry => fetchBy(selectedCountry))
  .subscribe( cities => cities$.next(cities.data));

Rx.Observable.from(citiesElem, "select");

Rx.Observable.from(restaurantsElem, "select");
```

So, here, we have a behavior of performing an AJAX request when we select a country; we get a filtered list of cities, and we introduce the new subject instance `cities$`. We call the `next()` method on it with our filtered cities as a parameter. Finally, we listen to changes to the `cities$` stream by calling the `subscribe()` method on the stream. As you can see, when data arrives, we rebuild our cities drop-down list there.

We realize that our next step is to react to changes from us doing a selection in the cities drop-down list. So, let's set that up:

```
// subjects/cascadingIII.js

let countriesElem = document.getElementById("countries");
let citiesElem = document.getElementBtyId("cities");
let restaurantsElem = document.getElementById("restaurants");

fetchCountries();

function buildList(list, items) {
  list.innerHTML = "";
  items.forEach(item => {
    let elem = document.createElement("option");
    elem.innerHTML = item;
    list.appendChild(elem);
  });
}

function fetchCountries() {
  return Rx.Observable.ajax("countries.json")
    .map(r => r.response)
    .subscribe(countries => buildList(countriesElem, countries.data));
}

function populateCountries() {
  fetchCountries()
    .map(r => r.response)
    .subscribe(countries => buildDropList(countriesElem, countries));
}

let cities$ = new Subject();
```

```
cities$.subscribe(cities => buildList(citiesElem, cities));

let restaurants$ = new Rx.Subject();
restaurants$.subscribe(restaurants => buildList(restaurantsElem,
restaurants));

Rx.Observable.fromEvent(countriesElem, "change")
  .map(ev => ev.target.value)
  .do( val => clearSelections())
  .switchMap(selectedCountry => fetchBy(selectedCountry))
  .subscribe( cities => cities$.next(cities.data));

Rx.Observable.from(citiesElem, "select")
  .map(ev => ev.target.value)
  .switchMap(selectedCity => fetchBy(selectedCity))
  .subscribe( restaurants => restaurants$.next(restaurants.data));

// talk to /book/restaurant/:restaurant, book selected restaurant
Rx.Observable.from(restaurantsElem, "select");
```

In the preceding code, we added some code to react to a selection being made in our cities drop-down list. We also added some code to listen to changes in the `restaurants$` stream, which finally led to our restaurants drop-down list being repopulated. The last step is to listen to changes on us selecting a restaurant in the restaurants drop-down list. What should happen here is up to you, dear reader. A suggestion is that we query some API for the selected restaurant's opening hours, or its menu. Use your creativity. We will leave you with some final subscription code, though:

```
// subjects/cascadingIV.js

let cities$ = new Rx.Subject();
cities$.subscribe(cities => buildList(citiesElem, cities));

let restaurants$ = new Rx.Subject();
restaurants$.subscribe(restaurants => buildList(restaurantsElem,
restaurants));

function buildList(list, items) {
  list.innerHTML = "";
  items.forEach(item => {
    let elem = document.createElement("option");
    elem.innerHTML = item;
    list.appendChild(elem);
  });
}

function fetchCountries() {
```

```
    return Rx.Observable.ajax("countries.json")
      .map(r => r.response)
      .subscribe(countries => buildList(countriesElem, countries.data));
}

function fetchBy(by) {
    return Rx.Observable.ajax(`${by}.json`)
    .map(r=> r.response);
}

function clearSelections() {
    citiesElem.innerHTML = "";
    restaurantsElem.innerHTML = "";
}

let countriesElem = document.getElementById("countries");
let citiesElem = document.getElementById("cities");
let restaurantsElem = document.getElementById("restaurants");

fetchCountries();

Rx.Observable.fromEvent(countriesElem, "change")
  .map(ev => ev.target.value)
  .do(val => clearSelections())
  .switchMap(selectedCountry => fetchBy(selectedCountry))
  .subscribe(cities => cities$.next(cities.data));

Rx.Observable.fromEvent(citiesElem, "change")
  .map(ev => ev.target.value)
  .switchMap(selectedCity => fetchBy(selectedCity))
  .subscribe(restaurants => restaurants$.next(restaurants.data));

Rx.Observable.fromEvent(restaurantsElem, "change")
  .map(ev => ev.target.value)
  .subscribe(selectedRestaurant => console.log("selected restaurant",
selectedRestaurant));
```

This became a quite long code example, and it should be said that this is not the best way of solving a problem like this, but it does demonstrate how a Subject works: it can add value to the stream when it wants, and it can be subscribed to.

BehaviorSubject

So far, we have been looking at the default type of Subject, and we have uncovered a little of its secrets. However, there are many more types of Subjects. One such interesting type of Subject is the BehaviorSubject. So, why do we need a BehaviorSubject, and for what? Well, when dealing with a default Subject, we are able to add values to the stream, as well as subscribe to the stream. The BehaviorSubject gives us some added capabilities, in the form of:

- A starter value, which is great if we are able to show something to the UI while waiting for an AJAX call to finish
- We can query on the latest value; in some situations, it is interesting to know what the last emitted value was

To address the first bullet, let's write some code and showcase this capability:

```
// subjects/behavior-subject.js

let behaviorSubject = new Rx.BehaviorSubject("default value");

// will emit 'default value'
behaviorSubject.subscribe(data => console.log(data));

// long running AJAX scenario
setTimeout(() => {
  return Rx.Observable.ajax("data.json")
    .map(r => r.response)
    .subscribe(data => behaviorSubject.next(data));
}, 12000);
```

ReplaySubject

With a normal Subject, it matters when we start subscribing. If we start emitting values before our subscription is set up, those values are simply lost. If we have a BehaviorSubject, we have a somewhat better scenario. Even if we are late in subscribing, so a value has already been emitted, the very last emitted value is still possible to gain access to. Then the following question arises: What if two or more values are emitted before a subscription happens and we care about those values – what then?

Let's illustrate this scenario and see what happens with a Subject and `BehaviorSubject`, respectively:

```
// example of emitting values before subscription

const Rx = require("rxjs/Rx");

let subject = new Rx.Subject();
subject.next("subject first value");

// emits 'subject second value'
subject.subscribe(data => console.log("subscribe - subject", data));
subject.next("subject second value");

let behaviourSubject = new Rx.BehaviorSubject("behaviorsubject initial
value");
behaviourSubject.next("behaviorsubject first value");
behaviourSubject.next("behaviorsubject second value");

// emits 'behaviorsubject second value', 'behaviorsubject third value'
behaviourSubject.subscribe(data =>
  console.log("subscribe - behaviorsubject", data)
);

behaviourSubject.next("behaviorsubject third value");
```

What we can see from the preceding code is that Subject is not a good candidate if we care about values prior to us subscribing. The `BehaviorSubject` constructors are slightly better for that scenario, but if we really care about prior values, and a lot of them, then we should have a look at the `ReplaySubject`. The `ReplaySubject` has the ability to specify two things: a buffer size and a window size. A buffer size is simply the amount of values it should remember from the past, and the window size specifies for how long it should remember them for. Let us demonstrate this in code:

```
// subjects/replay-subject.js

const Rx = require("rxjs/Rx");

let replaySubject = new Rx.ReplaySubject(2);

replaySubject.next(1);
replaySubject.next(2);
replaySubject.next(3);

// emitting 2 and 3
replaySubject.subscribe(data => console.log(data));
```

In the preceding code, we can see how we emit 2 and 3, that is, the two latest emitted values. This is due to the fact that we specify the buffer size in the `ReplaySubject` constructor to be 2. The only value we loose out on is 1. Had we, on the other hand, specified a 3 in our constructor, all three values would have reached the subscriber. So much for the buffer size and how that works; what about the window size property? Let's illustrate how that works with the following code:

```
// subjects/replay-subject-window-size.js

const Rx = require("rxjs/Rx");

let replaySubjectWithWindow = new Rx.ReplaySubject(2, 2000);
replaySubjectWithWindow.next(1);
replaySubjectWithWindow.next(2);
replaySubjectWithWindow.next(3);

setTimeout(() => {
  replaySubjectWithWindow.subscribe(data =>
    console.log("replay with buffer and window size", data));
  },
2010);
```

Here, we specify the window size as 2,000 milliseconds; that is how long the values should be held in the buffer. We can see below that we delay the creation of our subscription to occur after 2,010 milliseconds. The end result of this is that no values will be emitted, as the buffer will have been emptied before the subscription has time to occur. A higher value of the window size would have fixed this issue.

AsyncSubject

The `AsyncSubject` has a capacity of one, which means we can emit a ton of values, but only the latest one is something that is stored. It isn't really lost, either, but you won't see it unless you complete the stream. Let's look at a piece of code that illustrates just this:

```
// subjects/async-subject.js

let asyncSubject = new Rx.AsyncSubject();
asyncSubject.next(1);
asyncSubject.next(2);
asyncSubject.next(3);
asyncSubject.next(4);

asyncSubject.subscribe(data => console.log(data), err =>
console.error(err));
```

Earlier, we had fours values being emitted, but nothing seems to reach the subscriber. At this point, we don't know whether this is because it just acts like a subject and throws away all emitted values that happen before a subscription or not. Let's therefore call the `complete()` method and see how that plays out:

```
// subjects/async-subject-complete.js

let asyncSubject = new Rx.AsyncSubject();
asyncSubject.next(1);
asyncSubject.next(2);
asyncSubject.next(3);
asyncSubject.next(4);

// emits 4
asyncSubject.subscribe(data => console.log(data), err =>
console.error(err));
asyncSubject.complete();
```

This will emit a 4 due to the fact that `AsyncSubject` only remembers the last value and we are calling the `complete()` method, thereby signaling the completion of the stream.

Error handling

Error handling is a very big topic. It is an area that is easy to underestimate. Normally, when coding, we could be led to believe we just need to do certain things, such as ensure we don't have syntax errors or runtime errors. With streams, we mostly think of runtime errors. The question is, how should we act when an error occurs? Should we pretend like it rains and just throw the error away? Should we hope for a different outcome if we try the same code some time in the future, or should we maybe just give up when a certain type of error exists? Let's try to collect our thoughts and look at the different error approaches that exist within RxJS.

Catch and continue

Sooner or later, we will have a stream that will throw an error. Let's see what that can look like:

```
// example of a stream with an error

let stream$ = Rx.Observable.create(observer => {
  observer.next(1);
  observer.error('an error is thrown');
```

```
    observer.next(2);
});

stream$.subscribe(
  data => console.log(data), // 1
  error => console.error(error) // 'error is thrown'
);
```

In the preceding code, we set up a scenario where we first emit a value, followed by emitting an error. The first value is captured in our first callback in our subscribe method. The second emitted thing, the error, is captured by our error callback. The third emitted value does not get emitted to our subscriber because our stream has been interrupted by the error. There is something we can do here, and that is to use the `catch()` operator. Let's apply that to our stream and see what happens:

```
// error-handling/error-catch.js
const Rx = require("rxjs/Rx");

let stream$ = Rx.Observable.create(observer => {
  observer.next(1);
  observer.error("an error is thrown");
  observer.next(2);
}).catch(err => Rx.Observable.of(err));

stream$.subscribe(
  data => console.log(data), // emits 1 and 'error is thrown'
  error => console.error(error)
);
```

Here, we capture our error with the `catch()` operator. In the `catch()` operator, we take our error and emit it as a normal Observable using the `of()` operator. What happens to the 2 we emit, though? Still no luck with that one. The `catch()` operator is able to take our error and turn it into a normal emitted value; instead of an error, we don't get all the values from the stream.

Let's have a look at a scenario when we are dealing with multiple streams:

```
// example of merging several streams

let merged$ = Rx.Observable.merge(
  Rx.Observable.of(1),
  Rx.Observable.throw("err"),
  Rx.Observable.of(2)
);

merged$.subscribe(data => console.log("merged", data));
```

In the scenario above, we merge three streams. The first stream emits the number 1 and nothing else gets emitted. This is due to our second stream tearing everything down, as it emits an error. Let's try to apply our newfound `catch()` operator and see what happens:

```
// error-handling/error-merge-catch.js

const Rx = require("rxjs/Rx");

let merged$ = Rx.Observable.merge(
  Rx.Observable.of(1),
  Rx.Observable.throw("err").catch(err => Rx.Observable.of(err)),
  Rx.Observable.of(2)
);

merged$.subscribe(data => console.log("merged", data));
```

We run the above code and we notice that the 1 is emitted, the error is emitted as a normal value, and, finally, even the 2 is emitted. Our conclusion here is that it is a good idea to apply a `catch()` operator to a stream before it is being merged with our streams.

As before, we can also conclude that the `catch()` operator is able to stop the stream from just erroring out, but that other values that would have been emitted after the error are effectively lost.

Ignoring the error

As we saw in the former section, the `catch()` operator does a good job of ensuring that a stream that errors out doesn't cause any problems when being merged with another stream. The `catch()` operator enables us to take the error, investigate it, and create a new Observable that will emit a value as though nothing happened. Sometimes, however, you don't want to even deal with streams that error out. For such a scenario, there is a different operator, called `onErrorResumeNext()`:

```
// error-handling/error-ignore.js
const Rx = require("rxjs/Rx");

let mergedIgnore$ = Rx.Observable.onErrorResumeNext(
  Rx.Observable.of(1),
  Rx.Observable.throw("err"),
  Rx.Observable.of(2)
);

mergedIgnore$.subscribe(data => console.log("merge ignore", data));
```

The implication of using the `onErrorResumeNext()` operator is that the second stream, the one that emits an error, gets completely ignored, and the values 1 and 2 get emitted. This is a very nice operator to use if your scenario is only about caring for the streams that do not error out.

Retry

There are different reasons why you would want to retry a stream. It's easier to imagine why you would want to if your stream is dealing with AJAX calls. Network connections may be unreliable at times with the local network you are on, or the service you are trying to hit may be temporarily down for some reason. Regardless of the reason, you have a situation where hitting that endpoint will some of the time reply with an answer, and some of the time return a 401 error. What we are describing here is the business case for adding retry logic to your streams. Let's have a look at a stream designed to fail:

```
// error-handling/error-retry.js
const Rx = require("rxjs/Rx");

let stream$ = Rx.Observable.create(observer => {
  observer.next(1);
  observer.error("err");
})
.retry(3);

// emits 1 1 1 1 err
stream$
  .subscribe(data => console.log(data));
```

The output of the code above is the value 1 being emitted four times, followed by our error. What happens is that our streams' values are retried three times before the error callback is hit in the subscribe. Using the `retry()` operator delays when the error is actually treated as an error. The preceding example doesn't make sense to retry, though, as the error will always occur. Therefore, let's take a better example – an AJAX call where the network connection may come and go:

```
// example of using a retry with AJAX

let ajaxStream$ = Rx.Observable.ajax("UK1.json")
  .map(r => r.response)
  .retry(3);

ajaxStream$.subscribe(
  data => console.log("ajax result", data),
```

```
    err => console.error("ajax error", err)
);
```

Here, we are attempting an AJAX request towards a file that doesn't seem to exist. Having a look at the console, we are faced with the following result:

```
⊗ ▶GET http://localhost:8080/UK1.json 404 (Not Found)
⊗ ▶GET http://localhost:8080/UK1.json 404 (Not Found)
⊗ ▶GET http://localhost:8080/UK1.json 404 (Not Found)
⊗ ▶GET http://localhost:8080/UK1.json 404 (Not Found)
⊗ ▶ajax error ▶AjaxError {message: "ajax error 404", xhr: XMLHttpRequest, request: {…}, status: 404, responseType: "json", …}
```

What we see in the above logging are four failed AJAX requests that lead to an error. We have essentially just switched our simple stream to a more credible AJAX request stream, with the same behavior. Should the file suddenly start to exist, we may have a scenario with two failed attempts and one successful attempt. Our approach has a flaw, though: we retry our AJAX attempts far too often. If we are actually dealing with an intermittent network connection, we need to have some kind of delay between attempts. It is reasonable to set a delay between attempts of at least 30 seconds or more. We can accomplish that by using a slightly different retry operator that takes milliseconds rather than a number of attempts as an argument. It looks like the following:

```
// retry with a delay

let ajaxStream$ = Rx.Observable.ajax("UK1.json")
  .do(r => console.log("emitted"))
  .map(r => r.response)
  .retryWhen(err => {
    return err.delay(3000);
  });
```

What we do here is use the operator `retryWhen()`. The `retryWhen()` operator's mission in life is to return a stream. At this point, you can manipulate the stream it returns by appending a `.delay()` operator that takes a number of milliseconds. The result from doing so is that it will retry the AJAX call for all eternity, which may not be what you want.

Advanced Retry

What we most likely want is to combine the delay between retry attempts with being able to specify how many times we want to retry the stream. Let's have a look at how we can accomplish that:

```
// error-handling/error-retry-advanced.js

const Rx = require("rxjs/Rx");

let ajaxStream$ = Rx.Observable.ajax("UK1.json")
  .do(r => console.log("emitted"))
  .map(r => r.response)
  .retryWhen(err => {
    return err
    .delay(3000)
    .take(3);
});
```

The interesting part here is that we use the operator `.take()`. We specify the number of emitted values we want from this inner Observable. We have now accomplished a nice approach in which we are able to control the number of retries and the delay between retries. There is an aspect to this that we haven't tried, namely, how we want all the retries to end when it finally gives up. In the preceding code, the stream just completes after the stream is retried after *x* number of times with no successful result. However, we may want the stream to error out instead. We can accomplish this by just adding an operator to the code, like this:

```
// error-handling/error-retry-advanced-fail.js

let ajaxStream$ = Rx.Observable.ajax("UK1.json")
  .do(r => console.log("emitted"))
  .map(r => r.response)
  .retryWhen(err => {
    return err
    .delay(3000)
    .take(3)
    .concat(Rx.Observable.throw("giving up"));
});
```

Here, we are adding a `concat()` operator that adds a stream that just fails. So we are guaranteed, after three failed attempts, to have an error happen. This is usually a better approach than having the stream silently complete after *x* number of failed attempts.

This isn't a perfect approach, though; imagine that you want to investigate what type of error you get back. In the case of AJAX requests being made, it matters whether we get a 400-something error or a 500-something error back as HTTP status code. They mean different things. With 500 errors, something is very wrong on the backend, and we probably want to give up straight away. With a 404 error, however, this implies the resource isn't there, but in the case with an intermittent network connection, this means the resource can't be reached due to our connection being offline. For that reason, a 404 error might be worth retrying. To solve that in code, we need to inspect the value being emitted to determine what to do. We can inspect values using the do() operator.

In the following code, we investigate the type of HTTP status of the response and determine how to handle it:

```
// error-handling/error-retry-errorcodes.js

const Rx = require("rxjs/Rx");

function isOkError(errorCode) {
  return errorCode >= 400 && errorCode < 500;
}

let ajaxStream$ = Rx.Observable.ajax("UK1.json")
  .do(r => console.log("emitted"))
  .map(r => r.response)
  .retryWhen(err => {
    return err
      .do(val => {
        if (!isOkError(val.status) || timesToRetry === 0) {
          throw "give up";
        }
      })
      .delay(3000);
  });
```

Marble testing

Testing asynchronous code can be challenging. For one, we have the time factor. The way we specify what operators to use for our crafted algorithm leads to the algorithm taking anywhere from 2 seconds to 30 minutes to execute. Therefore, it will at first feel like there is no point in testing it, because it can't be done within a reasonable time. We have a way to test RxJS, though; it is called Marble testing and it allows us to control how fast time passes so we have a test that can execute it in milliseconds.

The idea of a Marble is known to us. We can represent one or many streams and the effect an operator has one two or more streams. We do this by drawing the streams as a line and values as circles on the lines. The operator is shown as verb below the input streams. Following operator is a third stream, the result of taking the input streams and applying the operator, a so - called marble diagram. The line represents a continuous timeline. We take this concept and bring it to testing. What this means is that we can express our incoming values as a graphical representation and apply our algorithm to it and assert on the result.

Set up

Let's set up our environment correctly so we can write marble tests. We need the following:

- The NPM library jasmine-marbles
- A scaffolded Angular application

With that we scaffold our Angular project, like so:

```
ng new MarbleTesting
```

After the project has been scaffolded, it's time to add our NPM library, like so:

```
cd MarbleTesting
npm install jasmine-marbles --save
```

Now we have finished the setup, so the time has come to write tests.

Writing your first marble test

Let's create a new file `marble-testing.spec.ts`. It should look like the following:

```
// marble-testing\MarbleTesting\src\app\marble-testing.spec.ts

import { cold } from "jasmine-marbles";
import "rxjs/add/operator/map";

describe("marble tests", () => {
  it("map - should increase by 1", () => {
    const one$ = cold("x-x|", { x: 1 });
    expect(one$.map(x => x + 1)).toBeObservable(cold("x-x|", { x: 2 }));
  });
});
```

A lot of interesting things are happening here. We import the function `cold()` from the NPM library marble-testing. Thereafter we set up a test suite by calling `describe()`, followed by a test specification, by calling `it()`. Then we call our `cold()` function and provide it a string. Let's have a close look at that function call:

```
const stream$ = cold("x-x|", { x: 1 });
```

The above code set up a stream that expects to values to be emitted followed by the stream ending. How do we know that? It's time to explain what x-x| means. x is just any value, the hyphen – means time has passed. The pipe | means our stream has ended. The second argument in the cold function is a mapping object that tells us what the x means. In this case, it has come to mean the value 1.

Moving on, let's have a look at the next line:

```
expect(stream$.map(x => x + 1)).toBeObservable(cold("x-x|", { x: 2 }));
```

The preceding code applies the operator `.map()` and increased the value with one for each value emitted in the stream. Thereafter, we call the `.toBeObservable()` helper method and verify it against an expected condition,

```
cold("x-x|", { x: 2 })
```

The previous condition states that we expect the stream to should emit two values, but that the values should now have the number 2. This makes sense, as our `map()` function performs just that.

Fleshing out with more tests

Let's write one more test. This time we will be testing the `filter()` operator. This one is interesting, as it filters away values that does not fulfill a certain condition. Our test file should now look like the following:

```
import { cold } from "jasmine-marbles";
import "rxjs/add/operator/map";
import "rxjs/add/operator/filter";

describe("marble testing", () => {
  it("map - should increase by 1", () => {
    const one$ = cold("x-x|", { x: 1 });
    expect(one$.map(x => x + 1)).toBeObservable(cold("x-x|", { x: 2 }));
  });

  it("filter - should remove values", () => {
```

```
      const stream$ = cold("x-y|", { x: 1, y: 2 });
      expect(stream$.filter(x => x > 1)).toBeObservable(cold("--y|", { y: 2
}));
    });
  });
});
```

This test is set up in pretty much the same way as our first test. This time we use the `filter()` operator but what stands out is our expected stream:

```
cold("--y|", { y: 2 })
```

`--y`, means that our first values is removed. Based on how the filter condition is defined, we are not surprised. The reason for the double hyphen, –, though, is that time still passes, but instead of an emitted value a hyphen takes its place.

To learn more about Marble testing, have a look at the following link from the official documentation, `https://github.com/ReactiveX/rxjs/blob/master/doc/writing-marble-tests.md`

Pipeable operators

We haven't mentioned it much so far, but the RxJS library weighs in quite heavily when used in an app. In today's world of mobile first, every kilobyte counts when it comes to libraries that you include in your app. They count because the user may be on a 3G connection, and if it takes too long to load, your user may leave, or just may end up not liking your app, as it feels slow to load, and this may cause you to have bad reviews or lose users. So far, we have used two different ways of importing RxJS:

- Importing the whole library; this one is quite costly in terms of size
- Importing only the operators we need; this ensures that the bundle decreases significantly

The different options have looked like this, for importing the whole library and all its operators:

```
import Rx from "rxjs/Rx";
```

Or like this, to only import what we need:

```
import { Observable } from 'rxjs/Observable';
import "rxjs/add/operator/map";
import "rxjs/add/operator/take";

let stream = Observable.interval(1000)
  .map(x => x +1)
  .take(2)
```

That looks good, right? Well, yes, but it is a flawed approach. Let's explain what happens when you type:

```
import "rxjs/add/operator/map";
```

By typing the preceding, we add to the prototype of the Observable. Looking in the source code for RxJS, it looks like this:

```
var Observable_1 = require('../../Observable');
var map_1 = require('../../operator/map');

Observable_1.Observable.prototype.map = map_1.map;
```

As you can see from the preceding code, we import the Observable as well as the operator in question and we add the operator to the prototype by assigning it to a map property on the prototype. What's flawed with that, you might wonder? The problem is tree shaking, a process we use to get rid of unused code. Tree shaking has a hard time determining what you use and don't use, respectively. You may actually import a map() operator and it gets added to the Observable. As the code changes over time, you may end up not using it anymore. You may argue that you should remove the import at that point, but you might have a lot of code, and it is easy to overlook. It would be better if only used operators were included in the final bundle. It is, as we mentioned before, hard for the tree-shaking process to know what is used and what is not, with the current approach. For that reason, a big rewrite has happened in RxJS, adding something called pipeable operators, which help us with the above problem. There is also another downside to patching the prototype, and that is the fact that it creates a dependency. If the library changes and the operator is no longer added when we patch it (calling the import), then we have a problem. We won't detect the problem until runtime. We would rather be told that the operator has gone through us importing and explicitly using it, like so:

```
import { operator } from 'some/path';

operator();
```

Creating reusable operators with let()

The let() operator lets you have the whole operator and operate on it, rather than just manipulating the values as you would do with the map() operator, for example. Using the let() operator could look like this:

```
import Rx from "rxjs/Rx";

let stream = Rx.Observable.of(0,1,2);
let addAndFilter = obs => obs.map( x => x * 10).filter(x => x % 10 === 0);
let sub3 = obs => obs.map(x => x - 3);

stream
  .let(addAndFilter)
  .let(sub3)
  .subscribe(x => console.log('let', x));
```

In the preceding example, we were able to define a group of operators such as addAndFilter and sub3 and use them on the stream with the let() operator. This enables us to create composable and reusable operators. It is with this very knowledge that we now move on to the concept of pipeable operators.

Shifting to pipeable operators

As we mentioned already, pipeable operators are here, and you can find them by importing the respective operators from the rxjs/operators directory, like so:

```
import { map } from "rxjs/operators/map";
import { filter } from "rxjs/operators/filter";
```

To use it, we are now relying on the pipe() operator that we use as the parent operator, if you will. Using the preceding operators will therefore look like this:

```
import { map } from "rxjs/operators/map";
import { filter } from "rxjs/operators";
import { of } from "rxjs/observable/of";
import { Observable } from "rxjs/Observable";

let stream = of(1,2);
stream.pipe(
  map(x => x + 1),
  filter(x => x > 1)
)
.subscribe(x => console.log("piped", x)); // emits 2 and 3
```

Summary

This chapter has taken us deep into RxJS by covering topics such as hot, cold, and warm Observables, and what that generally means in terms of when to subscribe to a stream and how they share their Producer under certain conditions. Next up, we covered Subjects, and the fact that Observable isn't the only thing you can subscribe to. Subjects also allow as to append values to the stream whenever we want, and we also learned that there exist different types of Subjects, depending on the situation at hand.

We ventured deeper into an important topic, testing, and tried to explain the difficulty in testing asynchronous code. We talked about the current state of the testing situation and what libraries to use here and now for your testing scenarios. Lastly, we covered pipeable operators, and our new preferred way of importing and composing operators to ensure we end up with the smallest possible bundle size.

With all this RxJS knowledge, it is now time to take on the Redux pattern and its core concepts in the coming chapter, so we are ready to tackle NgRx in the final chapter of this book. It's time to get excited, if you weren't before.

8
Redux

Maintaining and controlling state in an app is something that quickly becomes complicated as soon as our app is larger than a Todo app, especially if we have multiple views, models, and dependencies between them. The situation is complicated by multiple types of states, such as cached data, server responses, and data that only lives locally when you work with the app. Changing the state is made more complicated because multiple actors, synchronous, and asynchronous code can change the state. The end result with a growing app is, sooner or later, a non-deterministic system. The problem with such a system is that you lose predictability, which in turn means you may have bugs that are hard to produce, and it makes the app and its data hard to reason with. We crave order and predictability, but we get neither.

To try to address the problem, we covered the Flux pattern in a previous chapter. All is well and good, right? We don't need another pattern. Or do we? Well, Flux has problems. One of the problems is that your data is divided up into several stores. Why is that a problem, you wonder? Imagine you have an action that triggers in multiple stores. It's easy to forget to handle an action in all stores. So, that issue is more of a management problem. Another problem with multiple stores is that it's hard to get a good overview of what your state consists of. Updates are another problem we have with Flux. Sometimes you have a lot of updates; updating the state and the order matters. In Flux, this is handled with a construct called `waitFor`. The idea is that you should be able to specify what should happen in which order. That's all well and good, but imagine that this is spread out over many modules; it becomes hard to keep track of and is thereby error prone.

Mutation and asynchronous behavior are two concepts that are hard to deal with. Mutation means we change the data. Asynchronous means something takes time to complete; when it does it may mutate a state. Imagine mixing synchronous and asynchronous operations that all update state. We realize it's not easy to keep track of the code because of this, and mixing that in with state mutation makes it all the more complicated.

This leads us to what Redux can do for us, which is to make our mutations predictable, but it also gives us one store, one single source of truth.

In this chapter, you will learn:

- The core concepts
- How data flows
- How to put your skills into practice by building your own mini implementation of Redux
- How to deal with AJAX in the context of Redux
- Some sound best practices

Principles

Redux rests on three principles:

- Single source of truth: We have one place where all our data lives.
- State is read-only: No mutation; there is only one way to change state and that is through an action.
- Changes are made with pure functions: A new state is produced by taking the old state, applying the change, and producing the new state; the old state is never changed.

Let's explore these bullet points one by one.

Single source of truth

The data lives in a single store in Redux and not a multiple store like in Flux. The data is represented by one object tree. This brings about a lot of benefits, such as:

- It is easier to see what your application knows at any given point, so it is easy to serialize or deserialize it.
- It is easier to work with in development, and easier to debug and inspect.
- It easier to do things such as undo/redo if all applied actions produce a new state.

An example of a single store can look like the following:

```
// principles/store.js

class Store {
  getState() {
    return {
      jedis: [
        { name: "Yoda", id: 1 },
        { name: "Palpatine", id: 2 },
        { name: "Darth Vader", id: 3 }
      ],
      selectedJedi: {
        name: "Yoda",
        id: 1
      }
    };
  }
}

const store = new Store();
console.log(store.getState());

/*
{
  jedis: [
    { name: 'Yoda', id: 1 },
    { name: 'Palpatine', id: 2 },
    { name: 'Darth Vader', id: 3 }
  ],
  selectedJedi: {
    name: 'Yoda', id: 1
  }
}
*/
```

As you can see, this is just an object.

Read-only states

We want to ensure we only have one way to alter state, and that is through mediators called actions. An action should describe the intent of the action as well as the data that should be applied to the current state. An action is dispatched by us using a `store.dispatch(action)`. The action itself should look like the following:

```
// principles/action.js

// the action
let action = {
  // expresses intent, loading jedis
  type: "LOAD_JEDIS",
  payload:[
    { name: "Yoda", id: 1 },
    { name: "Palpatine", id: 2 },
    { name: "Darth Vader", id: 3 }
  ]
};
```

At this point, let's try to implement what a store might actually look like and what it initially contains:

```
// principles/storeII.js

class Store {
  constructor() {
    this.state = {
      jedis: [],
      selectedJedi: null
    }
  }
  getState() {
    return this.state;
  }
}

const store = new Store();

console.log(store.getState());
// state should now be
/*
{
  jedis : [],
  selectedJedi: null
}
*/
```

We can see that it is an object that consists of two properties, jedis, which is an array, and selectedJedi, which is an object holding an object that we select. At this point, we want to dispatch an action, which means we will take our old state, as shown in the preceding code, and produce a new state. The action we described earlier should change the jedis array and replace the empty array with the incoming array. Remember, though, we don't mutate the existing store object; we simply take it, apply our change, and produce a new object. Let's dispatch our action and see the end result:

```js
// principles/storeII-with-dispatch.js

class Store {
  constructor() {
    this.state = {
      jedis: [],
      selectedJedi: null
    }
  }

  getState() {
    return this.state;
  }

  dispatch(action) {
    // to be implemented in later sections
  }
}

// the action
let action = {
  type: 'LOAD_JEDIS',
  payload:[
    { name: 'Yoda', id: 1 },
    { name: 'Palpatine', id: 2 },
    { name: 'Darth Vader', id: 3 }
  ]
}

// dispatching the action, producing a new state
store.dispatch(action);

console.log(store.getState());
// state should now be
/*
{
  jedis : [
    { name: 'Yoda', id: 1 },
```

```
        { name: 'Palpatine', id: 2 },
        { name: 'Darth Vader', id: 3 }
    ],
    selectedJedi: null
  }
*/
```

The preceding code is pseudo code as it doesn't actually produce the intended result, yet. We will learn to implement a store in later chapters. OK, so now our state has changed and our incoming array has replaced the empty array we used to have. We again repeat that we have not mutated the existing state, but instead produced a new state given the old state and our action. Let's look at the next section on *pure functions* and further explain what we mean.

Changing states with pure functions

In the previous section, we introduced the concept of the action and how that was the mediator through which we were allowed to change our state. We didn't change the state, though, in the normal sense of the word, but rather took the old state, applied the action, and produced a new state. To accomplish this, we need to use a pure function. In the context of Redux those are called reducers. Let's write ourselves a `reducer`:

```
// principles/first-reducer.js

module.exports = function reducer(state = {}, action) {
  switch(action.type) {
    case "SELECT_JEDI":
      return Object.assign({}, action.payload);
    default:
      return state;
  }
}
```

We highlight the pure aspect of the preceding `reducer`. It takes our `selectedJedi` from the `action.payload`, it copies it using the `Object.assign()`, assigns it, and returns the new state.

What we have written is a `reducer` that switches, depending on the action we try to perform, and carries out the change. Let's put this pure function into use:

```
const reducer = require("./first-reducer");

let initialState = {};
let action = { type: "SELECT_JEDI", payload: { id: 1, name: "Jedi" } };
let state = reducer(initialState, action);
console.log(state);

/* this produces the following:
{ id: 1, name: 'Yoda' }
*/
```

Core concepts

In React, we are dealing with three core concepts, which we have already introduced the state, the action, and the reducer. Now, let's dive in deeper and really get a sense of how they fit together and how they work.

Immutability patterns

The whole point of the state is to take an existing state, apply an action to it, and produce a new state. It can be written like this:

```
old state + action = new state
```

Imagine, if you were performing basic calculations, then you would start writing it like this:

```
// sum is 0
let sum = 0;

// sum is now 3
sum +=3;
```

The Redux way of doing things, though, is to change the preceding to:

```
let sum = 0;
let sumWith3 = sum + 3;
let sumWith6 = sumWith3 + 3;
```

We don't mutate anything but rather produce a new state for everything we do. Let's look at different constructs and what it means in practice to not mutate.

Changing a list

There are two operations we can perform on a list:

- Add item(s) to a list
- Remove item(s) from a list

Let's take the first bullet point and make this change in the old way and then make the Redux way:

```
// core-concepts/list.js

// old way
let list = [1, 2, 3];
list.push(4);

// redux way
let immutablelist = [1, 2, 3];
let newList = [...immutablelist, 4];

console.log("new list", newList);
/*
  [1, 2, 3, 4]
*/
```

The preceding code takes the old list and its items and creates a new list containing the old list plus our new member.

For our next bullet, to remove an item, we do this:

```
// core-concepts/list-remove.js

// old way
let list = [1, 2, 3];
let index = list.indexOf(1);
list.splice(index, 1);

// redux way
let immutableList = [1, 2, 3];
let newList = immutableList.filter(item => item !== 1);
```

As you can see, we produce a list not containing our item.

Changing an object

Changing an object is about changing properties on it as well as adding properties to it. First off, let's look at how to change existing values:

```
// core-concepts/object.js

// the old way
let anakin = { name: "anakin" };
anakin.name = "darth";
console.log(anakin);

// the Redux way
let anakinRedux = { name: "anakin" };
let darth = Object.assign({}, anakinRedux, { name: "darth" });

console.log(anakinRedux);
console.log(darth);
```

That covers the existing case. What about adding a new property? We can do that like so:

```
// core-concepts/object-add.js

// the old way
let anakin = { name: "anakin" };
console.log("anakin", anakin);

anakin["age"] = "17";
console.log("anakin with age", anakin);

// the Redux way
let anakinImmutable = { name: "anakin" };
let anakinImmutableWithAge = Object.assign({}, anakinImmutable, { age: 17 });

console.log("anakin redux", anakinImmutable);
console.log("anakin redux with age", anakinImmutableWithAge);
```

Using reducers

In the previous section, we covered how to change state in the old way and how to do it in the new Redux-like way. The reducers are nothing more than pure functions; pure in the sense that they don't mutate but produce a new state. A reducer needs an action to work though. Let's deepen our knowledge on Reducers and Actions. Let's create an action meant to add things to a list and a reducer that goes with it:

```
// core-concepts/jedilist-reducer.js

let actionLuke = { type: "ADD_ITEM", payload: { name: "Luke" } };
let actionVader = { type: "ADD_ITEM", payload: "Vader" };

function jediListReducer(state = [], action) {
  switch(action.type) {
    case "ADD_ITEM":
      return [... state, action.payload];
    default:
      return state;
  }
}

let state = jediListReducer([], actionLuke);
console.log(state);
/*
[{ name: 'Luke '}]
*/

state = jediListReducer(state, actionVader);
console.log(state);
/*
[{ name: 'Luke' }, { name: 'Vader' }]
*/

module.exports = jediListReducer;
```

OK, so know we know how to deal with lists; what about objects? We again need to define an action and a reducer:

```
// core-concepts/selectjedi-reducer.js

let actionPerson = { type: "SELECT_JEDI", payload: { id: 1, name: "Luke" }
};
let actionVader = { type: "SELECT_JEDI", payload: { id: 2, name: "Vader" }
};

function selectJediReducer({}, action) {
```

```
  switch (action.type) {
    case "SELECT_JEDI":
      return Object.assign({}, action.payload);
    default:
      return state;
  }
}

state = selectJediReducer({}, actionPerson);
console.log(state);
/*
{ name: 'Luke' }
*/

state = selectJediReducer(state, actionVader);
console.log(state);
/*
{ name: 'Vader' }
*/

module.exports = selectJediReducer;
```

What we see here is how one object completely replaces the content of another object by invoking SELECT_JEDI. We also see how we use Object.assign() to ensure we only copy over the values from the incoming object.

Merging all reducers together

OK, so we now have a reducer for handling our list of jedis as well as a reducer dedicated to handling selections of a specific jedis. We mentioned before that, in Redux, we have a single store where all our data lives. Now it's time to create that single store. This can be easily accomplished by creating the following function store():

```
// core-concepts/merged-reducers.js

function store(state = { jedis: [], selectedJedi: null }, action) {
  return {
    jedis: jediListReducer(state.jedis, action),
    selectedJedi: selectJediReducer(state.selectedJedi, action)
  };
}

let newJediActionYoda = { type: "ADD_ITEM", payload: { name: "Yoda"} };
let newJediActionVader = { type: "ADD_ITEM", payload: { name: "Vader"} };
let newJediSelection = { type: "SELECT_JEDI", payload: { name: "Yoda"} };
```

```
let initialState = { jedis: [], selectedJedi: {} };

let state = store(initialState, newJediActionYoda);
console.log("Merged reducers", state);
/*
  {
    jedis: [{ name: 'Yoda' }],
    selectedJedi: {}
  }
*/

state = store(state, newJediActionVader);
console.log("Merged reducers", state);
/*
  {
    jedis: [{ name 'Yoda' }, {name: 'Vader'}],
    selectedJedi: {}
  }
*/

state = store(state, newJediSelection);
console.log("Merged reducers", state);

console.log(state);
/*
{
  jedis: [{ name: 'Yoda' }, { name: 'Vader'}],
  selectedJedi: { name: 'Yoda' }
}
*/
```

From what we can see here, our `store()` function does nothing more than return an object. The returned object is our current state. What we choose to call the properties of the state object is what we want to refer to when displaying the content of the store. If we want to change the state of our store, we need to invoke the `store()` function anew and provide it with an action that represents the intent of our change.

Data flow

OK, so we know about actions, reducers, and manipulating the state in a pure way. What about putting all this in practice in a real application? How would we do that? Let's try to model the data flow of our application. Imagine that we have a view that handles adding an item to a list and a view that handles showing the list. Then, our data flow could look like the following:

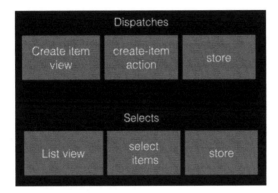

In the case of the create item view, we enter the data we need to create an item and then we dispatch an action, create-item, which ends up adding the item to the store. In our other data flow, we simply have a list view that selects the items from the store, which leads to the list view being populated. We realize that in a real application there may be the following steps:

1. User interaction
2. Creation of an action that represents our intent
3. Dispatching an action, which leads to our state changing its state

The preceding steps are true for our create item view. For our list view, we simply want to read from a store and display the data. Let's try to make this more tangible and turn at least the Redux part into actual code.

Creating the action

We will start by creating an action creator, a helper function that helps us create actions:

```
// dataflow/actions.js

export function createItem(title){
  return { type: "CREATE_ITEM", payload: { title: title } };
}
```

Creating a controller class – create-view.js

Now imagine that we are inside the code of the view that handles creating items; it may look something like this:

```
// dataflow/create-view.js

import { createItem } from "./actions";
import { dispatch, select } from "./redux";

console.log("create item view has loaded");

class CreateItemView {
  saveItem() {
    const elem = document.getElementById("input");
    dispatch(createItem(elem.value));
    const items = select("items");
    console.log(items);
  }
}

const button = document.getElementById("saveButton");
const createItemWiew = new CreateItemView();

button.addEventListener("click", createItemWiew.saveItem);

export default createItemWiew;
```

OK, so, in our `create-view.js` file we create a `CreateItemView` class that has a
method `saveItem()` method on it. The `saveItem()` method is the first responder to a
button click on a button with the ID `saveButton`. When the button is clicked, our
`saveItem()` method is invoked, which ends up calling our dispatch function with
the `createItem()` action method, which in turn is using the input elements value as input,
like so:

```
dispatch(createItem(elem.value));
```

Creating a store implementation

We have yet to create the `dispatch()` method, so we will do that next:

```
// dataflow/redux.js

export function dispatch(action) {
  // implement this
}
```

What we can see from the preceding code is that we have a `dispatch()` function, which is
one of the things we export from this file. Let's try to fill in the implementation:

```
// dataflow/redux-stepI.js

// 1)
function itemsReducer(state = [], action) {
  switch(action.type) {
    case "CREATE_ITEM":
      return [...state, Object.assign(action.payload) ];
    default:
      return state;
  }
}

// 2)
let state = {
  items: []
};

// 3
function store(state = { items: [] }, action) {
  return {
    items: itemsReducer(state.items, action)
  };
}
```

```
// 4)
export function getState() {
  return state;
}

// 5)
export function dispatch(action) {
  state = store(state, action);
}
```

Let's explain what we did there from the top. We first define a reducer 1)
called `itemsReducer`, which can produce a new state given a new item. Thereafter, we
create a state variable, which is our state 2). This is followed by the `store()` function 3),
which is a function to set up which property goes together with which reducer. Thereafter,
we define a function called `getState()` 4), which returns our current state. Lastly, we have
our `dispatch()` function 5), which just invokes the `store()` function with the action we
provide it.

Testing out our store

Now it is time to put our code to use; first, we will create a `redux-demo.js` file to test out
our Redux implementation, then we will polish it a bit, and lastly we will use it in the view
we created earlier:

```
// dataflow/redux-demo.js

import { dispatch, getState, select, subscribe } from "./redux";

const { addItem } = require("./actions");
subscribe(() => {
console.log("store changed");
});
console.log("initial state", getState());
dispatch(addItem("A book"));
dispatch(addItem("A second book"));
console.log("after dispatch", getState());
console.log("items", select("items"));

/*
this will print the following

state before: { items: [] }
state after: { items: [{ title: 'a new book'}] }
*/
```

Cleaning up the implementation

OK, so our Redux implementation seems to be working. It's time to clean it up a bit. We need to move the reducer out into its own file, like so:

```
// dataflow/reducer.js

function itemsReducer(state = [], action) {
  switch(action.type) {
    case "CREATE_ITEM":
      return [...state, Object.assign(action.payload) ];
    default:
      return state;
  }
}
```

It's also a good idea to add a `select()` function to the store as we sometimes don't want to move a full state back, only part of it. Our list view will benefit from the use of the `select()` function. Let's add that next:

```
// dataflow/redux-stepII.js

// this now refers to the reducers.js file we broke out
import { itemsReducer } from "./reducers";

let state = {
  items: []
};

function store(state = { items: [] }, action) {
  return {
    items: itemsReducer(state.items, action)
  };
}

export function getState() {
  return state;
}

export function dispatch(action) {
  state = store(state, action);
}

export function select(slice) {
  return state[slice];
}
```

Creating our second controller class – list-view.js

Let's now shift our focus to our `list-view.js` file that we are yet to create:

```javascript
// dataflow/list-view.js

import { createItem } from "./actions";
import { select, subscribe } from "./redux";

console.log("list item view has loaded");

class ListItemsView {
  constructor() {
    this.render();
    subscribe(this.render);
  }

  render() {
    const items = select("items");
    const elem = document.getElementById("list");

    elem.innerHTML = "";
    items.forEach(item => {
      const li = document.createElement("li");
      li.innerHTML = item.title;
      elem.appendChild(li);
    });
  }
}

const listItemsView = new ListItemsView();
export default listItemsView;
```

OK, so we utilize the `select()` method and get a slice of state from our state from the `redux.js` file we created. Thereafter, we render the response. As long as these views are on different pages, we will always get the latest version of `items` arrays from our state. However, if these views are visible at the same time, then we have a problem.

Adding subscription capability to our store

Somehow, the list view needs to listen to changes in the store so that it can rerender when a change happens. A way to do that is, of course, to set up some kind of listener that triggers an event when a change happens. If we, as a view, subscribe to such changes, then we can act accordingly and rerender our view. There are different ways of accomplishing this: we can either just implement an Observable pattern or use a library, such as EventEmitter. Let's update our redux.js file to make it so:

```
// dataflow/redux.js

import { itemsReducer } from "./reducer";
import EventEmitter from "events";
const emitter = new EventEmitter();

let state = {
  items: []
};

function store(state = { items: [] }, action) {
  return {
    items: itemsReducer(state.items, action)
  };
}

export function getState() {
  return state;
}

export function dispatch(action) {
  const oldState = state;
  state = store(state, action);
  emitter.emit("changed");
}

export function select(slice) {
  return state[slice];
}

export function subscribe(cb) {
  emitter.on("changed", cb);
}
```

Creating a program

So far, we have created a bunch of files, namely, the following:

- `redux.js`: Our store implementation.
- `create-view.js`: A controller that listens to inputs and button presses. The controller will read the input on a button press and dispatch the input's value so it is saved in the store.
- `list-view.js`: Our second controller, responsible for showing the content of the store.
- `todo-app.js`: The starter file that creates our entire application (we have yet to create this).
- `index.html`: The UI for our application (we are yet to create this).

Setting up our environment

Maybe you have noticed that we are using import statements used for ES6 modules? There are many ways to make that work, but we choose a modern option, namely, utilizing webpack. We will need to do the following to set up webpack successfully:

- Install the npm libraries `webpack` and `webpack-cli`
- Create a `webpack.config.js` file and specify the entry point of your application
- Add an entry to the `package.json` file so that we can build and run our app with a simple `npm start`
- Add a HTTP server so that we can show the app

We can install the needed libraries by typing:

```
npm install webpack webpack-cli --save-dev
```

Thereafter, we need to create our `config` file, `webpack.config.js`, like so:

```
// dataflow/webpack.config.js

module.exports = {
  entry: "./todo-app.js",
  output: {
    filename: "bundle.js"
  },
  watch: true
};
```

In the preceding code, we are stating that the entry point should be `todo-app.js` and also that the output file should be called `bundle.js`. We also ensure our bundle will be rebuilt by setting `watch` to `true`. Let's add the needed entry to `package.json` by adding the following to the `script` tag:

```
// dataflow/package.json excerpt

"scripts": {
  "start" : "webpack -d"
}
```

Here, we are defining a start command that invokes webpack with the flag -d, which means it will generate source maps, making for a nice debug experience.

For our last setup step, we need a HTTP server so that we can display our app. Webpack itself has one called, `webpack-dev-server`, or we could use `http-server`, which is an NPM package. This is a pretty simple application so either will do fine.

Creating the missing files and running our program

Our application needs a UI so let's create that:

```
// dataflow/dist/index.html

<html>
  <body>
    <div>
      <input type="text" id="input">
      <button id="saveButton">Save</button>
    </div>
    <div>
      <ul id="list"></ul>
    </div>
    <button id="saveButton">Save</button>
    <script src="bundle.js"></script>
  </body>
</html>
```

So, here we have an input element and a button that we can press to save a new item. This is followed by a list, where our content will be rendered.

Let's create the `todo-app.js` next. It should look like the following:

```
// dataflow/todo-app.js

// import create view
import createView from "./create-view";
// import list view
import listView from "./list-view";
```

Here, we are requiring in the two controllers so we can collect input as well as displaying store content. Let's try out our application by typing `npm start` in the Terminal window. This will create the `bundle.js` file in a dist folder. To display the app, we need to fire up another terminal window and place ourselves in the `dist` folder. Your dist folder should consist of the following files:

- `index.html`
- `bundle.js`

Now we are ready to launch the app by typing `http-server -p 5000`. You will be able to find your app at `http:localhost:5000` in your browser:

We see our expected application with an input element and a button, and we see our console to the right showing us that both our controllers were loaded. Additionally, we see the content of the items property of our store object, which points to an empty array. This is expected as we haven't added any items to it yet. Let's add an item to our store by adding a value to our input element and pressing the **Save** button:

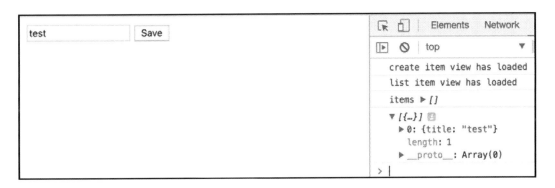

On the right, we can see that our store now contains an item but our UI is not updated. The reason for that is that we don't actually subscribe to changes. We can change that by adding the following piece of code to our list-view.js controller file:

```
// dataflow/list-view.js

import { createItem } from "./actions";
import { select, subscribe } from "./redux";

console.log("list item view has loaded");

class ListItemsView {
  constructor() {
    this.render();
    subscribe(this.render);
  }

  render() {
    const items = select("items");
    const elem = document.getElementById("list");
    elem.innerHTML = "";
    console.log("items", items);
    items.forEach(item => {
      const li = document.createElement("li");
      li.innerHTML = item.title;
      elem.appendChild(li);
    });
  }
}

const listItemsView = new ListItemsView();
export default listItemsView;
```

Now our app renders as it should and should look something like this, providing that you added a few items:

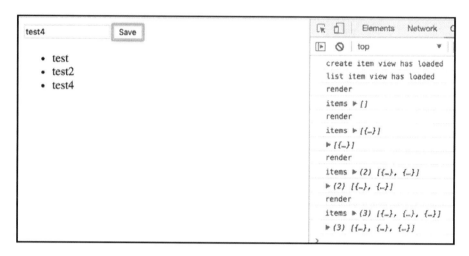

Dealing with asynchronous calls

Dispatching actions is always done synchronously. Data is fetched through AJAX asynchronously, so how do we get asynchronous to play well with Redux?

You should define your Redux states in the following way when setting up an asynchronous call:

- Loading: Here, we have the chance to show a spinner, not render part of the UI, or convey to the user in some other way that the UI is waiting for something
- Data successfully fetched: You should set a state for the fetched data
- Error happened: You should record the error somehow so that you are able to tell the user that an error occurred

You, by convention, use the word fetch to indicate that you are fetching data. Let's look at an example of what that might look like. First off, let's start by defining the steps we need to take:

1. Create a reducer. This should have the ability to set different states depending on whether we are waiting for the response, got the response, or an error happened.
2. Create actions. We need a file of actions that supports our states mentioned earlier; creating this is more about convenience.

3. Update our `redux.js` file to use our new reducer.

4. Test our creation out.

Let's say we are fetching a book from an API. We should have a reducer that looks like the following:

```
// async/book-reducer.js

let initialState = {
  loading: false,
  data: void 0,
  error: void 0
};

const bookReducer = (state = initialState, action) => {
  switch(action.type) {
    case 'FETCH_BOOK_LOADING':
      return {...state, loading: true };
    case 'FETCH_BOOK_SUCCESS':
      return {...state, data: action.payload.map(book => ({ ... book })) };
    case 'FETCH_BOOK_ERROR':
      return {...state, error: { ...action.payload }, loading: false };
  }
}

module.exports = bookReducer;
```

Now that we have covered the reducer bit, let's move on to the creation of actions. It will look like the following:

```
// async/book-actions.js

const fetchBookLoading = () => ({ type: 'FETCH_BOOK_LOADING' });
const fetchBookSuccess = (data) => ({ type: 'FETCH_BOOK_SUCCESS', payload:
data });
const fetchBookError = (error) => ({ type: 'FETCH_BOOK_ERROR', payload:
error });

module.exports = {
  fetchBookLoading,
  fetchBookSuccess,
  fetchBookError
};
```

Now we need to turn to our `store` file and update it:

```
// async/redux.js

const bookReducer = require('./book-reducer');
const EventEmitter = require('events');
const emitter = new EventEmitter();

let state = {
  book: {}
};

function store(state = {}, action) {
  return {
    book: bookReducer(state.book, action)
  };
}

function getState() {
  return state;
}

function dispatch(action) {
  const oldState = state;
  state = store(state, action);
  emitter.emit('changed');
}

function select(slice) {
  return state[slice];
}

function subscribe(cb) {
  emitter.on('changed', cb);
}

module.exports = {
  getState, dispatch, select, subscribe
}
```

Creating a demo with Redux and asynchronous

Now the time has come to test everything out. What we are interested in here is ensuring that our store state behaves the way we want it to. We want the store to reflect the fact that we are loading the data, receiving the data, and if there is an error, that should be reflected as well. Let's start out by mimicking an AJAX call:

```
const { fetchBookLoading, fetchBookSuccess, fetchBookError } =
require('./book-actions');
const { dispatch, getState } = require('./redux');

function fetchBook() {
  return new Promise(resolve => {
    setTimeout(() => {
      resolve({ title: 'A new hope  - the book' });
    }, 1000);
  })
}
```

As our next order of business, let's set up some logging for the state and dispatch our first action, `fetchBookLoading`, which indicates that an AJAX request is underway. This is where, ideally, we would want to reflect this state in the UI and show a spinner or similar:

```
console.log(getState());
// { book: {} }

dispatch(fetchBookLoading());

console.log(getState());
// { book: { loading: true } }
```

The last step is about a call to our `fetchBook()` method and setting the store state appropriately:

```
async function main() {
try {
  const book = await fetchBook();
  dispatch(fetchBookSuccess(book));
  console.log(getState());
  // { book: { data: { title: 'A new hope - the book'}, loading: false } }
} catch(err) {
  dispatch(fetchBookError(err));
  console.log(getState());
```

```
// { book: { data: undefined, error: { title: 'some error message' } } }
  }
}

main();
```

We have so far described our demo in pieces from top to bottom. The full code should read like this:

```
// async/demo.js

const { fetchBookLoading, fetchBookSuccess, fetchBookError } =
require('./book-actions');
const { dispatch, getState } = require('./redux');

function fetchBook() {
  return new Promise(resolve => {
    setTimeout(() => {
      resolve({ title: 'A new hope - the book' });
    }, 1000);
  })
}

console.log(getState());
dispatch(fetchBookLoading());
console.log(getState());

async function main() {
  try {
    const book = await fetchBook();
    dispatch(fetchBookSuccess(book));
    console.log(getState());
  } catch(err) {
    dispatch(fetchBookError(err));
    console.log(getState());
  }
}

main();
```

As you can see, there is really not much to dealing with asynchronous, you just need to dispatch the suitable state once the asynchronous action has run its course. There are libraries for dealing with asynchronous though. If you are a React user it might be worth looking into Sagas and if Angular is your flavor, then NgRx and effects is your go-to. The reason for separate libraries existing for this is to say that asynchronous interactions, especially AJAX ones, are considered side-effects and as such they are outside the *normal* flow. Ultimately, it's up to you if you feel you need such a library.

Best practices

So far, we have gone through a lot. We have covered principles, core concepts, and even got to build our own Redux implementation. We should be mighty proud of ourselves at this point. There is something we have yet to cover, though, and that is how we use Redux in an optimal way. There are some key rules we can follow.

Organize your file system optimally. You should not have a few files when building an app but rather many, and usually organized by feature. This leads to the following file setup for a feature:

- **Reducer**: We should have one file, per reducer, for this
- **Actions**: We should have a file describing all the actions we could possibly dispatch
- **View/component file**: This has nothing to do with Redux but, regardless of the framework we go with, we usually have a file describing the component we are trying to build

There is another aspect that is worth doing as well, and that is optimizing the setup process of our store. The store normally needs to be initialized with a number of reducers. We could write some code that looks like this:

```
const booksReducer = require("./books/reducer");
const personReducer = require("./reducer");

function combineReducers(config) {
  const states = Object.keys(config);
  let stateObject = {};

  states.forEach(state => {
    stateObject[state] = config[state];
  });

  return stateObject;
}

const rootReducer = combineReducers({
  books: booksReducer,
  person: personReducer
});

const store = createStore(rootReducer);

store.reduce({ type: "SOME_ACTION", payload: "some data" });
```

There is nothing wrong with the setup here, but it you have many features, and a reducer in each, you will end up with a lot of imports, and your call to `combineReducers()` will be longer and longer. An approach that will solve that is having each reducer register itself with the `rootReducer`. This way, we can switch the following call:

```
const rootReducer = combineReducers({
  books: booksReducer,
  person: personReducer
});

const store = createStore(rootReducer);
```

It will be switched with this:

```
const store = createStore(getRootReducer());
```

This forces us to create a new `root-reducer.js` file, which will look like the following:

```
// best-practices/root-reducer.js

function combineReducers(config) {
  const states = Object.keys(config);
  let stateObject = {};
  states.forEach(state => {
    stateObject[state] = config[state];
  });

  return stateObject;
}

let rootReducer = {};

function registerReducer(reducer) {
  const entry = combineReducers(reducer);
  rootReducer = { ...rootReducer, ...entry };
}

function getRootReducer() {
  return rootReducer;
}

module.exports = {
  registerReducer,
  getRootReducer
};
```

We have highlighted the important part here, the `registerReducer()` method, which a reducer can now use to register itself with the `rootReducer`. At this point, it's worth going back to our reducer and updating it to use the `registerReducer()` method:

```
// best-practies/books/reducer.js

const { registerReducer } = require('../root-reducer');

let initialState = [];

function bookReducer(state = initialState, action) {
  switch(action.type) {
    case 'LIST_BOOKS':
      return state;
    case 'ADD_BOOK':
      return [...state, {...action.payload}];
  }
}

registerReducer({ books: bookReducer });
```

Summary

This chapter has been a wild ride, going from describing principles to core concepts, to being able to understand and even build our own Redux. Time was spent looking at how to deal with AJAX calls and suitable state patterns for that. We learned that there was really nothing much to it. We finished off the chapter by looking at best practices as well. At this point, we are in a considerably better position to be able to understand and appreciate NgRx because we know its underlying patterns and reasons for existing. We can say farewell to this chapter knowing that we will take on NgRx in the last chapter of the book. The aim is to cover the principles and concepts that govern it, how to use it in practice, and also to cover some necessary tooling that will ensure we become really successful.

9

NgRx – Reduxing that Angular App

We have reached the last chapter of this book. The time has come to understand the NgRx library. So far, different topics have been covered, making you as a reader more used to thinking about things such as immutable data structures and reactive programming. We did all this so it would be easier for you to digest what is to come in this chapter. NgRx is an implementation of Redux made for Angular, so concepts such as store, action creators, actions, selectors, and reducers are well used. What you have hopefully picked up on by reading the past chapters is how Redux works. By reading the previous chapter, you will have discovered how what you learned about Redux translates to NgRx and its principles on how to organize your code. This chapter aims to describe the core library `@ngrx-store`, how to handle side effects with `@ngrx-effects`, and how to debug like a pro with `@ngrx/store-devtools`, among other things.

In this chapter, we will learn:

- State management with `@ngrx/store`
- Handling side effects with `@ngrx/effects`
- How to debug with `@ngrx/store-devtools`
- How to capture and transform the router state with `@ngrx/router-store`

NgRx overview

NgRx consists of the following parts:

- `@ngrx/store`: This is the core that contains a way for us to maintain state and dispatch actions.
- `@ngrx/effects`: This will handle side effects such as, AJAX requests, for example.
- `@ngrx/router-store`: This ensures we can integrate NgRx with the Angular routing.
- `@ngrx/store-devtools`: This will install a tool that gives us the opportunity to debug NgRx by, for example, giving us a time travel debugging functionality.
- `@ngrx/entity`: This is a library that helps us manage record collections.
- `@ngrx/schematics`: This is a scaffolder library that helps you when using NgRx.

A word on state management

Some components must have state. When there is a need for another component to know about that very same state, the first component needs to find a way to communicate that to the other component. There are many ways to achieve this. One way is to ensure that all state that should be shared lives in a centralized store. Think of this store as a single source of truth, from which all components can read. Every state does not necessarily need to end up in the centralized store, as the state may only concern a specific component. Before NgRx and Redux, one way of solving this was to put everything in a globally accessible object or service. The store, as we mentioned, is just that. It is globally accessible in the sense that it can be injected into any component that might need it. A word of caution; even though it is tempting to put all of our state in our store, we really shouldn't. State that we notice needs to be shared between components is worth putting there.

Another benefit we get from having a centralized store is that it is very easy to save down the application's state for later recovery. If state only lives in one place, a user, or the system, can easily persist that state to a backend so that next time, if they want to continue from where they left off, they can easily do so by querying the backend for that state. So, there does exist another reason for wanting a centralized store other than wanting to share the data between many components.

@ngrx/store – state management

All of the files in this section points to `Chapter9/State` project.

This is the moment we have been waiting for. How do we actually get started? It's really easy. Let's first ensure we have installed Angular CLI. We do so by typing the following in our terminal:

```
npm install -g @angular/cli
```

At this point, we need an Angular project. We use the Angular CLI for that, and scaffold ourselves a new project using the following command:

```
ng new <my new project>
```

Once the scaffolding process is done, we navigate to our newly created director project with a simple `cd <project dir>`. We want to use the core functionality provided in the `@ngrx/store` library, therefore we install it by typing the following:

```
npm install @ngrx/store --save
```

Let's now open up the `app.module.ts` file in our scaffolded project. The time has come to import and register NgRx with `AppModule`:

```
// app.module.ts

import { BrowserModule } from "@angular/platform-browser";
import { NgModule } from "@angular/core";
import { StoreModule } from "@ngrx/store";
import { AppComponent } from "./app.component";
import { counterReducer } from "./reducer";

@NgModule({
  declarations: [AppComponent],
  imports: [
    BrowserModule,
    StoreModule.forRoot({ counter: counterReducer }),
  ],
  bootstrap: [AppComponent]
})
export class AppModule {}
```

In the preceding code, we've highlighted the important part, which is importing `StoreModule` and registering it with `AppModule` by typing:

```
StoreModule.forRoot({ counter: counterReducer })
```

Here, we are telling the store what state should exist, which is `counter`, and that `counterReducer` is the reducer meant to take care of that slice of state. As you can see, the code doesn't quite work yet because we haven't created `counterReducer` yet, let's do that next:

```
// reducer.ts

export function counterReducer(state = 0, action) {
  switch(action.type) {
    case 'INCREMENT':
      return state + 1;
    case 'DECREMENT':
      return state -1;
    default:
      return state;
  }
}
```

Hopefully, you have read Chapter 8, *Redux*, and understand why we write the reducer file as we have done. Let's recap a bit, and declare that a reducer is just a function that takes a state and produces a new state given an action. It's also important to stress that reducers are so called pure functions that do not change the state, but produce a new state, given the old state plus the incoming action. Let's show here how we would theoretically use our reducer if we wanted to use it outside of Redux. We do this just to demonstrate how reducers work:

```
let state = counterReducer(0, { type: 'INCREMENT' });
// state is 1
state = counterReducer(state, { type: 'INCREMENT' });
// state is 2
```

As we can see from this, we start off with an initial value of 0, and it computes a new value that results in 1. Upon the second execution of the function, we provide it with the existing state, which has the value 0. This results in our state now being 2. This may look simple, but this is pretty much as complicated as a reducer can get. Normally, you wouldn't execute the reducer function yourself but rather register it with the store and dispatch actions towards the store. This will lead to the reducer being invoked. So, how do we tell the store to dispatch? Simple, we use the function `dispatch()` on the store. For this code, let's move to the `app.component.ts` file. We also need to create a file called `app-state.ts`, which is an interface, a typed representation of our store:

```
// app-state.ts
export interface AppState {
  counter: number;
}
```

```
// app.component.ts
import { Component } from "@angular/core";
import { Store } from "@ngrx/store";
import { Observable } from "rxjs/Observable";
import { AppState } from "./app-state";

@Component({
  selector: "app-root",
  template: `
  {{ counter$ | async }}
  `
})
export class AppComponent {
  counter$;

  constructor(private store: Store<AppState>) {
    this.counter$ = store.select("counter");
  }
}
```

What we can see from the preceding code is how we inject a store service into the constructor, like so:

```
constructor(private store: Store<AppState>) {
  this.counter$ = store.select("counter");
}
```

Thereafter, we call `store.select("count")`, which means we are asking our store for the `count` property part of its state as that's all this component cares about. A call `store.select()` returns an `Observable` that when resolved contains a value. We can easily show this value by adding it to the template markup, like so:

```
{{ counter$ | async }}
```

That takes care of getting and displaying the state. What about dispatching an action? The store instance has a method on it called `dispatch()`, which takes an object containing the property type. So the following is perfectly good input:

```
// example input to a store

store.dispatch({ type: 'INCREMENT' });
store.dispatch({ type: 'INCREMENT', payload: 1 });
store.dispatch({})
// will throw an error, as it is missing the type property
```

Now, let's build out our component a little, and create some methods and markup that will allow us to dispatch actions and see the end result of doing so:

```
// app.component.ts

import { Component } from "@angular/core";
import { Store } from "@ngrx/store";
import { AppState } from "./app-state";

@Component({
  selector: "app-root",
  template: `
  {{ counter$ | async }}
  <button (click)="increment()" >Increment</button>
  <button (click)="decrement()" >Decrement</button>
  `
})
export class AppComponent {
  counter$;

  constructor(private store: Store<AppState>) {
    this.counter$ = store.select("counter");
  }

  increment() {
    this.store.dispatch({ type: 'INCREMENT' });
  }

  decrement() {
    this.store.dispatch({ type: 'DECREMENT' });
  }
}
```

We added the `increment()` and `decrement()` methods to the class body, and also added two buttons to the markup that invoke said functions. Trying this out, we can see how our UI is updated for every press of the button. The reason for this working is, of course, that each dispatched action calls our `counterReducer` implicitly, and also because we hold a reference to our state in the form of the `counter$` variable. As this is an `Observable`, it means it will be updated when a change happens. The change is then pushed out to our `counter$` variable when an action is dispatched. It's simple, but powerful.

A more complex example – a list

We have so far learned how to set up NgRx by importing and registering its module. We have also been taught about the `select()` function that gives us a slice of state, and the `dispatch()` function that allows us to dispatch an action. These are the basics, we will use these very same basics and create a new reducer to reinforce what we already know, while introducing the concept payload.

We need to do the following:

- Tell the store we have a new state, `jedis`
- Create a `jediListReducer` and register it with the store
- Create a component that supports showing our `jediList`, but is also able to dispatch actions that will change our slice of state `jedis`

Let's get down to business by defining our reducer, `jediListReducer`:

```
// jedi-list.reducer.ts
export function jediListReducer(state = [], action) {
  switch(action.type) {
    case 'ADD_JEDI':
      return [ ...state, { ...action.payload }];
    case 'REMOVE_JEDI':
      return state.filter(jedi => jedi.id !== action.payload.id);
    case 'LOAD_JEDIS':
      return action.payload.map(jedi => ({...jedi}));
    default:
      return state;
  }
}
```

Let's explain what goes on here for each case in our switch. First off, we have ADD_JEDI. We take our `action.payload` and add it to the list. Or technically, we take our existing list and construct a new list based on the old list, plus our new list item found in `action.payload`. Secondly we have REMOVE_JEDI that uses the `filter()` function to take away the list item that we don't want to see. Lastly we have LOAD_JEDIS that takes in an existing list and replaces our state. Now, let's demo this reducer by invoking it here:

```
let state = jediListReducer([], { type: 'ADD_JEDI', payload : { id: 1,
name: 'Yoda' });
// now contains [{ id: 1, name: 'Yoda' }]

state = jediListReducer(state, { type: 'ADD_JEDI', payload: { id: 2, name:
'Darth Vader'} });
```

```
// now contains [{ id: 1, name: 'Yoda' }, { id: 2, name: 'Darth Vader'}];

state = jediListReducer(state, { type: 'REMOVE JEDI', payload: { id: 1 }
});
// now contains [{ id: 2, name: 'Darth Vader'}];

state = jediListReducer(state, { type: 'LOAD_JEDIS', payload: [] });
// now contains []
```

Now, let's register this reducer with the store. We will therefore return to `app.module.ts`:

```typescript
// app.module.ts

import { BrowserModule } from "@angular/platform-browser";
import { NgModule } from "@angular/core";
import { StoreModule } from "@ngrx/store";
import { AppComponent } from "./app.component";
import { counterReducer } from "./reducer";
import { jediListReducer } from "./jedi-list-reducer";

@NgModule({
  declarations: [AppComponent],
  imports: [
    BrowserModule,
    StoreModule.forRoot({
      count: counterReducer,
      jediList: jediListReducer }),
  ],
  bootstrap: [AppComponent]
})
export class AppModule {}
```

Because we just added a new state to our store, we should make the `app-state.ts` file aware of it, and we should also create a `Jedi` model so we can use that in our component later on:

```typescript
// jedi.model.ts

export interface Jedi {
  id: number;
  name: string;
}

// app-state.ts

import { Jedi } from "./jedi.model";
```

```
export interface AppState {
  counter: number;
  jediList: Array<Jedi>;
}
```

From the preceding code, we can see that `jediListReducer`, as well as the state `jediList`, is added to the object that serves as input to the `StoreModule.forRoot()` function. This means that NgRx is aware of this state and will let us retrieve it and dispatch actions to it. To do so, let's build a component with just that. We need to create the `jedi-list.component.ts` file:

```
// jedi-list.component.ts

import { Component } from "@angular/core";
import { Store } from "@ngrx/store";
import { AppState } from "../app-state";
import { Jedi } from "./jedi.model";

@Component({
  selector: "jedi-list",
  template: `
  <div *ngFor="let jedi of list$ | async">
    {{ jedi.name }}<button (click)="remove(jedi.id)" >Remove</button>
  </div>
  <input [(ngModel)]="newJedi" placeholder="" />
  <button (click)="add()">Add</button>
  <button (click)="clear()" >Clear</button>
  `
})
export class JediListComponent {
  list$: Observable<Array<Jedi>>;
  counter = 0;
  newJedi = "";

  constructor(private store: Store<AppState>) {
    this.list$ = store.select("jediList");
  }

  add() {
    this.store.dispatch({
      type: 'ADD_JEDI',
      payload: { id: this.counter++, name: this.newJedi }
    });
    this.newJedi = '';
  }

  remove(id) {
```

```
    this.store.dispatch({ type: 'REMOVE_JEDI', payload: { id } });
  }

  clear() {
    this.store.dispatch({ type: 'LOAD_JEDIS', payload: [] });
    this.counter = 0;
  }
}
```

The last thing we need to do is to register this component with our module, and we should have a working application:

```
// app.module.ts

import { BrowserModule } from "@angular/platform-browser";
import { NgModule } from "@angular/core";
import { StoreModule } from "@ngrx/store";
import { AppComponent } from "./app.component";
import { counterReducer } from "./reducer";
import { jediListReducer } from "./jedi-list.reducer";
import { JediListComponent } from './jedi-list.component';

@NgModule({
  declarations: [AppComponent, JediListComponent ],
  imports: [
    BrowserModule,
    StoreModule.forRoot({ count: counterReducer, jediList: JediListReducer
}),
  ],
  bootstrap: [AppComponent]
})
export class AppModule {}
```

Best practices

The following files points to the demo project `Chapter9/BestPractices`.

So far, we have created some working code, but it could look a lot better, and be less error prone as well. There are steps we can take to improve the code, those are:

- Get rid of so-called magic strings and rely on constants
- Add a default state to your reducer

- Create so-called action creators
- Move everything into a dedicated module and split up it up into several components

Let's have a look at our first bullet point. Given the type of actions we perform on our `jediList`, we can create a `constants.ts` file for them, like so:

```
// jedi.constants.ts

export const ADD_JEDI = 'ADD_JEDI';
export const REMOVE_JEDI = "REMOVE_JEDI";
export const LOAD_JEDIS ="LOAD_JEDIS";
```

Now, when we refer to these actions we can instead import this file and use these constants instead, decreasing the risk of us mistyping.

The second thing we can do is to simplify the creation of actions by creating the so-called action creator. We are so far used to typing the following to create an action:

```
const action = { type: 'ADD_JEDI', payload: { id: 1, name: 'Yoda' } };
```

A better habit here is to create a function that does this for us. For the case with the list reducer, there are three possible actions that can take place, so let's put all these in a `actions.ts` file:

```
// jedi.actions.ts

import {
  ADD_JEDI,
  REMOVE_JEDI,
  LOAD_JEDIS
} from "./jedi.constants";

export const addJedi = (id, name) => ({ type: ADD_JEDI, payload: { id, name
} });
export const removeJedi = (id) => ({ type: REMOVE_JEDI, payload:{ id } });
export const loadJedis = (jedis) => ({ type: LOAD_JEDIS, payload: jedis });
```

The point of creating the `actions.ts` file was so that we would have to write less code when we dispatch actions. Instead of writing the following:

```
store.dispatch({ type: 'ADD_JEDI', payload: { id: 3, name: 'Luke' } });
```

We can now write this as:

```
// example of how we can dispatch to store using an actions method

import { addJedi } from './jedi.actions';
store.dispatch(addJedi(3, 'Luke'));
```

A cleanup example

The following scenario can be found in the `Chapter9/BestPractices` folder of the code repository.

Let's explain where we are coming from, and why there might be a need to clean up your code. If you are starting out with a very simple app, you might add the reducer, the actions, and components in the root module of your project. This might create a mess as soon as you want to add another component. Let's illustrate what our file structure might look like before we start cleaning up:

```
app.component.ts
app.module.ts
jedi-list-reducer.ts
jedi-constants.ts
jedi-list-actions.ts
jedi-list-component.ts
```

From this, it's pretty clear that this will only hold up if our app will only consist of that one component. As soon as we add more components, things will start to look messy.

Let's list what we need to do to create a better file structure, but also utilize the action creator, constants, and reducers in the best way possible:

- Create a dedicated feature module and directory
- Create action constants that the reducer and actions file can use
- Create an action creator file with all the actions we mean to perform
- Create a reducer that handles dispatches
- Create a `JediList` component that is able to handle all actions we mean to use
- Register our reducer and state with the store

Create a dedicated directory and feature module

For that reason, we want to place everything in a dedicated directory, `jedi`. The easiest way to do that is to use the Angular CLI and run the following commands:

```
ng g module jedi
```

The preceding code will generate the following files:

```
jedi/
  jedi.module.ts
```

Place yourself in your newly created `jedi` directory and type the following:

```
ng g component jedi-list
```

This will add the following structure to your `jedi` directory:

```
jedi/
  jedi.module.ts
  jedi-list/
    jedi-list.component.html
    jedi-list.component.ts
    jedi-list.component.css
    jedi-list.component.spec.ts
```

However, we have created the `jedi-list.component` and its belonging files in a previous section, so we will remove those scaffolded files for now and just move in the already created files under the `jedi-list` directory. So, your directory should look like:

```
jedi/
  jedi.module.ts
  jedi-list/
```

Add reducer and constants

Let's create our reducer, like so:

```
// jedi/jedi-list/jedi-list.reducer.ts

import {
  ADD_JEDI,
  REMOVE_JEDI,
  LOAD_JEDIS
} from './jedi-list.constants.ts'
```

```
const initialState = [];

export function jediListReducer(state = initialState, action) {
  switch(action.type) {
    case ADD_JEDI:
      return [ ...state, { ...action.payload }];
    case REMOVE_JEDI:
      return state.filter(jedi => jedi.id !== action.payload.id);
    case LOAD_JEDIS:
      return action.payload.map(jedi => ({ ...jedi}));
    default:
      return state;
  }
}
```

Our next order of business is our constants file, which has already been created and just need to move, like so:

```
// jedi/jedi-list/jedi-list-constants.ts

export const ADD_JEDI = 'ADD_JEDI';
export const REMOVE_JEDI = "REMOVE_JEDI";
export const LOAD_JEDIS ="LOAD_JEDIS";
```

A general tip is if you find the number of components and files growing, consider creating a dedicated directory for it.

Next up is the action creator file that we have also already created, and that we just need to move to our `jedi` directory, like so:

```
// jedi/jedi-list/jedi-list-actions.ts

import { ADD_JEDI, REMOVE_JEDI, LOAD_JEDIS } from "./jedi-list-constants";

let counter = 0;

export const addJedi = (name) => ({ type: ADD_JEDI, payload: { id:
counter++, name }});
export const removeJedi = (id) => ({ type: REMOVE_JEDI, payload: { id } });
export const loadJedis = (jedis) => ({ type: LOAD_JEDIS, payload: jedis });
```

Our directory should now look like this:

```
jedi/
  jedi.module.ts
  jedi-list/
    jedi-list.reducer.ts
    jedi-list.actions.ts
```

Moving the component to our jedi directory

The next point is about moving our JediListComponent to our jedi directory, like so:

```
// jedi/jedi-list/jedi-list.component.ts

import { Component } from "@angular/core";
import { Store } from "@ngrx/store";
import { Observable } from "rxjs/Observable";
import { AppState } from "../app-state";
import {
  addJedi,
  removeJedi,
  loadJedis
} from './jedi-list-actions';

@Component({
  selector: "jedi-list",
  template: `
  <div *ngFor="let jedi of list$ | async">
    {{ jedi.name }}<button (click)="remove(jedi.id)" >Remove</button>
  </div>
  <input [(ngModel)]="newJedi" placeholder="" />
  <button (click)="add()">Add</button>
  <button (click)="clear()" >Clear</button>
  `
})
export class JediListComponent {
  list$: Observable<number>;
  counter = 0;
  newJedi = "";

  constructor(private store: Store<AppState>) {
    this.list$ = store.select("jediList");
  }

  add() {
    this.store.dispatch(addJedi(this.newJedi));
```

```
    this.newJedi = '';
  }

  remove(id) {
    this.store.dispatch(removeJedi(id));
  }

  clear() {
    this.store.dispatch(loadJedis([]));
    this.counter = 0;
  }
}
```

After moving our `jedi-list` component, our directory should now look like the following:

```
jedi/
  jedi.module.ts
  jedi-list/
    jedi-list.reducer.ts
    jedi-list.actions.ts
    jedi-list.component.ts
```

Registering our reducer with the store

Lastly, we just need to do a slight update to the `app.module.ts` file to have it point correctly to our `JediListReducer`, like so:

```
// app.module.ts

import { BrowserModule } from "@angular/platform-browser";
import { NgModule } from "@angular/core";
import { StoreModule } from "@ngrx/store";
import { AppComponent } from "./app.component";
import { counterReducer } from "./reducer";
import { JediModule } from './jedi/jedi.module';
import { jediListReducer } from "./jedi/jedi-list/jedi-list.reducer";

@NgModule({
  declarations: [AppComponent],
  imports: [
    BrowserModule,
    StoreModule.forRoot({
      counter: counterReducer,
      jediList: JediListReducer
    }),
    JediModule
```

```
  ],
  bootstrap: [AppComponent]
})
export class AppModule {}
```

Leveraging types and feature modules

The following files is pointing to the demo project `Chapter9/FeatureModules`.

OK, one thing we can definitely improve is how we tell the `StoreModule` about what state and reducers exist in our app. Let's do a quick recap and look at its current state:

```
// from app.module.ts

StoreModule.forRoot({ count: counterReducer, jediList: JediListReducer })
```

So, we are essentially feeding the `forRoot()` method an object. What's wrong with that? Well, imagine you have ten different feature modules and every feature module may have three to four states, then the object you pass to `forRoot()` will grow in size and the number of imports that you need to do in your `app.module.ts` will grow. It will look something like this:

```
StoreModule.forRoot({
  featureModuleState1: featureModuleState1Reducer,
  featureModuleState2 : featureModuleState2Reducer
  .
  .
  .
  .
  .
  .
  .
  .
})
```

Going from forRoot() to forFeature()

To solve the mess we are creating in `app.module.ts`, we will now use a method called `forFeature()` on `StoreModule` that will allow us to set up the states we need per feature module. Let's take the existing setup and refactor that:

```
// app.module.ts

StoreModule.forRoot({  }) // this would be empty
```

We move our two reducer entries to their respective feature modules, `counter.module.ts` and `jedi.module.ts`. That would now look like this:

```
// counter.module.ts
@NgModule({
  imports: [StoreModule.forFeature(
    // add reducer object here
  )]
})

// jedi.module.ts
@NgModule({
  imports : [StoreModule.forFeature(
  // add reducer here
  )]
})
```

We left out the implementation on purpose here because we need to take a step back. Remember when we called `StoreModule.forRoot()`, we could just pass it an object. It doesn't look quite the same with `forFeature()`. There is a little bit of difference, so let's try to explain what that difference is. We are used to setting up our store by passing it an object, which looks like this:

```
{
  sliceOfState : reducerFunction,
  anotherSliceOfState: anotherReducerFunction
}
```

Setting up forFeature() from string to selection function

We can set it up in pretty much the same way, but we need to pass it the name of a feature as well. Let's take our `counter.module.ts` and add a little code to it:

```
// counter.module.ts
```

```
@NgModule({
  imports: [
    StoreModule.forFeature('counter',{
      data: counterReducer
    })
  ]
})
```

This will change how we select our state, though. Imagine we are inside of
counter.component.ts with the current implementation looking like the following:

```
// counter.component.ts

@Component({
  selector: 'counter',
  template: `{{ counter$ | async }}`
})
export class CounterComponent {
  counter$;

  constructor(private store: Store<AppState>) {
    // this needs to change..
    this.counter$ = this.store.select('counter');
  }
}
```

Because we changed what the state looked like in counter.module.ts, we now need to
reflect that in counter.component.ts, like so:

```
// counter.component.ts
@Component({
  selector: 'counter',
  template: `{{ counter$ | async }}`
})
export class CounterComponent {
  counter$;

  constructor(private store: Store<AppState>) {
    this.counter$ = this.store.select((state) => {
      return state.counter.data;
    });
  }
}
```

Introducing NgRx types for setting up the state

Up to this point, we have learned how we move the store state declaration from
`app.module.ts` and register it in each feature module instead. This will provide us with a
little more order. Let's take a close look at the types used for registering state.
`ActionReducerMap` is a type we have been using implicitly so far. We have been using it
every time we call `StoreModule.forRoot()` or `StoreModule.forFeature()`. We have
been using it in the sense that, the object we pass containing state and their reducers
consists of this type. Let's prove that is the case by turning to our `counter.module.ts`:

```
// counter.module.ts

@NgModule({
  imports: [
    StoreModule.forFeature('counter',{
      data: counterReducer
    })
  ]
})
```

Let's change that a bit, to this:

```
// counter.reducer.ts

export interface CounterState = {
  data: number
};

export reducer: ActionReducerMap<CounterState> = {
  data: counterReducer
}

// counter.module.ts

@NgModule({
  imports: [
    StoreModule.forFeature('counter', reducer)
  ]
})
```

Now, we can see that we are leveraging `ActionReducerMap`, which is a generic that forces
us to provide it with a type. In this case, the type is `CounterState`. Running this code
should just work. So, why use `ActionReducerMap` explicitly like this?

Giving forFeature() a type

Well, the `forFeature()` method is a generic as well, and we can specify this one explicitly like so:

```
// counter.module.ts

const CounterState = {
  data: number
};

const reducers: ActionReducerMap<CounterState> = {
  data: counterReducer
}

@NgModule({
  imports: [
    StoreModule.forFeature<CounterState, Action>('counter', reducers)
  ]
})
```

This protects us from adding a state mapping object that it does not expect to the `forFeature()` method. For instance, the following would render an error:

```
// example of what NOT to do

interface State {
  test: string;
}

function testReducer(state ="", action: Action) {
  switch(action.type) {
    default:
      return state;
  }
}

const reducers: ActionReducerMap<State> = {
  test: testReducer
};

@NgModule({
  imports: [
    BrowserModule,
    StoreModule.forFeature<CounterState, Action>('counter', reducers)
  ],
  exports: [CounterComponent, CounterListComponent],
```

```
    declarations: [CounterComponent, CounterListComponent],
    providers: [],
})
export class CounterModule { }
```

The reason for this is that we are providing the wrong type to the `forFeature()` method. It expects a reducer parameter to be something of type `ActionReducerMap<CounterState>`, which it clearly is not, as we are sending in `ActionReducerMap<State>`.

Several states in the same feature module

The following scenario can be found in the `Chapter9/TypesDemo` folder of the code repository.

OK, so now we know about the `ActionReducerMap` type, and we also know that we can provide a type to the `forFeature()` method and make it safer to use. What happens if we've got several states in our feature module, what then? The answer is quite simple, but let's first have a closer look at what we mean exactly by several states. Our counter module contains the `counter.value` state. This is displayed in our `counter.component.ts`. If we want to add a `counter.list` state, we need to add the supporting constants, reducers, actions, and a component file so we can properly display it. Our file structure should therefore look like the following:

```
/counter
    counter.reducer.ts
    counter.component.ts
    counter.constants.ts
    counter.actions.ts
    /counter-list
        counter-list.reducer.ts
        counter-list.component.ts
        counter-list.constants.ts
        counter-list.action.ts
        counter.model.ts
    counter.module.ts
```

We need to add implementation for all of these bold files.

Adding the counter-list reducer

Let's start off with the reducer:

```
// counter/counter-list/counter-list.reducer.ts

import {
  ADD_COUNTER_ITEM,
  REMOVE_COUNTER_ITEM
} from "./counter-list.constants";
import { ActionPayload } from "../../action-payload";
import { Counter } from "./counter.model";

export function counterListReducer(state = [], action:
ActionPayload<Counter>) {
  switch (action.type) {
    case ADD_COUNTER_ITEM:
      return [...state, Object.assign(action.payload)];
    case REMOVE_COUNTER_ITEM:
      return state.filter(item => item.id !== action.payload.id);
    default:
      return state;
  }
}
```

This reducer supports two types, ADD_COUNTER_ITEM and REMOVE_COUNTER_ITEM, which will let us add and remove items from the list.

Adding the component

This one comes in two parts, the HTML template and the class file. Let's start with the class file:

```
// counter/counter-list/counter-list.component.ts

import { Component, OnInit } from "@angular/core";
import { AppState } from "../../app-state";
import { Store } from "@ngrx/store";
import { addItem, removeItem } from "./counter-list.actions";

@Component({
  selector: "app-counter-list",
  templateUrl: "./counter-list.component.html",
  styleUrls: ["./counter-list.component.css"]
})
export class CounterListComponent implements OnInit {
```

```
    list$;
    newItem: string;
    counter: number;

    constructor(private store: Store<AppState>) {
      this.counter = 0;
      this.list$ = this.store.select(state => state.counter.list);
    }

    ngOnInit() {}

    add() {
      this.store.dispatch(addItem(this.newItem, this.counter++));
      this.newItem = "";
    }

    remove(id) {
      this.store.dispatch(removeItem(id));
    }
}
```

The HTML template file is quite simple, and looks like this:

```
// counter/counter-list/counter-list.component.html

<div>
  <input type="text" [(ngModel)]="newItem">
  <button (click)="add()">Add</button>
</div>
<div *ngFor="let item of list$ | async">
  {{item.title}}
  <button (click)="remove(item.id)">Remove</button>
</div>
```

In the preceding code, we are supporting the following:

- Showing a list of counter objects
- Adding an item to the list
- Removing an item from the list

Adding the constants

Next up is adding the constants. Constants are a nice thing to have; they protect us from making mistakes due to us mistyping when we deal with action creators as well as reducers:

```
// counter/counter-list/counter-list.constants.ts

export const ADD_COUNTER_ITEM = "add counter item";
export const REMOVE_COUNTER_ITEM = "remove counter item";
```

Adding the action methods

We also need to define the action methods. These are just functions that will help us create our actions, so it's less for us to type:

```
// counter/counter-list/counter-list.actions.ts

import {
  ADD_COUNTER_ITEM,
  REMOVE_COUNTER_ITEM
} from "./counter-list.constants";

export const addItem = (title, id) => ({
  type: ADD_COUNTER_ITEM,
  payload: { id, title }
});

export const removeItem = id => ({
  type: REMOVE_COUNTER_ITEM,
  payload: { id }
});
```

Adding the model

We need to type what our counter-list should contain. For that we need to create a model:

```
// counter/counter-list/counter.model.ts

export interface Counter {
  title: string;
  id: number;
}
```

Register our reducers

We do need to add and implement all the files in bold, but we also need to update the `counter.module.ts` file so we are able to handle the added state:

```
// counter/counter.module.ts

import { NgModule } from "@angular/core";
import { CommonModule } from "@angular/common";
import { CounterComponent } from "./counter.component";
import { StoreModule, ActionReducerMap } from "@ngrx/store";
import { counterReducer } from "./counter.reducer";
import { CounterListComponent } from "./counter-list/counter-
list.component";
import { Counter } from "./counter-list/counter.model";
import { counterListReducer } from "./counter-list/counter-list.reducer";
import { FormsModule } from "@angular/forms";

export interface CounterState {
  data: number;
  list: Array<Counter>;
}

const combinedReducers: ActionReducerMap<CounterState> = {
  data: counterReducer,
  list: counterListReducer
};

@NgModule({
  imports: [
    CommonModule,
    StoreModule.forFeature("counter", combinedReducers),
    FormsModule
  ],
  declarations: [CounterComponent, CounterListComponent],
  exports: [CounterComponent, CounterListComponent]
})
export class CounterModule {}
```

We need to add a `CombinedState` interface that represents all of our reducers with their state. Lastly, we change the call to `StoreModule.forFeature()`. That concludes how we deal with several states and reducers within the same module.

Component architecture

There are different kinds of components. Two types of components are of interest in the context of NgRx: smart components and dumb components.

Smart components are also called container components. They should be on the highest level of your application, and handle routes. For example, `ProductsComponent` should be a container component if it handles the `route/products`. It should also know about the store.

The definition of a dumb component is that it has no knowledge of a store and relies solely on the `@Input` and `@Output` properties—it's all about presentation, which is why it is also called a presentational component. A presentational component in this context can therefore be a `ProductListComponent` or a `ProductCreateComponent`. A quick overview of a feature module could therefore look like this:

```
ProductsComponent // container component
ProductsListComponent // presentational component
ProductsCreateComponent // presentational component
```

Let's look at a small code example so you get the idea:

```
// products.component.ts  – container component
@Component({
  template: `
    <products-list [products]="products$ | async">
  `
})
export class ProductsComponent {
  products$: Observable<Product>;

  constructor(private store: Store<AppState>) {
    this.products$ = this.store.select('products');
  }
}

// products-list.component.ts  – dumb component
@Component({
  selector: 'products-list',
  template : `
  <div *ngFor="let product of products">
  {{ products.name }}
  </div>
  `
})
```

```
export class ProductsListComponent {
  @Input() products;
}
```

Our `ProductsComponent` is responsible for handling the route to
`/products`. `ProductsListComponent` is a dumb component and just gets a list assigned
to it that it is more than happy to render to the screen.

@ngrx/store-devtools – debugging

The following scenario can be found in the code repository under `Chapter9/DevTools`.

There are three things we need to do to get DevTools to work:

- Install the NPM package: `npm install @ngrx/store-devtools --save`.
- Install the Chrome extension: `http://extension.remotedev.io/`. This is
  called the Redux DevTools extension.
- Set it up in your Angular module: this requires us to import DevTools into our
  Angular project.

Providing we have done the two first steps, we should only have the set up stage left, so we
need to open up the `app.module.ts` file for that:

```
import { BrowserModule } from "@angular/platform-browser";
import { NgModule } from "@angular/core";
import { StoreModule } from "@ngrx/store";
import { AppComponent } from "./app.component";
import { counterReducer } from "./reducer";
import { StoreDevtoolsModule } from '@ngrx/store-devtools';

@NgModule({
  declarations: [AppComponent],
  imports: [
    BrowserModule,
    StoreModule.forRoot({
      counter: counterReducer,
      StoreDevtoolsModule.instrument({
        maxAge: 25 // Retains last 25 states
      })
    ],
  bootstrap: [AppComponent]
})
export class AppModule {}
```

Ok, so now everything is set up and we are ready to take our application for a spin and see what our debug tool can tell us. Let's start up our application with `ng serve` and surf to `http://localhost:4200/`. First thing we want to do is open developer tools in Chrome and click on a tab called **Redux**. You should see something like this:

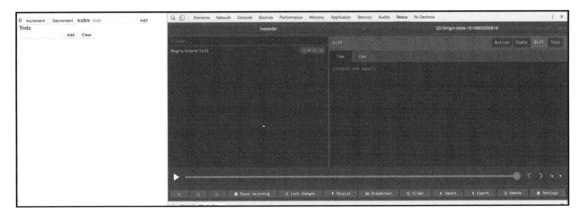

Redux tab

To the left we have our application UI, and to the right we have our Redux plugin. At this point, no actions have been carried out other than the initialization of the store, which we can see under the plugin part marked as **Inspector**. There is but one log entry, `@ngrx/store/init`. Let's interact with the UI by clicking on the **Increment** button and see what happens with our store:

Increment button

As you can see, we have a new entry called **INCREMENT**. Two things are of interest now from a debug perspective:

- What actions were dispatched?
- What impact did these actions have on the store?

We learn the answer to both these questions by interacting with the tab buttons on the right-hand side of our plugin. The button called **Action** will tell us what action was dispatched and what payload it had, if any:

Action button

Here, it is clearly stated that an action with type value **Increment** was dispatched. Now to our second question; what was the impact to our store? To find that out, we simply click the **State** button:

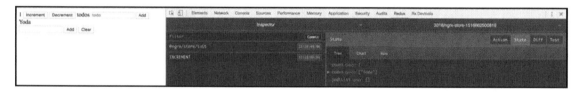

State button

Our state tells us it consists of three properties, `count`, `todos` and `jediList`.
Our `count` property has the value **1**, and is the one affected by us clicking the **Increment** button. Let's hit the **Increment** button a few more times to see that really is the case:

Increment button

We now see that our `count` property has the value 3, and we have three entries of **Increment** actions.

Now let's talk about a really cool feature, time-travel debugging. Yes, you read that correctly, we can control time in our store by replaying dispatched actions, and even change history by removing dispatched actions, all in the name of debugging. The Redux plugin gives us several ways to do this:

- Click on a specific dispatched action on your left, and choose to skip dispatching it
- Use a slider to control and replay all the events, and traverse back and forth in time as you see fit

Let's investigate the first way — click on a specific action:

Click on a specific action

Here we've clicked on the **Skip** button for one dispatch action and the end result is that this dispatched action is removed, which is indicated by the action being overstricken. We can also see that our `count` property now has the value 2, as the action never took place. We can easily toggle this back if we want to by hitting **Skip** again.

We mentioned there was another way to control the flow of dispatched actions, namely by using a slider. There is a button called **Slider** that toggles the slider. Clicking it results in us being shown a slider control with a **Play** button, like so:

Play button

If you press the **Play** button, it will simply play all the dispatched actions. However, if you choose to interact with the cursor on the slider itself you are able to pull it both to the left, to move back in time, and to the right, to move forward in time.

As you can see, the Redux plugin is a truly powerful tool to use in order to quickly gain an understanding of the following aspects:

- What your app's state is at a given point in time
- What part of the UI leads to what effects in the store

@ngrx/effects – working with side effects

At this point, we have a basic understanding of NgRx. We know how to set up our state and create all the artifacts that go with it such as actions, action creators, and reducers. Additionally, we have also gained familiarity with the Redux plugin for Chrome and understood what a valuable tool it can be to help us quickly gain an understanding of the state in our app, and most importantly how it can aid us in debugging any problems we may have related to NgRx.

Now, the time has come to talk about something that doesn't quite fit in to our organized and synchronous world of reducers and actions. I am talking about something called side effects. Side effects are operations such as accessing files or network resources, and is not really related to our applications state even though they may be the vessels that contain the data we want, or be the place we persist data to. As we just said, a dispatched action is dispatched in a synchronous way and the change to our state happens straight away. A side effect is something that may take time. Imagine that we access a large file or ask for a resource over the network using AJAX. This request will finish sometime in the future and, when done, it may affect our state. How do we make these time consuming and asynchronous operations fit in with our synchronous and momentary world? The answer in NgRx is a library called `@ngrx/effects`.

Installing and setting it up

Installing it is as easy as performing the following command in your terminal:

```
npm install @ngrx/effects --save
```

The next step is to set it up. The setup can be seen as consisting of two steps:

- Create our effect
- Register the effect with the `EffectsModule`

An effect is just an injectable service that listens for a specific action. Once the effect is in focus, it can carry out a number of operations and transformations before leaving over control. It leaves over control by dispatching an action.

Creating our first effect – a realistic scenario

The following scenario can be found in the code repository under `Chapter9/DemoEffects`.

This sounds a bit cryptic, so let's take a realistic scenario. You want to fetch products using AJAX from an endpoint. If you think about what you are about to undertake in the following steps:

1. Dispatch a `FETCHING_PRODUCTS`, this sets up our state so we can see that an AJAX request is under way and we can thereby use this to display a spinner for as long as the AJAX request is waiting to complete.
2. Perform an AJAX call and retrieve your products.
3. If successfully retrieving the products, then dispatch `FETCHING_PRODUCTS_SUCCESSFULLY`.
4. If there is an error, then dispatch `FETCHING_PRODUCTS_ERROR`.

Let's solve this task in the following steps:

1. Create a reducer for it.
2. Create actions and action creators.
3. Create an effect.
4. Register the preceding effect with our effects module.

To perform all of this, we will create a feature module. To do so, we create the `product/` directory with the following files:

- `product.component.ts`
- `product.actions.ts`
- `product.constants.ts`
- `product.reducer.ts`
- `product.selectors.ts`
- `product.module.ts`
- `product.effect.ts`

All of these files are known to us before, except for `product.effect.ts`.

Creating our constants

Let's start with our constants file. What we need are constants that will support us firing away an AJAX request. We also need a constant for when we get our data back successfully, but we also need to cater to any error that might occur. This means we need the following three constants:

```
// product/product.constants.ts

export const FETCHING_PRODUCTS = "FETCHING_PRODUCTS";
export const FETCHING_PRODUCTS_SUCCESSFULLY =
"FETCHING_PRODUCTS_SUCCESSFULLY";
export const FETCHING_PRODUCTS_ERROR = "FETCHING_PRODUCTS_ERROR";
```

Action creators

We need to expose a number of functions that can build objects for us containing a type and a payload property. Depending on what function we invoke, we will assign it with a different constant, and of course a different payload, if using one. The action creator `fetchProducts()` will create an object where only the type is set. This is followed by a `fetchSuccessfully()` action creator, which will be invoked once the data comes back from an endpoint. Lastly, we have the `fetchError()` action creator, which we will invoke if an error occurs:

```
// product/product.actions.ts

import {
  FETCHING_PRODUCTS_SUCCESSFULLY,
  FETCHING_PRODUCTS_ERROR,
  FETCHING_PRODUCTS
} from "./product.constants";

export const fetchSuccessfully = (products) => ({
  type: FETCHING_PRODUCTS_SUCCESSFULLY,
  payload: products
});

export const fetchError = (error) => ({
  type: FETCHING_PRODUCTS_ERROR,
  payload: error
});
```

```
export const fetchProductsSuccessfully = (products) => ({
  type: FETCHING_PRODUCTS_SUCCESSFULLY,
  payload: products
});

export const fetchProducts =() => ({ type: FETCHING_PRODUCTS });
```

Reducer with a new type of default state

At first glance, the following reducer is just like any reducer you have written before. It is a function that takes a parameters' state and action, and it contains a switch construct that switches between different actions. So far, everything is familiar. The `initialState` variable is different though. It contains the `loading`, `list`, and `error` properties. `loading` is simply a Boolean that indicates whether our AJAX request is still pending. `list` is our data property that will contain our list of products once they are are returned. The `error` property is simply a property that contains the error if any comes back from the AJAX request:

```
// product/product.reducer.ts

import {
  FETCHING_PRODUCTS_SUCCESSFULLY,
  FETCHING_PRODUCTS_ERROR,
  FETCHING_PRODUCTS
} from "./product.constants";
import { Product } from "./product.model";
import { ActionReducerMap } from "@ngrx/store/src/models";

const initialState = {
  loading: false,
  list: [{ name: "init" }],
  error: void 0
};

export interface ProductState {
  loading: boolean;
  list: Array<Product>;
  error: string;
}

export interface FeatureProducts {
  products: ProductState;
}

export const ProductReducers: ActionReducerMap<FeatureProducts> = {
```

```
    products: productReducer
};

export function productReducer(state = initialState, action) {
  switch (action.type) {
    case FETCHING_PRODUCTS_SUCCESSFULLY:
      return { ...state, list: action.payload, loading: false };
    case FETCHING_PRODUCTS_ERROR:
      return { ...state, error: action.payload, loading: false };
    case FETCHING_PRODUCTS:
      return { ...state, loading: true };
    default:
      return state;
  }
}
```

The effect – listening to a specific dispatched action

So we come to the effect. Our effect acts like a listener to a dispatched action. This gives us the opportunity to carry out a unit of work, but also to dispatch an action once that work is done.

We have created all the usual bits that we are used to, so now it is time to create our effect that will handle the entire workflow:

```
// product/product.effect.ts

import { Actions, Effect } from "@ngrx/effects";

@Injectable()
export class ProductEffects {
  @Effect() products$: Observable<Action>;

  constructor(
    private actions$: Actions<Action>>
  ) {}
}
```

The effect is just a class decorated with the `@Injectable` decorator. It also contains two members: one member of `Actions` type and another of the `Observable<Action>` type. Actions come from the `@ngrx/effects` module and are nothing more than a specialized `Observable` with the `ofType()` method on it. `ofType()` is the method that takes a string constant, which is the event we are listening for. In the previous code, the `products$` is the `Observable` that we decorate with the `@Effect` decorator. Our next step is to connect `products$` with `actions$`, and define how our effect should work. We do that with the following code:

```
// product/product.effect.ts, starting out..

import { Actions, Effect, ofType } from "@ngrx/effects";
import { switchMap } from "rxjs/operators";
import { Observable } from "rxjs/Observable";
import { Injectable } from "@angular/core";

@Injectable()
export class ProductEffects {
  @Effect() products$: Observable<Action> = this.actions$.pipe(
    ofType(FETCHING_PRODUCTS),
    switchMap(action => {
      // do something completely else that returns an Observable
    })
  );

  constructor(
    private actions$: Actions<Action>>
  ) {}
}
```

Ok, so we have set up our effect a little more. The call to `ofType()` ensures we set ourselves up to listen to a specific dispatched action. The call to `switchMap()` ensures we are able to take the current `Observable` that we are currently on, and turn it into something completely different, such as a call to an AJAX service.

Let's now return back to our example and see how we can fit in some product-related logic in there:

```
// product/product.effect.ts

import { Actions, Effect, ofType } from "@ngrx/effects";
import { HttpClient } from "@angular/common/http";
import { FETCHING_PRODUCTS } from "./product.constants";
import { Injectable } from "@angular/core";
import { Observable } from "rxjs/Observable";
```

```
import { delay, map, catchError, switchMap } from "rxjs/operators";
import { fetchProductsSuccessfully, fetchError } from "./product.actions";
import { Action } from "@ngrx/store";

@Injectable()
export class ProductEffects {
  @Effect()
  products$ = this.actions$.pipe(
    ofType(FETCHING_PRODUCTS),
    switchMap(action =>
      this.http
      .get("data/products.json")
      .pipe(
        delay(3000),
        map(fetchProductsSuccessfully),
        catchError(err => of(fetchError(err)))
      )
    )
  );

  constructor(private actions$: Actions<Action>, private http: HttpClient)
{}
}
```

What we do in the preceding code is listen to our FETCHING_PRODUCTS action and carry out a call to an AJAX service. We added a call to the `delay()` operator so as to simulate that our AJAX call takes some time to carry out. This will give us a chance to show a loading spinner. The `map()` operator ensures we dispatch an action when we get the AJAX response back. We can see that we call the action creator, `fetchProductsSuccessfully()`, which implicitly calls the reducer and sets a new state on the products property.

At this point, we need to register the effect before moving on. We can do so in the root module or in the feature module. It's a very similar call, so let's describe both ways of doing it:

```
// app.module.ts - registering our effect in the root module, alternative I

/* omitting the other imports for brevity */
import { EffectsModule } from "@ngrx/effects";
import { ProductEffects } from "./products/product.effect";

@NgModule({
  declarations: [AppComponent],
  imports: [
    BrowserModule,
    StoreModule.forRoot({}),
```

```
      ProductsModule,
      StoreDevtoolsModule.instrument({
        maxAge: 25 // Retains last 25 states
      }),
      EffectsModule.forRoot([ ProductEffects ])
    ],
    bootstrap: [AppComponent]
})
export class AppModule {}
```

If we have a feature module, on the other hand, we could be using
the forFeature() method on the EffectsModule and call that in our feature module like
so:

```
// product/product.module.ts, registering in the feature module,
alternative II

import { NgModule } from "@angular/core";
import { ProductComponent } from "./product.component";
import { BrowserModule } from "@angular/platform-browser";
import { ProductEffects } from "./product.effect";
import { EffectsModule } from "@ngrx/effects";
import { StoreModule, Action } from "@ngrx/store";
import { ProductReducers } from "./product.reducer";
import { HttpClientModule } from "@angular/common/http";
import { ActionReducerMap } from "@ngrx/store/src/models";

@NgModule({
  imports: [
    BrowserModule,
    StoreModule.forFeature("featureProducts", ProductReducers),
    EffectsModule.forFeature([ProductEffects]),
    HttpClientModule
  ],
  exports: [ProductComponent],
  declarations: [ProductComponent],
  providers: []
})
export class ProductModule {}
```

Adding a component – introducing selectors

That's it, thats all you need to create an effect. We're not done here though, we need a component to display our data, as well as a spinner, while we are waiting for the AJAX request to finish.

Ok, first things first: what do we know of components that should be using NgRx? The obvious answer is that they should be injecting the store so we can listen to a slice of state from the store. The way we listen to a slice of state is by calling the stores `select()` function. This will return an `Observable`. We know we can easily show Observables in the template through the use of the async pipe. So let's start sketching our component:

```
// product/product.component.ts

import { Component, OnInit } from "@angular/core";
import { AppState } from "../app-state";
import { Store } from "@ngrx/store";

@Component({
  selector: "products",
  template: `
    <div *ngFor="let product of products$ | async">
      Product: {{ product.name }}
    </div>
  </div>
  `
})
export class ProductsComponent {
  products$;
  loading$;

  constructor(private store: Store<AppState>) {
    this.products$ = this.store.select((state) => {
      return state.products.list;
    });
  }
}
```

This part of our component here shouldn't come as too much of a surprise; we inject the store into the constructor, call `select()`, and get an Observable back. But, there is a *but* here, we are calling the `select()` method differently. We used to pass a string to the `select()` function, and now we pass it a function. Why is that? Well, because we changed how our state looked. Let's show our new state again, for clarity:

```
const initialState = {
   loading: false,
   list: [],
   error: void 0
}
```

The preceding code shows that we can't just do `store.select("products")` because that would give us the whole object back. So we need a way to dig into the previous object in order to get a hold of the list property that should contain our list of products. The way to do that is to use the variant of the `select` method that takes a function instead. We do just that with the following code:

```
this.products$ = this.store.select((state) => {
   return state.products.list;
});
```

Ok, but will this really be type safe? Won't the `AppState` interface complain? Does it know of our changed state structure? Well, we can tell it knows about it, but we need to ensure that our reducer exports an interface that represents our new state structure. We therefore change the reducer to look like the following:

```
// product/products-reducer.ts

import {
   FETCHING_PRODUCTS_SUCCESSFULLY,
   FETCHING_PRODUCTS_ERROR,
   FETCHING_PRODUCTS
} from "./product-constants";

export interface ProductsState {
   loading: boolean;
   list: Array<Product>;
   error: string;
}

const initialState: ProductsState = {
   loading: false,
   list: [],
   error: void 0
}
```

```
export function productReducer(state = initialState, action) {
  switch(action.type) {
    case FETCHING_PRODUCTS_SUCCESSFULLY:
      return { ...state, list: action.payload, loading: false };
    case FETCHING_PRODUCTS_ERROR:
      return { ...state, error: action.payload, loading: false };
    case FETCHING_PRODUCTS:
      return { ...state, loading: true };
    default:
      return state;
  }
}
```

And of course, we need to update the `AppState` interface to look like this:

```
// app-state.ts

import { FeatureProducts } from "./product/product.reducer";

export interface AppState {
  featureProducts: FeatureProducts;
}
```

Ok, this made our `AppState` know what kind of beast our `products` property really is, and is thereby what makes the `store.select(<Fn>)` call possible. The function we gave the `select` method is called a selector, and is actually something that doesn't have to live inside the component. The reason for this is that we might want to access that slice of state somewhere else. Let's therefore create a `product.selectors.ts` file. We will add to this later as we keep supporting CRUD:

```
// product/product.selectors.ts
import { AppState } from "../app-state";

export const getList = (state:AppState) =>
state.featureProducts.products.list;
export const getError = (state:AppState) =>
state.featureProducts.products.error;
export const isLoading = (state:AppState) =>
state.featureProducts.products.loading;
```

Ok, so now we have created our selectors file, and we can immediately start improving our components code and clean it up a bit before we continue to add things to it:

```
// product/product.component.ts

import { Component, OnInit } from "@angular/core";
import { AppState } from "../app-state";
```

```
import { Store } from "@ngrx/store";
import { getList } from './product.selectors';

@Component({
  selector: "products",
  template: `
    <div *ngFor="let product of products$ | async">
      Product: {{ product.name }}
    </div>
  `
})
export class ProductsComponent {
  products$;

  constructor(private store: Store<AppState>) {
    this.products$ = this.store.select(getList);
  }
}
```

Our code looks much better. It's time to start caring about the other aspect of this; what if our HTTP service takes a few seconds, or even one second to return? This is a real concern especially with our users being potentially on a 3G connection. To take care of this, we grab the `loading` property from our products state and use that as a conditional in our template. We will basically say that if the HTTP call is still pending, show some text or an image that indicates to the user that something is loading. Let's add that piece of functionality to the component:

```
import { Component, OnInit } from "@angular/core";
import { AppState } from "../app-state";
import { Store } from "@ngrx/store";
import { getList, isLoading } from "./products.selectors";

@Component({
  selector: "products",
  template: `
    <div *ngFor="let product of products$ | async">
      Product: {{ product.name }}
    </div>
    <div *ngIf="loading$ | async; let loading">
      <div *ngIf="loading">
      loading...
      </div>
    </div>
  `
})
export class ProductsComponent {
  products$;
```

```
  loading$;

  constructor(private store: Store<AppState>) {
    this.products$ = this.store.select(getList);
    this.loading$ = this.store.select(isLoading);
  }
}
```

Let's also ensure that we show any errors by subscribing to `products.error`. We simply update the component with the following alterations:

```
import { Component, OnInit } from '@angular/core';
import { AppState } from "../app-state";
import { Store } from "@ngrx/store";
import { getList, isLoading, getError } from "./products.selectors";

@Component({
  selector: "products",
  template: `
    <div *ngFor="let product of products$ | async">
      Product: {{ product.name }}
    </div>
    <div *ngIf="loading$ | async; let loading">
      <div *ngIf="loading">
      loading...
      </div>
    </div>
    <div *ngIf="error$ | async; let error" >
      <div *ngIf="error">{{ error }}</div>
    </div>
  `
})
export class ProductsComponent {
  products$;
  loading$;
  error$;

  constructor(private store: Store<AppState>) {
    this.products$ = this.store.select(getList);
    this.loading$ = this.store.select(isLoading);
    this.error$ = this.store.select(getError);
  }
}
```

Ok, we fire up our application at this point. There is just one teeny tiny problem; we don't see any products at all. Why is that? The explanation is simple. We don't actually dispatch an action that will lead to the AJAX call being made. Let's fix that by adding the following code to our component:

```
import { Component, OnInit } from '@angular/core';
import { AppState } from "../app-state";
import { Store } from "@ngrx/store";
import { getList, isLoading, getError } from "./products.selectors";
import { fetchProducts } from "./products.actions";

@Component({
  selector: "products",
  template: `
    <div *ngFor="let product of products$ | async">
      Product: {{ product.name }}
    </div>
    <div *ngIf="loading$ | async; let loading">
      <div *ngIf="loading">
      loading...
      </div>
    </div>
    <div *ngIf="error$ | async; let error" >
      <div *ngIf="error">{{ error }}</div>
    </div>
  `
})
export class ProductsComponent implements OnInit {
  products$;
  loading$;
  error$;

  constructor(private store: Store<AppState>) {
    this.products$ = this.store.select(getList);
    this.loading$ this.store.select(isLoading);
    this.error$ = this.store.select(getError);
  }

  ngOnInit() {
    this.store.dispatch(fetchProducts);
  }
}
```

This will of course trigger our effect, which will lead to our HTTP call, which will lead to `fetchProductsSuccessfully()` being called, and thereby our state will be updated and `products.list` will no longer be an empty array, meaning our UI will show a list of products. Success!

Extending our example with the create effect

So far, we have gone through the full flow of adding an effect, building a component, and improved the code with selectors. To make sure we really understand how to work with effects and how the application scales with it, let's add another effect, this time let's add an effect to support an HTTP POST call. What we want to happen from an application standpoint is that we add another product to the list. This should update the UI and show our added product. What happens data-wise is that our store should reflect that change and, as a side effect, a HTTP POST should be carried out. We need the following to accomplish this:

- A reducer that supports adding a product to our products list
- An effect that listens to a product being added action and that carries out a HTTP POST
- We also need to register the created effect

Updating the constants file

Just like with the fetching of products, we need to support one action that triggers everything. We need another action for when the HTTP request succeeds and one last action to support error handling:

```
// product.constants.ts

export const FETCHING_PRODUCTS = "FETCHING_PRODUCTS";
export const FETCHING_PRODUCTS_SUCCESSFULLY =
"FETCHING_PRODUCTS_SUCCESSFULLY";
export const FETCHING_PRODUCTS_ERROR = "FETCHING_PRODUCTS_ERROR";
export const ADD_PRODUCT = "ADD_PRODUCT";
export const ADD_PRODUCT_SUCCESSFULLY = "ADD_PRODUCT_SUCCESSFULLY";
export const ADD_PRODUCT_ERROR ="ADD_PRODUCT_ERROR";
```

Updating the reducer

At this point we take our existing `reducer.ts` file and add what we need to support adding a product:

```
// products.reducer.ts

import {
  FETCHING_PRODUCTS_SUCCESSFULLY,
  FETCHING_PRODUCTS_ERROR,
  FETCHING_PRODUCTS,
  ADD_PRODUCT,
  ADD_PRODUCT_SUCCESSFULLY,
  ADD_PRODUCT_ERROR
} from "./product.constants";

import { Product } from "./product.model";

const initialState = {
  loading: false,
  list: [],
  error: void 0
}

export interface ProductsState {
  loading: boolean;
  list: Array<Product>,
  error: string;
}

function addProduct(list, product) {
  return [ ...list, product];
}

export function productsReducer(state = initialState, action) {
  switch(action.type) {
    case FETCHING_PRODUCTS_SUCCESSFULLY:
      return { ...state, list: action.payload, loading: false };
    case FETCHING_PRODUCTS_ERROR:
    case ADD_PRODUCT_ERROR:
      return { ...state, error: action.payload, loading: false };
    case FETCHING_PRODUCTS:
    case ADD_PRODUCT:
      return { ...state, loading: true };
    case ADD_PRODUCT_SUCCESSFULLY:
      return { ...state, list: addProduct(state.list, action.payload) };
    default:
```

```
        return state;
    }
}
```

It's worth noting how we create the help function, `addProduct()`, which allows us to create a new list containing the old content and our new product. It's also worth noting that we can group `FETCHING_PRODUCTS_ERROR` and `ADD_PRODUCT_ERROR` actions, and also `ADD_PRODUCT` and `ADD_PRODUCT_SUCCESSFULLY`.

Additional actions

The next order of business is to update our `products.actions.ts` file with the new methods that we need to support the preceding code:

```
// products.actions.ts

import {
  FETCHING_PRODUCTS_SUCCESSFULLY,
  FETCHING_PRODUCTS_ERROR,
  FETCHING_PRODUCTS,
  ADD_PRODUCT,
  ADD_PRODUCT_SUCCESSFULLY,
  ADD_PRODUCT_ERROR
} from "./product.constants";

export const fetchProductsSuccessfully = (products) => ({
  type: FETCHING_PRODUCTS_SUCCESSFULLY,
  payload: products
});

export const fetchError = (error) => ({
  type: FETCHING_PRODUCTS_ERROR,
  payload: error
});
export const fetchProductsLoading = () => ({ type: FETCHING_PRODUCTS });
export const fetchProducts = () => ({ type: FETCHING_PRODUCTS });
export const addProductSuccessfully (product) => ({
  type: ADD_PRODUCT_SUCCESSFULLY },
  payload: product
);
export const addProduct = (product) => ({
  type: ADD_PRODUCT,
  payload: product
});
export const addProductError = (error) => ({
```

```
    type: ADD_PRODUCT_ERROR,
    payload: error
});
```

What is worth noting with the created actions is that the `addProduct()` method takes a product as a parameter. The reason for that is that we want the side effect to use that as body data for the forthcoming HTTP POST.

Adding another effect

Now we are finally ready to construct our effect. It's going to look very similar to the existing one:

```
import { Injectable } from "@angular/core";
import { HttpClient } from "@angular/common/http";
import { Action } from "@ngrx/store";
import { Actions, Effect, ofType } from "@ngrx/effects";
import { Observable } from "rxjs/Observable";
import { of } from "rxjs/observable/of";
import "rxjs/add/observable/of";
import {
  catchError,
  map,
  mergeMap,
  delay,
  tap,
  switchMap
} from "rxjs/operators";
import { FETCHING_PRODUCTS, ADD_PRODUCT } from "./product.constants";
import {
  fetchProductsSuccessfully,
  fetchError,
  addProductSuccessfully,
  addProductError
} from "./product.actions";
import { Product } from "./product.model";
import { ActionPayload } from "../interfaces";

@Injectable()
export class ProductEffects {
  @Effect() productsAdd$: Observable<Action> = this.actions$.pipe(
    ofType(ADD_PRODUCT),
    switchMap(action =>
      this.http.post("products/", action.payload).pipe(
        map(addProductSuccessfully),
        catchError((err) => of(addProductError(err)))</strong>
```

```
      )
    )
  );

  @Effect() productsGet$: Observable<Action> = this.actions$.pipe(
    ofType(FETCHING_PRODUCTS),
    switchMap(action =>
      this.http.get("data/products.json").pipe(
        delay(3000),
        map(fetchProductsSuccessfully),
        catchError((err) => of(fetchError(err)))
      )
    )
  );

  constructor(
    private http: HttpClient,
    private actions$: Actions<ActionPayload<Product>>
  ) {}
}
```

The first thing we do here is to reuse our ProductEffects class and add a new member productsAdd$ to it. While at it, we rename products$ to productsGet$. As long as we are dealing with products we can keep on adding to this class.

The similarities we see with the existing effect is that we set up our ofType() operator to listen for a dispatched action of our choice. Thereafter, we continue with our side effect, that is the call to the HttpClient service that ends up being an HTTP POST call.

Supporting the effect in our component

We don't need to do much in our component. Of course, we need to add some things in the template to support adding a product. In terms of NgRx, we just need to dispatch the ADD_PRODUCT action. Let's have a look at the code:

```
import { Component, OnInit } from "@angular/core";
import { AppState } from "../app-state";
import { Store } from "@ngrx/store";
import { fetchProducts, addProduct } from "./product.actions";
import { getList, isLoading, getError } from "./products.selectors";

@Component({
selector: "products",
  template: `
```

```
<div>
  <input [(ngModel)]="newProduct" placeholder="new product..." />
  <button (click)="addNewProduct()"></button>
</div>
<div *ngFor="let product of products$ | async">
Product: {{ product.name }}
</div>
<div *ngIf="loading$ | async; let loading">
  <div *ngIf="loading">
  loading...
  </div>
</div>
<div *ngIf="error$ | async; let error">
{{ error }}
</div>
`
})
export class ProductsComponent implements OnInit {
  products$;
  loading$;
  error$;
  newProduct: string;

  constructor(private store: Store<AppState>) {
    this.products$ = this.store.select(getList);
    this.loading$ = store.select(isLoading);
    this.error$ = store.select(getError);
  }

  ngOnInit() {
    this.store.dispatch(fetchProducts());
  }

  addNewProduct() {
    this.store.dispatch(addProduct(this.newProduct));
    this.newProduct = "";
  }
}
```

Ok, from this code we set up an input control and a button to be able to handle the user inputting a new product. For the class, we added the `newProduct` field and we also added the `addNewProduct()` method that, in its body, invokes the `addProduct()`, method and thereby passes an `ADD_PRODUCT` action. We really don't need to do more. Our product addition sets the loading state before carrying out the HTTP call, so we can show a spinner if we want, and our error state picks up on any errors that might occur and presents them in the UI. Lastly, don't forget to add the `FormsModule` to the `import` property in the `product.module.ts`.

Running a demo of the app

To try out our app, we can simply run the `ng serve` command in the terminal. What we expect to see is a screen that for three seconds states it is loading, just to be replaced by the fetched data. This will demonstrate both the dispatch of the loaded state, as well as us dispatching the data to the store once it arrives. The following is the initial screen when our data is yet to arrive. We fire off the `FETCHING_PRODUCTS` action, which makes our loading text appear:

 The next screen is when our data arrives. Subsequently, we fire off `ADD_PRODUCT_SUCCESSFULLY` to ensure that the fetched data is placed in the store:

Summary

We have gone through a lot in this chapter. Among the things covered have been installing and using the store. To that knowledge, we have added some sound best practices to organize your code. It's important to note that consistency is key. There are many ways to organize code, so as long as that chosen way remains consistent throughout the app, that is the most important factor. With that said, organizing your code by domain is what is prescribed for most things Angular. Whether that holds true for NgRx is up to you, dear reader. See best practices as a guide rather than a rule. Furthermore, we covered side effects and how to handle those with `@ngrx/effects`. `@store-devtools` was another thing we covered, which lets us use our browser to easily debug our store. In the next, and final, chapter, we will cover `@ngrx/schematics` and `@ngrx/entity`, so we really cover everything NgRx has to offer us. Also, we will showcase how you can build NgRx yourself to gain further understanding on what goes on under the hood. If knowing what goes on under the hood isn't exciting to you, then you are in the wrong profession! Everything is really set up to make the final chapter a very interesting one.

10
NgRx – In Depth

This chapter will go into more advanced NgRx topics. As you implement your first applications using NgRx, you will notice that it means creating a lot of boilerplate and you may not feel as fast as when you were NOT using NgRx. For that reason, the entity library exists to help alleviate some of the boilerplate creation—more on that later in this chapter.

The router and its state is another thing that can be interesting to keep track of. The URL of where you are currently, the router parameter, as well as query parameters are all interesting pieces of information that might come in handy. They might come in handy should you be in a situation where you might want to reinstate the app, also called **rehydration**.

Next, we will dive into how to build your own micro implementation of NgRx using RxJS, so you get a feel for what's going on. Hopefully, that will be a real eye-opening moment in understanding the underlying ideas of what makes NgRx and Redux tick.

To round off this chapter and this book, we will explain what schematics is and how it will help you quickly scaffold the various parts that you need to be a really efficient user of NgRx.

In this chapter, you will learn how to:

- Leverage the entity library and how it makes our life easier using NgRx
- Capture the router state as well as customize what gets saved down by writing our own customization code
- Build a micro implementation of NgRx
- Demystify schematics and see how it can make us an even faster and more efficient user of NgRx

@ngrx/entity

The demo code for this section can be found in the code repository for this book under `Chapter10/Entity`.

The entity library is here to help us manage collections and basically, write less and do more. This means that so far we have been writing a lot of code when creating reducers and selectors that we simply won't need to do when we leverage the full power of the entity library.

Setting it up

We start by downloading the entity library. To do this, we need to run the following command:

```
npm install @ngrx/entity
```

We then need to perform the following steps:

1. Create a model.
2. Create an entity state based on the model.
3. Create an entity adapter.
4. Create the initial state.
5. Create the reducer and set up the state in the `StoreModule`.

Let's start off by creating our model:

```
// user.model.ts

export interface User {
  id: number;
  name: string;
}
```

The preceding code is just a simple model with fields `id` and `name`. We then create our entity state, like so:

```
// excerpt from app.module.ts

import {
  EntityState,
  createEntityAdapter,
  EntityAdapter
```

```
} from "@ngrx/entity";

export interface State extends EntityState
  selectedUserId: number | null;
}
```

This will be the return type our reducer needs to abide by. Type `EntityState` looks like the following, if you peek into the NgRx source code:

```
// from NGRX source code

export interface EntityState<T> {
  ids: string[] | number[];
  entities: Dictionary<T>;
}
```

By extending the preceding interface `EntityState,` when we create type `State` we will also get the properties `ids` and `entities`. We will see later in this section how these properties are populated, once we start using the utility methods the entity library gives us.

The next step is to create our adapter. An instance of the adapter sits on a range of methods, allowing us to write a great deal less code. We create the adapter with the following code:

```
// excerpt from app.module.ts

import {
  EntityState,
  createEntityAdapter,
  EntityAdapter
} from "@ngrx/entity";

const userAdapter: EntityAdapter<User> = createEntityAdapter<User>();
```

At this point, we are almost ready; we just need to get the initial state from the adapter and provide that to our reducer.

To get the initial state, we need to talk to our adapter, like so:

```
// excerpt from app.module.ts

const initialState: State = {
  ids: [],
  entities: {},
  selectedUserId: null
};

const initial = userAdapter.getInitialState(initialState);
```

What's happening here is that we need to create an object representing the initial state. It needs to be of type `State` and therefore it needs to have the properties `ids`, `entities`, and `selectedUserId` defined. Then, we call `getInitialState()` on the adapter to produce our initial state. So, what do we need the initial state for? We'll need to set it as the default value of our reducer's state.

Next, we create our reducer and set its default state to our initial state instance, created previously:

```
// interfaces.ts

import { Action } from "@ngrx/store";

export interface ActionPayload<T> extends Action {
  payload: T;
}

// excerpt from app.module.ts

function userReducer(state = initial, action: ActionPayload<User>): State {
  switch (action.type) {
    case "ADD_USER":
      return userAdapter.addOne(action.payload, state);
    default:
      return state;
    }
  }
}
```

Note here how we call our `userAdapter` and invoke the method `addOne()`; this means that we don't have to write code that looks like this:

```
// example of what a reducer could look like that is NOT using @ngrx/entity

function reducer(state = [], action: ActionPayload<User>) {
  switch (action.type) {
    case "ADD_USER":
      return [
        ...state.users
        Object.assign({}, action.payload)
      ];
    default:
      return state;
    }
  }
}
```

The last step to setting everything up is to add the state to the `StoreModule` so that NgRx knows about it:

```
// excerpt from app.module.ts

@NgModule({
  declarations: [AppComponent, EditUserComponent],
  imports: [
    BrowserModule,
    FormsModule,
    StoreModule.forRoot({
      users: userReducer
    })
  ],
  providers: [],
  bootstrap: [AppComponent]
})
export class AppModule {}
```

That concludes the required setup. The next steps we want to take in the following sections are how to display the data in a component, and also how to perform a full CRUD and thereby leveraging more of what the `EntityAdapter` has to offer.

Selecting our data

We have learnt by now that to select data in NgRx, we need to inject the store service and call `select` on it, either with a string as an argument or with a function. Let's inject the store service and have a look at the state that comes back:

```
// app.component.ts  - a first draft

import { Component } from "@angular/core";
import { AppState } from "./app-state";
import { Store } from "@ngrx/store";

@Component({
  selector: "app-root",
  template: `
  User list view

  `
})
export class AppComponent {
  title = "app";
  users$;
```

```
constructor(private store: Store<AppState>) {
  this.users$ = this.store
    .select(state => state);

  this.users$
    .subscribe(data => console.log("users", data));
}
}
```

The preceding component won't display the users in a neat list just yet; we will explain why later. In the meantime, we will just focus on what is logged to the console:

```
users  ▼ {users: {…}}  🔢
           ▼ users:
               ▶ entities: {}
               ▶ ids: []
                 selectedUserId: null
               ▶ __proto__: Object
           ▶ __proto__: Object
```

What we see here is the state of our store, which contains a user's property at the highest level, it has `entities`, `ids` and `selectedUserId` as properties. This is to be expected so far. What does surprise us a little is the fact that the entities dictionary is an object and not a list. How do we output that in a list form using `*ngFor`? Well, we can easily solve that with a `map()` operator, like so:

```
// app.component.ts adding more UI and selecting the correct slice of state

import { Component } from "@angular/core";
import { AppState } from "./app-state";
import { Store } from "@ngrx/store";
import { map } from "rxjs/operators";

@Component({
  selector: "app-root",
  template: `
  <div style="border: solid 1px black; padding: 10px;"
      *ngFor="let user of users$ | async">
  {{ user.name }}
  </div>
  `
})
export class AppComponent {
  title = "app";
  users$;
```

```
constructor(private store: Store<AppState>) {
  this.users$ = this.store
    .select(state => state.users.entities)
    .pipe(
      map(this.toArray)
    );
  this.users$.subscribe(data => console.log("users", data));
}

toArray(obj) {
  const keys = Object.keys(obj);
  return keys.map(key => obj[key]);
}
}
```

OK, so now we drill down to `state.users.entities` to get to our users but we need to add the `map()` operation to turn our entities dictionary into a list. So, the console now shows us an empty array as the initial value of `users$`, which makes perfect sense. The UI is still empty, as we have an empty array and therefore nothing to show. In the following section, we will cover how to add, remove, and update the state using the `EntityAdapter`.

Adding the full CRUD

What we mean by CRUD is the ability to add, edit, read, and delete the data from the store. The point of using the entity library is for it to do most of the heavy lifting. The time has come to revisit our reducer:

```
// excerpt from app.module.ts

function userReducer(
  state = initial,
  action: ActionPayload<User>): State {

  switch (action.type) {
    case "ADD_USER":
      return userAdapter.addOne(action.payload, state);
    default:
      return state;
  }
}
```

Here, we are using the `userAdapter` instance to carry out adding one item to the store. There is a lot more the adapter can do for us though—here is a full list of its capabilities:

```
// description of the interface for EntityStateAdapter,
// the interface our userAdapter implements

export interface EntityStateAdapter<T> {
  addOne<S extends EntityState<T>>(entity: T, state: S): S;
  addMany<S extends EntityState<T>>(entities: T[], state: S): S;
  addAll<S extends EntityState<T>>(entities: T[], state: S): S;
  removeOne<S extends EntityState<T>>(key: string, state: S): S;
  removeOne<S extends EntityState<T>>(key: number, state: S): S;
  removeMany<S extends EntityState<T>>(keys: string[], state: S): S;
  removeMany<S extends EntityState<T>>(keys: number[], state: S): S;
  removeAll<S extends EntityState<T>>(state: S): S;
  updateOne<S extends EntityState<T>>(update: Update<T>, state: S): S;
  updateMany<S extends EntityState<T>>(updates: Update<T>[], state: S): S;
}
```

Creating users

As we can see, `EntityStateAdapter` has methods for the full CRUD. Let's look at adding the capability to add a user to our component. We need to make the following additions to our component:

- Add an input field
- Dispatch an `ADD_USER` action with our new user as payload

The required code changes are in bold, as follows:

```
// app.component.ts - adding the capability to add users

import { Component } from "@angular/core";
import { AppState } from "./app-state";
import { Store } from "@ngrx/store";
import { map } from "rxjs/operators";

@Component({
selector: "app-root",
template: `
  <div style="border: solid 1px black; padding: 10px;"
      *ngFor="let user of users$ | async">
    {{ user.name }}
  </div>
  <div>
```

```
    <input [(ngModel)]="user" /> <button (click)="add()">Add</button>
  </div>

})
export class AppComponent {
  title = "app";
  users$;
  user;
  id = 1;

  constructor(private store: Store<AppState>) {
    this.users$ = this.store
      .select(state => state.users.entities)
      .pipe(map(this.toArray));
    this.users$.subscribe(data => console.log("users", data));
  }

  toArray(obj) {
    const keys = Object.keys(obj);
    return keys.map(key => obj[key]);
  }

  add() {
    const newUser = { id: this.id++, name: this.user };
    this.store.dispatch({
      type: "ADD_USER",
      payload: newUser
    });
  }
}
```

This code demonstrates how we add an input element and connect that to the field   user
on our class through ngModel. We also added the add() method that dispatches a user to
our reducer. Adding a user should now look like the following in the UI:

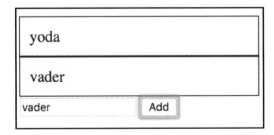

Updating users

There are two things we need to do to support updating users:

- Add a component that supports updating
- Adding a CASE to our reducer that listens to an action and calls the appropriate `adapter` method

Let's start with our component:

```typescript
// edit-user.component.ts

import {
  Component,
  OnInit,
  Output,
  Input,
  EventEmitter
} from "@angular/core";

@Component({
  selector: "edit-user",
  template: `
  <div>
    <input [(ngModel)]="user.name" />
    <button (click)="save.emit(user)" >Save</button>
  </div>
  `
})
export class EditUserComponent implements OnInit {
  private _user;

  @Input()
  get user() {
    return this._user;
  }

  set user(val) {
    this._user = Object.assign({}, val);
  }

  @Output() save = new EventEmitter();

  constructor() {}
  ngOnInit() {}
}
```

Here, we have a component that takes a `user` as input and is able to invoke a `save` as output thereby calling the parent component. In short, this component allows us to edit a user.

Now we need to add this component to `app.module.ts` so that other components within this module can use it:

```
// excerpt from app.module.ts

@NgModule({
  declarations: [AppComponent, EditUserComponent],
  imports: [
    BrowserModule,
    FormsModule,
    StoreModule.forRoot({
      users: userReducer
    })],
  providers: [],
  bootstrap: [AppComponent]
})
export class AppModule {}
```

Now we are ready to add the component to the parent components template, like so:

```
// app.component.ts - adding EditUserComponent to the markup

import { Component } from "@angular/core";
import { AppState } from "./app-state";
import { Store } from "@ngrx/store";
import { map } from "rxjs/operators";

@Component({
  selector: "app-root",
  template: `
    <div style="border: solid 1px black; padding: 10px;"
        *ngFor="let user of users$ | async">
      {{ user.name }}
      <edit-user [user]="user" (save)="update($event)" ></edit-user>
    </div>
    <div>
      <input [(ngModel)]="user" /> <button (click)="add()">Add</button>
    </div>
  `
})
export class AppComponent {
  title = "app";
  users$;
```

```
    user;
    id = 1;

    constructor(private store: Store<AppState>) {
      this.users$ = this.store
        .select(state => state.users.entities)
        .pipe(map(this.toArray));
      this.users$.subscribe(data => console.log("users", data));
    }

    toArray(obj) {
      const keys = Object.keys(obj);
      return keys.map(key => obj[key]);
    }

    add() {
      const newUser = { id: this.id++, name: this.user };
      this.store.dispatch({
        type: "ADD_USER",
        payload: newUser
      });
    }

    update(user) {
      console.log("updating", user);
      this.store.dispatch({ type: "UPDATE_USER", payload: user });
    }
  }
```

This code shows us how we add the EditUserComponent to the markup, as well as us adding the update() method that, when invoked, dispatches the action UPDATE_USER. This will lead to our reducer being invoked which leads us to our final piece of the puzzle, the required changes we need to make to the reducer:

```
// excerpt from app.module.ts

function userReducer(state = initial, action: ActionPayload<User>): State {
  switch (action.type) {
    case "ADD_USER":
      return userAdapter.addOne(action.payload, state);
    case "UPDATE_USER":
      return userAdapter.updateOne({
        id: action.payload.id,
        changes: action.payload
      },
      state
    );
```

```
      default:
        return state;
    }
  }
```

We now support the ability to update our users list.

Deleting users

The last piece of supporting CRUD is the ability to remove users from the list. This case is very similar to all the other cases:

- We need to add support for it to `app.component.ts`
- We need to update the reducer, and the reducer needs to call the appropriate adapter method

Let's start with the component and add support in the markup, as well as adding a `remove()` method to the component class, like so:

```
// app.component.ts - adding remove capability

import { Component } from "@angular/core";
import { AppState } from "./app-state";
import { Store } from "@ngrx/store";
import { map } from "rxjs/operators";

@Component({
  selector: "app-root",
  template: `
  <div style="border: solid 1px black; padding: 10px;"
      *ngFor="let user of users$ | async">
    {{ user.name }}
    <button (click)="remove(user.id)" >Remove</button>
    <edit-user [user]="user" (save)="update($event)" ></edit-user>
  </div>
  <div>
    <input [(ngModel)]="user" /> <button (click)="add()">Add</button>
  </div>
  `
})
export class AppComponent {
  title = "app";
  users$;
  user;
  id = 1;
```

```
constructor(private store: Store<AppState>) {
  this.users$ = this.store
    .select(state => state.users.entities)
    .pipe(map(this.toArray));
  this.users$.subscribe(data => console.log("users", data));
}

toArray(obj) {
  const keys = Object.keys(obj);
  return keys.map(key => obj[key]);
}

add() {
  const newUser = { id: this.id++, name: this.user };
  this.store.dispatch({
    type: "ADD_USER",
    payload: newUser
  });
}

remove(id) {
  console.log("removing", id);
  this.store.dispatch({ type: "REMOVE_USER", payload: { id } });
}

update(user) {
  console.log("updating", user);
  this.store.dispatch({ type: "UPDATE_USER", payload: user });
}
}
```

The remaining part is updating our reducer to say the following:

```
// excerpt from app.module.ts

function userReducer(state = initial, action: ActionPayload<User>): State {
  switch (action.type) {
    case "ADD_USER":
      return userAdapter.addOne(action.payload, state);
    case "REMOVE_USER":
      return userAdapter.removeOne(action.payload.id, state);
    case "UPDATE_USER":
      return userAdapter.updateOne(
        {
          id: action.payload.id,
          changes: action.payload
        },
        state
```

```
    );
  default:
    return state;\
  }
}
```

@ngrx/router-store

We want to be able to trace where we are in the application—*where*—is represented by our route, route parameters, as well as by query parameters. By saving where we are, down to our store, we are able to easily serialize the stores information to a storage for later retrieval and deserialization, which means we can re-instate the app with not only the state, but also our page location.

Installation and set up

The router store is in an NPM package and we can therefore type the following to install it:

```
npm install @ngrx/router-store --save
```

The next thing we need to do is to import the correct modules and set those up in the `import` properties of our root module, like so:

```
import { BrowserModule } from '@angular/platform-browser';
import { NgModule, Injectable } from '@angular/core';
import { StoreModule, Action } from '@ngrx/store';
import { AppComponent } from './app.component';
import { counterReducer } from './reducer';
import { TodoModule } from './todo/todo.module';
import { todosReducer } from './todo/reducer';
import { JediModule } from './jedi/jedi.module';
import { jediListReducer } from './jedi/list.reducer';
import { productsReducer } from './products/products.reducer';
import { StoreDevtoolsModule } from '@ngrx/store-devtools';
import { ProductsModule } from './products/products.module';
import { StoreRouterConnectingModule, routerReducer } from '@ngrx/router-store';
import { RouterModule } from '@angular/router';
import { TestingComponent } from './testing.component';
import { Effect, ofType, Actions } from '@ngrx/effects';
import { Observable } from 'rxjs/Observable';
import { switchMap } from 'rxjs/operators';
import { of } from 'rxjs/observable/of';
```

```
import { EffectsModule } from '@ngrx/effects';

@NgModule({
  declarations: [AppComponent, TestingComponent],
  imports: [
    BrowserModule,
    StoreModule.forRoot({
      count: counterReducer,
      todos: todosReducer,
      jediList: jediListReducer,
      products: productsReducer,
      router: routerReducer
    }),
    EffectsModule.forRoot([]),
    RouterModule.forRoot([{ path: 'testing', component: TestingComponent
}]),
    StoreRouterConnectingModule.forRoot({
      stateKey: 'router' // name of reducer key
    }),
    StoreDevtoolsModule.instrument({
      maxAge: 25 // Retains last 25 states
    }),
    TodoModule,
    JediModule,
    ProductsModule
  ],
  bootstrap: [AppComponent]
})
export class AppModule {}
```

We don't do a lot here. We call the `forRoot()` method on
the `StoreRouterConnectingModule`, and we also add a new reducer entry in the form of
a router that points to `routerReducer` as the reducer that will handle any changes to
the `router` property.

Investigating the router state

We have just set up the router store. This means that we automatically write to a
property `router` in our store every time we navigate. We can prove this is the case by
editing the `app.component.ts` to subscribe to that slice of state:

```
import { Component } from '@angular/core';
import { Store } from '@ngrx/store';
import { Observable } from 'rxjs/Observable';
import { Increment, Decrement } from './actions';
```

```
import { AppState } from './app-state';

@Component({
  selector: 'app-root',
  template: `
    {{ count$ | async }}
    <button (click)="increment()">Increment</button>
    <button (click)="decrement()">Decrement</button>
    <app-todos></app-todos>
    <jedi-list></jedi-list>
    <div>
      <a routerLink="/testing" routerLinkActive="active">Testing</a>
    </div>
    <router-outlet></router-outlet>`,
  styleUrls: ['./app.component.css']
})
export class AppComponent {
  count$: Observable<number>;

  constructor(private store: Store<AppState>) {
    this.count$ = store.select('count');
    store
      .select(state => state.router)
      .subscribe(route => console.log('router obj', route));
  }

  increment() {
    this.store.dispatch(Increment());
  }

  decrement() {
    this.store.dispatch(Decrement());
  }
}
```

Here, we subscribe to the state router and thereby listen to every time the route changes. We log the said object and it looks like this:

```
▼ Object 🔵
    navigationId: 1
  ▼ state: RouterStateSnapshot
    ▶ root: ActivatedRouteSnapshot
      url: "/"
    ▼ _root: TreeNode
      ▶ children: []
      ▶ value: ActivatedRouteSnapshot {url: Array(0), params: {…}, queryParams: {…}, fragment: null, data: {…}, …}
      ▶ __proto__: Object
    ▶ __proto__: Tree
  ▶ __proto__: Object
```

This screenshot shows us the object our router state now contains. We can see the url property points to / which means our default route has been loaded. We can also see that this object contains router parameters and query parameters in the root property. So, there is some interesting information in there.

Let's see what happens when we route somewhere like /testing:

```
▼ {state: RouterStateSnapshot, navigationId: 2} 🔘
    navigationId: 2
  ▼ state: RouterStateSnapshot
      root: (...)
      url: "/testing"
    ▶ _root: TreeNode {value: ActivatedRouteSnapshot, children: Array(1)}
    ▶ __proto__: Tree
  ▶ __proto__: Object
```

Our router state has been updated and we can see that our url property points to /testing.

So far, we have subscribed to the router state and listened to when the route is changing. There is a second way. We could be listening to when a specific action is being dispatched. The action being dispatched for routing is the string ROUTER_NAVIGATION. We can therefore easily build an effect for this so we can carry out side effects when the route changes. We may want to carry out AJAX requests or store things in a local cache. Only you know what you want to do. Let's build that effect. We will return back to an existing file, routing.effects.ts, and extend it:

```
import { Injectable } from '@angular/core';
import { Effect, Actions, ofType } from '@ngrx/effects';
import { Router } from '@angular/router';
import { map, tap, switchMap } from 'rxjs/operators';
import { Action } from '@ngrx/store';
import { PRODUCTS, RoutingAction } from './routing.constants';
import { Observable } from 'rxjs/Observable';

@Injectable()
export class RoutingEffects {
  @Effect({ dispatch: false })
  gotoProducts$ = this.actions$.ofType(PRODUCTS).pipe(
    tap(action => {
      this.router.navigate([action.payload.url]);
    })
  );

  @Effect({ dispatch: false })
```

```
locationUpdate$: Observable<Action> =
  this.actions$.ofType('ROUTER_NAVIGATION').pipe(
    tap((action: any) => {
      console.log('router navigation effect', action);
    })
  );

constructor(
  private router: Router,
  private actions$: Actions<RoutingAction>) {}
}
```

Custom serialization

The object being stored is a bit verbose though. It contains a lot of information and we may only be interested in parts of it. We can actually solve that by building our own custom serializer. We need to do the following to accomplish that:

- Create a class that implements the interface RouterStateSerializer and decide what we want to return
- Replace the router key RouterStateSerializer with our custom implementation

Let's begin. We first create a class, like so:

```
// my-serializer.ts

import { RouterStateSerializer } from '@ngrx/router-store';
import { RouterStateSnapshot } from '@angular/router';

interface MyState {
  url: string;
}

export class MySerializer implements RouterStateSerializer<MyState> {
  serialize(routerState: RouterStateSnapshot): MyState {
    return <MyState>{};
    // todo: implement
  }
}
```

The `RouterStateSeralizer` interface forces us to specify a `type` T, which could be anything. T is what we want to return from the routing object. Remember the reason for doing what we are doing is to grab a subset of interesting information from the routing object. The full routing information is contained within our input parameter `routerState` that is of type `RouterStateSnapshot`. A comment though is that `MyState` is a bit anemic, as it only contains a single property, `url`. You can of course extend this according to the needs of your application. You most likely want to grab the `router` and `query` parameters. We will grab those as well before we are done with this section but let's start with this to showcase how it works. The next step is to grab the data from the `routerState` parameter. For now, we dig out the `url`—let's update the code to reflect that:

```
// my-serializer.ts
import { RouterStateSerializer } from '@ngrx/router-store';
import { RouterStateSnapshot } from '@angular/router';

interface MyState {
  url: string;
}

export class MySerializer implements RouterStateSerializer<MyState> {
  serialize(routerState: RouterStateSnapshot): MyState {
    const { url } = routerState;
    return { url };
  }
}
```

Let's now tell the provider to use our implementation instead. We need to go to the `app.module.ts` file:

```
import { BrowserModule } from '@angular/platform-browser';
import { NgModule, Injectable } from '@angular/core';
import { StoreModule, Action } from '@ngrx/store';
import { AppComponent } from './app.component';
import { counterReducer } from './reducer';
import { TodoModule } from './todo/todo.module';
import { todosReducer } from './todo/reducer';
import { JediModule } from './jedi/jedi.module';
import { jediListReducer } from './jedi/list.reducer';
import { productsReducer } from './products/products.reducer';
import { StoreDevtoolsModule } from '@ngrx/store-devtools';
import { ProductsModule } from './products/products.module';
import { StoreRouterConnectingModule, routerReducer, RouterStateSerializer
} from '@ngrx/router-store';
import { RouterModule } from '@angular/router';
import { TestingComponent } from './testing.component';
```

```
import { Effect, ofType, Actions } from '@ngrx/effects';
import { Observable } from 'rxjs/Observable';
import { switchMap } from 'rxjs/operators';
import { of } from 'rxjs/observable/of';
import { EffectsModule } from '@ngrx/effects';
import { RoutingEffects } from './routing.effects';
import { ProductsTestComponent } from './productstest.component';
import { MySerializer } from './my-serializer';

@NgModule({
  declarations: [AppComponent, TestingComponent, ProductsTestComponent],
  imports: [
    BrowserModule,
    StoreModule.forRoot({
      count: counterReducer,
      todos: todosReducer,
      jediList: jediListReducer,
      products: productsReducer,
      router: routerReducer}),
    EffectsModule.forRoot([RoutingEffects]),
    RouterModule.forRoot([
      { path: 'testing', component: TestingComponent },
      { path: 'products', component: ProductsTestComponent }
    ]),
    StoreRouterConnectingModule.forRoot({
      stateKey: 'router' // name of reducer key
    }),
    StoreDevtoolsModule.instrument({
      maxAge: 25 // Retains last 25 states
    }),
    TodoModule,
    JediModule,
    ProductsModule
  ],
  providers: [{ provide: RouterStateSerializer, useClass: MySerializer }],
  bootstrap: [AppComponent]
})
export class AppModule {}
```

We have now imported the MySerializer class and the RouterStateSeralizer interface and we are replacing the provider key using the following line:

```
providers: [{ provide: RouterStateSerializer, useClass: MySerializer }]
```

Now it's time to take this for a spin. So, we fire up the app and see what happens if we navigate around in the app. Here is a quick reminder of what our app looks like right now:

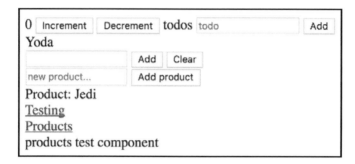

Clicking either the **Testing** or **Products** link will take us to /testing or /products, respectively. Let's do just that and see what that looks like. We have a look at the console and lo and, behold! Our router object is considerably smaller:

```
router obj  ▼ {state: {…}, navigationId: 1}
                navigationId: 1
              ▼ state:
                  url: "/testing"
              ►   __proto__: Object
          ►   __proto__: Object
```

Our object now contains pretty much only the url property. This is what gets stored down in the state of our application. If we want more things stored than that, then we can easily extend the MySerializer class—suggested additions are router and query parameters. Let's make the following alterations to the MySerializer class:

```
// my-serializer.ts
import { RouterStateSerializer } from '@ngrx/router-store';
import { RouterStateSnapshot } from '@angular/router';

interface MyState {
  url: string;
  queryParams;
}

export class MySerializer implements RouterStateSerializer<MyState> {
  serialize(routerState: RouterStateSnapshot): MyState {
    const { url, root: { queryParams } } = routerState;
    return { url, queryParams };
  }
}
```

Navigating to `http://localhost:4200/products?page=1` will now produce the following in the console:

```
router obj ▼ {state: {…}, navigationId: 1}
               navigationId: 1
             ▼ state:
               ▶ queryParams: {page: "1"}
                 url: "/products?page=1"
               ▶ __proto__: Object
           ▶ __proto__: Object
```

The difference is now that we have a `queryParams` property, which points to an object with content `{ page: 1 }`. This is what we expected. Digging out the router parameters is equally easy. But for us to have router parameters that are populated in the first place, we need to have a route with a routing parameter. Instead of `/products`, we need something such as `products/:id`. Let's start by adding that to our list of routes:

```
// products/products.module.ts

import { NgModule } from '@angular/core';
import { BrowserModule } from '@angular/platform-browser';
import { EffectsModule } from '@ngrx/effects';
import { ProductEffects } from './products.effect';
import { HttpClientModule } from '@angular/common/http';
import { ProductsComponent } from './products.component';
import { FormsModule } from '@angular/forms';
import { ProductsHttpActions } from './products-http.actions';
import { RouterModule } from '@angular/router';
import { ProductsDetailComponent } from './products-detail.component';

@NgModule({
  imports: [
    BrowserModule,
    HttpClientModule,
    FormsModule,
    EffectsModule.forFeature([ProductEffects]),
    RouterModule.forChild([{
      path: 'products',
      component: ProductsComponent
    }, {
      path: 'products/:id',
      component: ProductsDetailComponent
    }])
  ],
```

```
    exports: [ProductsComponent],
    declarations: [ProductsComponent, ProductsDetailComponent],
    providers: [ProductsHttpActions]
})
export class ProductsModule {}
```

And we of course need to add a component. It does nothing special other than exist for our demo purposes. Remember the emphasis is on understanding the serialization process:

```
// products-detail.component.ts

import { Component, OnInit } from '@angular/core';

@Component({
selector: 'app-products-detail',
  template: `
  products detail
`
})
export class ProductsDetailComponent{
  constructor() {}
}
```

At this point, it's time to return back to our browser and enter the `url`, `products/1?page=1`. Let's have a look at the console now:

```
router obj  ▼ {state: {…}, navigationId: 1} ▣
                navigationId: 1
              ▼ state:
                ▶ params: {id: "1"}
                ▶ queryParams: {page: "1"}
                  url: "/products/1?page=1"
                ▶ __proto__: Object
              ▶ __proto__: Object
```

Here, we see how our `params` property has been added to our custom object.

Navigating through dispatch

Now that we have our router store properly set up, we can actually start thinking in terms of dispatching actions, even for routes. OK, what does that mean? Well, imagine we are thinking more and more in dispatching actions; it makes our world simpler. When you dispatch an action, an HTTP call happens, and, in dispatching an action, the application routes you where you want to go.

This isn't really a feature of the router store, but a way you can look at it. A way to implement this is by writing your own effect that responds to a route action, and, as a result, you call the router service and perform the navigation. Let's summarize what we just said in a bullet list and carry out the resulting steps:

1. Set up some routing constants.
2. Set up some routing actions.
3. Write an effect that listens to routing actions and performs routing inside of the effect.

Here is Step 1:

```
// routing-constants.ts
export const PRODUCTS = 'Navigation products';
export const TODOS = 'Navigation todos';

export interface RoutingAction implements Action {
  type: string;
  payload: { url: string, query: { page: number } ; }
}
```

OK, our next step is to define a set of action creators so we can set off a certain behavior when a specific action occurs:

```
// router-actions.ts
import { PRODUCTS, TODOS } from './routing-constants';

export const gotoProducts = (pageNo) => ({
  type: PRODUCTS,
  payload: { url: '/products', query: { page: pageNo } }
});

export const gotoTodo = (pageNo) => ({
  type: TODOS,
  payload: { url: '/todos', query: { page: pageNo } }
})
```

Our next step is our effect, which would now be able to respond to the preceding actions:

```
// routing-effects.ts
import { PRODUCTS, TODOS } from './routing-constants';
import { gotoProducts, gotoTodo }

export class RoutingEffects {
  @Effect({ dispatch: false }) routingProducts$ = this.actions$
  .ofType(PRODUCTS)
```

```
.tap(action => {
  this.router.navigate('/products')
})

@Effect({ dispatch: false }) routingTodos$ = this.actions$
.ofType(TODOS)
.tap(action => {
  this.router.navigate('/todos');
})

constructor(
  private router: Router,
  private actions$: Actions) {
}
}
```

Understanding NgRx – building our own micro implementation

We have done this experiment once before in `Chapter 8`, *Redux*. The point was to gain a deeper understanding of what goes on behind the scenes. The difference between implementing Redux and implementing NgRx is the use of a library for publish/ subscribe, which is the way you choose to convey to a listener that a change has occurred. In our Redux implementation in `Chapter 8`, *Redux*, we gave you the choice between implementing the Gang of Four publish-subscribe pattern without the help of a library, or using `EventEmitter` to achieve the same thing. In NgRx, that component is RxJS. So, let's crack on with the implementation. Before doing so, let's describe what we aim to implement:

- We aim to implement a store that holds a state
- It should be possible to dispatch an action to said store so that its inner state changes
- Any change to the store should go through a reducer
- We will learn to handle side effects

Adding a store

A store at its heart is just a class wrapping a state. A store needs to be able to deal with changes; the change should come via method dispatch. The following pseudo code represents what the store might look like:

```
// NGRX-light/storeI.js

class Store {
  constructor() {
    this.state = {};
  }
  dispatch() {
    // calculate the new state and replace the old one
  }
}
```

We mentioned in the beginning of this main section that NgRx uses RxJS at its core. We mentioned that it was so the store could convey changes to its listeners. Let's mention the core concepts of RxJS that might fit the preceding problem description. In RxJS, we have:

- **Observable**: It is able to emit values and you can attach subscribers to it
- **Observer**: This is the object that is called so that we end up getting the values as a subscriber
- **Subscriber**: This is a combination of an Observable and an Observer in that it can be subscribed to but it is also possible to add values to it after the subscription has happened.

Thinking about the store for a bit, we realize we need to be able to add values to it at any point and we need to be able to subscribe to it. This seems to fit the behavior of the `Subject`. Let's continue our pseudo coding of the `Store` but let a `Subject` be part of it now:

```
// NGRX-light/storeII.js

class Store {
  constructor() {
    this.state = {};
  }

  dispatch(newState) {
    this.state = newState;
  }
}
```

We implemented the `dispatch()` method with the following code:

```
this.innerSubject.next(newState);
```

For now, let's care about implementing subscription functionality. Let's imagine the store will be used in the following way:

```
const store = new Store();
store.subscribe(data => {
  console.log('data', data);
})
```

For that to be possible, we could just add the `subscribe()` method to our store. If we were to do that ourselves, we would have to take care of a list of listeners and ensure listeners are told when a change happens to the state. A better option is to just let our store inherit from `Subject`. That would take care of the subscription bit. Let's see what that might look like:

```
// NGRX-light/storeIII.js

const Rx = require('rxjs');

class Store extends Rx.Subject {
  constructor() {
    super();
    this.state = {};
    this.subscribe(data => this.state = data);
  }

  dispatch(newState) {
    this.next(newState);
  }
}

const store = new Store();
store.subscribe(data => console.log('store', data));

store.dispatch({});
store.dispatch({ user: 'chris' });

// store {}
// store { user: 'chris' }
```

The preceding code reimplements the `dispatch()` method and we also set up a subscription in the constructor to ensure our latest state is updated. There is a thing we need to improve here and that is how we add state to our store. With Redux, the incoming state change should be reduced into the old state, like so:

```
const store = new Store();
store.subscribe(data => console.log('store', data));
// desired behavior:  store { name: 'chris' }
// desired behavior: store { name: 'chris', address: 'London' }

store.dispatch({ name : 'chris' });
store.dispatch({ address : 'London' });
```

The way to achieve this is to refactor our code a little and create another `Subject` that will be the target of a call to dispatch, like so:

```
// NGRX-light/storeIV.js

const Rx = require('rxjs');

class Store extends Rx.Subject {
  constructor() {
    super();
    this.dispatcher = new Rx.Subject();
    this.state = {};
    this.dispatcher.subscribe(data => {
      this.state = Object.assign({}, this.state, data);
      this.next(this.state);
    });
  }

  dispatch(newState) {
    this.dispatcher.next(newState);
  }
}

const store = new Store();
store.subscribe(data => console.log('store', data));

// store { name: 'chris' }
// store { address: 'London' }

store.dispatch({ name: 'chris' });
store.dispatch({ address: 'London' });
```

Merging the states in a better way

In the preceding code, we used an `Object.assign()` to merge the old state with the new state. We can do this even better by using the `scan()` operator on our dispatcher member, like so:

```
// NGRX-light/storeV.js

const Rx = require('rxjs');

class Store extends Rx.Subject {
  constructor() {
    super();
    this.dispatcher = new Rx.Subject();
    this.dispatcher
      .scan((acc, curr) => ({ ...acc, ...curr }))
      .subscribe(data => this.next(data));
  }

  dispatch(newState) {
    this.dispatcher.next(newState);
  }
}

const store = new Store();
store.subscribe(data => console.log('store', data));

store.dispatch({ name: 'chris' });
store.dispatch({ address: 'London' });
```

An important thing to note in the preceding code is that we removed the state member from the store. It's simply not needed as we only care about the latest value being emitted anyway.

Implementing a reducer and integrating it with the store

An important concept of Redux is to guard who and what can affect your store. The *who* is reducers. By allowing only reducers to affect your store, we are more in control of what happens. A simple reducer is just a function that takes a state and action as parameters and is able to produce a new state based on the old state and existing state, like so:

```
// example reducer
```

```
function countReducer(state = 0, action) {
  switch(action.type) {
    case "INCREMENT":
      return state + 1;
    default:
      return state;
  }
}

let state = countReducer(0, { type: "INCREMENT" });
// 1
state = countReducer(state, { type: "INCREMENT" });
// 2
```

So, where does a reducer come into the picture in Redux? Well, the state of the store is made up of an object, like so:

```
{
  counter: 1
  products : []
}
```

The way a store goes about calculating the next state of a store is by creating a function that looks something like this:

```
// calculate state
function calcState(state, action) {
  return {
    counter: counterReducer(state.counter, action),
    products: productsReducer(state.products, action)
  }
}
```

With the preceding code, we are able to let different reducer functions handle different parts of our state. Let's add such a function to our store along with some reducers:

```
// NGRX-light/storeVI.js

const Rx = require('rxjs');

function counterReducer(state = 0, action) {
  switch(action.type) {
    case "INCREMENT":
      return state + 1;
    default:
      return state;
  }
}
```

```
function productsReducer(state = [], action) {
  switch(action.type) {
    case 'ADD_PRODUCT':
      return [ ...state, Object.assign({}, action.payload) ]
    default:
      return state;
  }
}

class Store extends Rx.BehaviorSubject {
  constructor() {
    super({ counter: 0, products: [] });
    this.dispatcher = new Rx.Subject();
    this.state = {};
    this.dispatcher
      .scan((acc, curr) => ({ ...acc, ...curr }))
      .subscribe(data => this.next(data));
  }

  calcState(state, action) {
    return {
      counter: counterReducer(state.counter, action),
      products: productsReducer(state.products, action)
    }
  }

  dispatch(action) {
    const newState = this.calcState(this.value, action);
    this.dispatcher.next(newState);
  }
}

const store = new Store();
store.subscribe(data => console.log('store', data));

store.dispatch({ type: 'INCREMENT' });
store.dispatch({ type: 'INCREMENT' });
store.dispatch({ type: 'ADD_PRODUCT', payload: { id: 1, name: 'Yoda' } });
```

We have made quite a few changes to our store at this point:

- We have added two reducers
- Now we inherit from a `BehaviorSubject`; this is so we can remember what the old state was so when we call `calcState()` we are able to produce a new state based on the old state + action
- We added the method `calcState()` that takes the old state and an action

- The dispatcher now takes an action instead of a state
- The `super()` constructor in the constructor now takes an initial value

We have set ourselves up quite well for our next step, namely on how to get a part of the state.

Dealing with slices of state

The reason for wanting only part of the state is that we will use NgRx in a context where there will be many components that only care about rendering a little part of the application's full state. For example, we may have a product list component, a product detail component, and so on. For that reason, we need to implement support for getting a slice of state. Thanks to the fact that our store inherits from a `BehaviorSubject`, implementing a slice of state is child's play:

```
// NGRX-light/storeVII.js

const Rx = require('rxjs');

function counterReducer(state = 0, action) {
  switch(action.type) {
    case "INCREMENT":
      return state + 1;
    default:
      return state;
  }
}

function productsReducer(state = [], action) {
  switch(action.type) {
    case 'ADD_PRODUCT':
      return [ ...state, Object.assign({}, action.payload) ]
    default:
      return state;
  }
}

class Store extends Rx.BehaviorSubject {
  constructor() {
    super({ counter: 0, products: [] });
    this.dispatcher = new Rx.Subject();
    this.state = {};
    this.dispatcher
      .scan((acc, curr) => ({ ...acc, ...curr }))
```

```
          .subscribe(data => this.next(data));
    }

    calcState(state, action) {
      return {
        counter: counterReducer(state.counter, action),
        products: productsReducer(state.products, action)
      }
    }

    dispatch(action) {
      const newState = this.calcState(this.value, action);
      this.dispatcher.next(newState);
    }

    select(slice) {
      return this.map(state => state[slice]);
    }
  }

const store = new Store();
store
  .select('products')
  .subscribe(data => console.log('store using select', data));

// store using select, []
// store using select, [{ id: 1, name: 'Yoda' }]

store.subscribe(data => console.log('store', data));
store.dispatch({ type: 'INCREMENT' });
store.dispatch({ type: 'INCREMENT' });
// store 0
// store 1

store.dispatch({ type: 'ADD_PRODUCT', payload: { id: 1, name: 'Yoda' } });
```

Should we want a more advanced `select` method, we can let it take a function instead, like so:

```
// excerpt from the Store class
select(fn) {
  return this.map(fn);
}

// usage - if there were such a state as 'state.products.list'
store
  .select(state => state.products.list);
```

Handling side effects

What is a side effect? A side effect is something that isn't part of the normal code flow but something that accesses outside resources, such as filesystems or resources on other networks. In the context of Redux, side effects are most often used for carrying out AJAX calls. Once that call comes back, we most likely need to update the state of the store because something has changed. How would we implement such a function? One is add a method `effect()` that would take a function. The said function would take dispatch method as a parameter so that the parameter function can carry out a dispatch, should it have a need for it, once the side effect has run its course. Let's imagine it is being used in the following way:

```
// pseudo code

const store = new Store();

store.effect( async(dispatch) => {
  const products = await getProducts();
  dispatch({ type: 'LOAD_PRODUCTS', payload: products });
})
```

The preceding code shows how we in our side effect would want to carry out an AJAX call and fetch our products. Once we are done with our fetch, we want to dispatch the fetched products so they become part of the store's state. Let's attempt to implement the preceding `effect()` function:

```
// NGRX-light/storeVIII.js

const Rx = require('rxjs');

function counterReducer(state = 0, action) {
  switch(action.type) {
    case "INCREMENT":
      return state + 1;
    default:
      return state;
  }
}

function productsReducer(state = [], action) {
  switch(action.type) {
    case 'ADD_PRODUCT':
      return [ ...state, Object.assign({}, action.payload) ];
    case 'LOAD_PRODUCTS':
      return action.payload.map(p => Object.assign({}, p));
```

```
      default:
        return state;
    }
  }

  class Store extends Rx.BehaviorSubject {
    constructor() {
      super({ counter: 0, products: [] });
      this.dispatcher = new Rx.Subject();
      this.state = {};
      this.dispatcher
        .scan((acc, curr) => ({ ...acc, ...curr }))
        .subscribe(data => this.next(data));
    }

    calcState(state, action) {
      return {
        counter: counterReducer(state.counter, action),
        products: productsReducer(state.products, action)
      }
    }

    dispatch(action) {
      const newState = this.calcState(this.value, action);
      this.dispatcher.next(newState);
    }

    select(slice) {
      return this.map(state => state[slice]);
    }

    effect(fn) {
      fn(this.dispatch.bind(this));
    }
  }

  const store = new Store();
  store
    .select('products')
    .subscribe(data => console.log('store using select', data));

  store.subscribe(data => console.log('store', data));
  store.dispatch({ type: 'INCREMENT' });
  store.dispatch({ type: 'INCREMENT' });
  store.dispatch({ type: 'ADD_PRODUCT', payload: { id: 1, name: 'Yoda' } });

  const getProducts = () => {
    return new Promise(resolve => {
```

```
    setTimeout(() => {
      resolve([{ id: 1, name: "Vader" }]);
    }, 3000);
  });
}

store.effect(async(dispatch) => {
  const products = await getProducts();
  dispatch({ type: 'LOAD_PRODUCTS', payload: products });
});
```

The preceding code does the following:

- Adds a new case LOAD_PRODUCTS to the productsReducer
- Implements the effect() method on the Store class
- Defines a getProducts() method to simulate AJAX calls
- Demonstrates the use of the effect method by carrying out a call to getProducts and ends up dispatching the fetched products to the store

We have now fully implemented the store and effects libraries for NgRx—we should be proud of ourselves.

@ngrx/schematics

Schematics is dependent on all of the libraries you can possibly use with NgRx; it's therefore a good idea to start out by installing these libraries before we do anything else. Just type the following:

```
npm install @ngrx/effects --save
npm install @ngrx/entity --save
npm install @ngrx/store --save
npm install @ngrx/store-devtools
```

Schematics itself is a library that Angular-CLI uses to generate different constructs needed for Angular development, such as components services, filters, and much more. @ngrx/schematics provides blueprints to schematics so you can get help generating constructs that you need when working with NgRx, in other words it makes development a lot faster. You can get help with generating the following things:

- Actions
- Container
- Effect

- Entity
- Feature
- Reducer
- Store

Setting it up

`@ngrx/schematics` is an NPM library and as such can be easily installed by typing:

```
npm install @ngrx/schematics --save-dev
```

That's it. That's all that was needed to do the set up. To use it, you just need a terminal window and enter the appropriate commands. We will look at that next.

Generating constructs

Generating what you need is as simple as typing:

```
ng generate <what> <name>
```

This will create files in the appropriate place. This is a real time saver, so learn to use it. Almost all of the commands come with a lot of options so it's worth checking out how they can be configured in the official documentation, which can be found here `https://github.com/ngrx/platform/tree/master/docs/schematics`.

Generating actions

Do this by typing the following:

```
ng generate action jedis
```

It will generate an actions file for us called `jedi.actions.ts` with the following content:

```
// jedis.actions.ts

import { Action } from '@ngrx/store';

export enum JedisActionTypes {
  JedisAction = '[Jedis] Action'
}
```

```
export class Jedis implements Action {
  readonly type = JediActionTypes.JediAction;
}

export type JediActions = Jedi;
```

The preceding code gives us nice scaffolded files with some nice defaults and it creates a enum type that we can use in conjunction with reducers and selectors. Looking at the preceding code, we realize that we need to extend JedisActionTypes if we want things such as ADD, CREATE, and other CRUD operations.

Generating a container

This will inject a store into your component and create the component itself—the typical way to call this one is by typing:

ng generate container jedis

This will create the following files:

- jedis.component.ts
- jedis.component.html
- jedis.component.css
- jedis.component.spec.ts

And in jedis.component.ts and the store will be injected in the constructor, like so:

```
// jedis.component.ts

import { Component, OnInit } from '@angular/core';
@Component({
  selector: 'app-jedis',
  templateUrl: './jedis.component.html',
  styleUrls: ['./jedis.component.css']
})
export class JedisComponent implements OnInit {
  constructor(private store: Store<any>) { } }
  ngOnInit() {}
}
```

Generating an effect

You generate an effect by typing the following:

```
ng generate effect jedis
```

This will produce the files:

- jedis.effect.ts
- jedis.effect.spec.ts

The effects file looks like this:

```
import { Injectable } from '@angular/core';
import { Actions, Effect } from '@ngrx/effects';

@Injectable()
export class JedisEffects {
  constructor(private actions$: Actions) {}
}
```

Generating an entity

This generates a whole bunch of files that you can think of to work with an entity. To run the command, type:

```
ng generate entity product
```

The following files are generated:

- product.actions.ts
- product.model.ts
- product.reducer.ts
- product.reducer.spec.ts

It's worth mentioning that the product.reducer.ts file not only generates the full reducer function but also creates and initializes the EntityAdapter. That's a lot of boilerplate that you don't have to write. You also get all the actions and all selectors—a truly powerful command.

Generating a feature

Generating a feature gives you a lot of files. Let's have a look at what the command looks like:

```
ng generate feature category
```

This generates the following files:

- `category.actions.ts`
- `category.reducer.ts`
- `category.reducer.spec.ts`
- `category.effects.ts`
- `category.effects.spec.ts`

This again is a lot of files you don't have to write by hand.

Generating a reducer

This generates a reducer and a test file. If all you want is a reducer then this command is for you. To use it, type the following:

```
ng generate reducer travel
```

This produces the following files:

- `travel.reducer.ts`
- `travel.reducer.spec.ts`

Generating a store

This command sets you up completely for using the `@ngrx/store`. It also allows you to set up feature stores. So, by typing the following two commands, you can generate a whole lot of files:

```
ng generate module country
ng generate store country
```

The preceding code will generate a module as well as add a feature state. Running the following command will add the set up needed to work with the store, as well as set up the devtools that come with NgRx:

```
ng generate store State --root --module app.module.ts
```

Summary

In this, the final chapter of the book, we have looked at how to truly master NgRx and all its accompanying helper libraries. We have also gone through how to build your own micro implementation of NgRx to establish that we really know what is going on behind the scenes. We have looked at various ways to improve our speed and productivity by looking at the entity library and schematics library, respectively.

You, as a reader, have been taken through a long journey of Flux and Redux patterns throughout the course of this book. In addition, Functional programming, Reactive Programming, and deep RxJS knowledge have been added to your tool belt. This has built up to two full chapters covering everything NgRx has to offer. The aim of this book was to give you a broad and deep enough context of the underlying thoughts and paradigms behind NgRx and the library itself. The hope is that after, reading this book, you will feel full of confidence and know how to tackle existing and future projects using Angular and NgRx.

Thank you for taking the time to read this book, and do not hesitate to reach out with queries in any way, shape, or form.

Other Books You May Enjoy

If you enjoyed this book, you may be interested in these other books by Packt:

Learning Angular - Second Edition
Christoffer Noring, Pablo Deeleman

ISBN: 978-1-78712-492-9

- Set up the workspace and the project using webpack and Angular-Cli
- Explore the features of TypeScript and organize the code in ES6 modules
- Work with HTTP and Data Services and understand how data can flow in the app
- Create multiple views and learn how to navigate between them
- Make the app beautiful by adding Material Design
- Implement two different types of form handling and its validation
- Add animation to some standard events such as route change, initialization, data load, and so on
- Discover how to bulletproof your applications by introducing smart unit testing techniques and debugging tools

ASP.NET Core 2 and Angular 5
Valerio De Sanctis

ISBN: 978-1-78829-360-0

- Use ASP.NET Core to its full extent to create a versatile backend layer based on RESTful APIs
- Consume backend APIs with the brand new Angular 5 HttpClient and use RxJS Observers to feed the frontend UI asynchronously
- Implement an authentication and authorization layer using ASP.NET Identity to support user login with integrated and third-party OAuth 2 providers
- Configure a web application in order to accept user-defined data and persist it into the database using server-side APIs
- Secure your application against threats and vulnerabilities in a time efficient way
- Connect different aspects of the ASP. NET Core framework ecosystem and make them interact with each other for a Full-Stack web development experience

Leave a review - let other readers know what you think

Please share your thoughts on this book with others by leaving a review on the site that you bought it from. If you purchased the book from Amazon, please leave us an honest review on this book's Amazon page. This is vital so that other potential readers can see and use your unbiased opinion to make purchasing decisions, we can understand what our customers think about our products, and our authors can see your feedback on the title that they have worked with Packt to create. It will only take a few minutes of your time, but is valuable to other potential customers, our authors, and Packt. Thank you!

Index

C

D

E

about 197
Advanced Retry 202
catch 197
error, ignoring 199
retry 200
ES2015 modules
Angular example 27
consuming 27
default import/export 29
imports, renaming 29
multiple exports 28
service 30
using 26
existing construct
constants, overriding 39
dependencies, resolving with @Injectable 39
override at runtime 38
overriding 37

F

feature module
action methods, adding 267
component, adding 265
constants, adding 267
counter-list reducer, adding 265
model, adding 267
reducers, registering 268
several states 264
fetch API
reference 40
first-class higher-order functions 101
Flux pattern
core concepts 47
for-loops
avoiding 106
forFeature()
setting up, from string to selection function 260
forRoot()
migrating, to forFeature() 260
functional programming paradigm, combining with
streams
combining, with streams 116
filtering 117
mindsets, combining 117
projection 116

functional programming
about 99
versus imperative programming 100
Functional Reactive Programming (FRP) 7, 99

G

generators
reference 94
grouping operators, streams
about 166
buffer() operator 176
bufferTime() operator 176

H

hot Observables 180
hot stream
creating 182, 184

I

immutability patterns
about 217
list, changing 218
object, changing 219
imperative programming
versus declarative programming 100

J

JS Bin
reference 151

L

lists
comparing, to async streams 115

M

marble test
about 203
environment, setting up 204
reference 206
writing 204, 205
mathematical operators, streams
about 165, 171
max () 171

Printed in Great Britain
by Amazon